iOS Architecture Patterns

MVC, MVP, MVVM, VIPER, and VIP in Swift

Raúl Ferrer García

Apress®

iOS Architecture Patterns: MVC, MVP, MVVM, VIPER, and VIP in Swift

Raúl Ferrer García
Barcelona, Spain

ISBN-13 (pbk): 978-1-4842-9068-2   ISBN-13 (electronic): 978-1-4842-9069-9
https://doi.org/10.1007/978-1-4842-9069-9

Managing Director, Apress Media LLC: Welmoed Spahr
Acquisitions Editor: Aaron Black
Development Editor: James Markham
Coordinating Editor: Jessica Vakili

Cover image designed by Freepik (www.freepik.com)

Distributed to the book trade worldwide by Springer Science+Business Media New York, 1 New York Plaza, Suite 4600, New York, NY 10004-1562, USA. Phone 1-800-SPRINGER, fax (201) 348-4505, e-mail orders-ny@springer-sbm.com, or visit www.springeronline.com. Apress Media, LLC is a California LLC and the sole member (owner) is Springer Science + Business Media Finance Inc (SSBM Finance Inc). SSBM Finance Inc is a **Delaware** corporation.

For information on translations, please e-mail booktranslations@springernature.com; for reprint, paperback, or audio rights, please e-mail bookpermissions@springernature.com.

Apress titles may be purchased in bulk for academic, corporate, or promotional use. eBook versions and licenses are also available for most titles. For more information, reference our Print and eBook Bulk Sales web page at http://www.apress.com/bulk-sales.

Any source code or other supplementary material referenced by the author in this book is available to readers on the Github repository: https://github.com/Apress/iOS-Architecture-Patterns. For more detailed information, please visit http://www.apress.com/source-code.

Printed on acid-free paper

We're here to put a dent in the universe. Otherwise, why else even be here?

—Steve Jobs

They didn't know it was impossible, so they did it.

—Mark Twain

Table of Contents

About the Author

 **Raúl Ferrer García** holds a doctorate in chemistry, but he has always had a great interest in the world of computer science and software development, where he began his foray programming with a ZX Spectrum at the age of 14. For just over ten years, and in a self-taught way, he has entered the world of mobile development, first as an iOS Developer and then as Mobile Tech Lead at Editorial Vicens Vives, and he has dedicated himself completely to the development and management of mobile applications. He also maintains a blog in which he tries to explain everything he's learned and studied about the world of mobile development.

About the Technical Reviewer

Massimo Nardone has more than 25 years of experience in security, web and mobile development, cloud, and IT architecture. His true IT passions are security and Android. He has been programming and teaching how to program with Android, Perl, PHP, Java, VB, Python, C/C++, and MySQL for more than 20 years. He holds a Master of Science degree In Computing Science from the University of Salerno, Italy.

He has worked as a CISO, CSO, security executive, IoT executive, project manager, software engineer, research engineer, chief security architect, PCI/SCADA auditor, and senior lead IT security/cloud/SCADA architect for many years. His technical skills include security, Android, cloud, Java, MySQL, Drupal, Cobol, Perl, web and mobile development, MongoDB, D3, Joomla, Couchbase, C/C++, WebGL, Python, Pro Rails, Django CMS, Jekyll, Scratch, and more.

He worked as visiting lecturer and supervisor for exercises at the Networking Laboratory of the Helsinki University of Technology (Aalto University). He holds four international patents (PKI, SIP, SAML, and Proxy areas). He is currently working for Cognizant as head of cybersecurity and CISO to help both internally and externally with clients in areas of information and cybersecurity, like strategy, planning, processes, policies, procedures, governance, awareness, and so forth. In June 2017, he became a permanent member of the ISACA Finland Board.

Massimo has reviewed more than 45 IT books for different publishing companies and is the co-author of *Pro Spring Security: Securing Spring Framework 5 and Boot 2-based Java Applications* (Apress, 2019), *Beginning EJB in Java EE 8* (Apress, 2018), *Pro JPA 2 in Java EE 8* (Apress, 2018), and *Pro Android Games* (Apress, 2015).

Acknowledgments

First of all, I would like to thank my family for their support, their words of encouragement, their inspiration... during the preparation and writing of this book and, in general, ever since. This book is dedicated to them.

Second, I would like to thank the entire Apress team for the opportunity to write this book, starting with Aaron Black who contacted me and raised the possibility of writing a book on iOS development, and not forgetting Jessica Vakili and Nirmal Selvaraj for their great work in managing and editing this book.

Learning is a journey that never ends, so I would also like to thank the work of all those who in one way or another teach us something new every day.

Finally, thanks to you, reader. I hope that once you have read this book you consider it a wise decision and that, to a greater or lesser extent, it has helped you in your evolution as a developer.

Introduction

As we will see throughout the book, various architectural patterns have been developed to apply in the development of our applications – some well known (and older), such as MVC or MVVM, and others more innovative, such as VIPER or VIP.

If you are just starting to develop applications or have been at it for some time, you have surely searched for information on how an application is built and what architecture pattern is the best to apply. But possibly you have also reached the same conclusion as me: from a global point of view, there is no perfect architecture pattern, they all have advantages and disadvantages, and it almost always depends on how we apply said pattern that our code is readable, testable, and scalable.

In addition, you will also have noticed that an architecture pattern comes to mark some kind of application rules, but that later many developers adapt or modify it looking to improve its features or solve some of its possible drawbacks.

Who Is This Book For?

This book is aimed both at those developers who are starting now and who want to know what architecture patterns they can apply to their applications, as well as those developers who have been developing applications for some time but who want to know other possible architectures to apply.

Therefore, this book is for you if what you want is

- Learn to develop applications following some of the architecture patterns explained

- Understand the advantages and disadvantages of each of the architecture patterns explained and choose the one that suits you best

- Understand the advantages of developing a readable, testable, and scalable code

In this book I have not sought to delve into the use of each of the architectures explained, but rather to serve as a point of introduction to their use, to understand why they are important, and from here on you will be able to choose one or those that suit you best, know how to delve into them, apply them, and evolve in your career as a developer.

How to Use This Book?

Apart from a theoretical introduction to each of the architectural patterns presented (there are numerous articles for each of the architectures that we will cover that talk about their features, advantages, and disadvantages), this book is eminently practical. In Chapters 2–6 (MVC, MVP, MVVM, VIPER, and VIP architecture patterns), the development of an application (MyToDos) following each of these patterns is presented.

For the sake of simplicity, although the main parts of the code are presented (depending on the concept explained), you will be able to observe omitted parts of the code (marked with "..."). However, you can find the full code for each of the projects in this book's repository.

Therefore, I am going to assume that you have some knowledge of both Swift and Xcode that should allow you to follow the course of the book without problems.

CHAPTER 1

Introduction

Assume the following situation: you and your team have received a new project to develop a mobile application. A project, whether it originates from our idea or is commissioned by a client, will present a series of specifications, functionalities, behaviors, etc.

Continuing with our assumption, we are going to consider that all these specifications and functionalities have already been studied and transformed into user stories (i.e., how a functionality would be described from the point of view of a user: for example, "As a user, I want to login in the application") and that we could already start developing the application by writing the first lines of code.

It has happened to all of us that when we have a new project, we want to start writing code. However, if we work in this way, without proposing a project structure or taking into account the type of application, we can end up developing an application that works, but whose code is later difficult to maintain.

To avoid this situation, before starting to write code we have to determine what structure we are going to give it, what the Software Architecture is going to be, and what architecture pattern is the most suitable for our project.

Before starting to see the most used architecture patterns in the development of iOS applications, we are going to make an introduction to what Software Architecture is, what architecture patterns are, why their use is necessary, and how to choose the most suitable one for our projects.

© Raúl Ferrer García 2023
R. Ferrer García, *iOS Architecture Patterns*, https://doi.org/10.1007/978-1-4842-9069-9_1

What Is Software Architecture?

The Software Architecture defines how the software structure is, what are the components that form it, how they are joined, and how they communicate with each other.

All these points that intervene in the definition of the Software Architecture can be represented according to different models or views, the following three being the main ones (and an example of their application is one of the architectures that we will study later, the MVVM or Model–View–ViewModel):

- **Static view**: It indicates which components make up the structure. In MVVM, these components would be View, Model, and ViewModel.

- **Dynamic view**: It establishes the behavior of the different components and the communication between them over time.

- **Functional view**: It shows us what each component does. For example, in the example we are seeing, each of the components would have the following functionalities:

  - **Model**: It contains the classes and structures responsible for storing and transferring an application's data. It also includes business logic.

  - **View**: It represents the interface with the elements that form it, the interaction with the user, and how it is updated to show the user the information received.

- **ViewModel**: It acts as an intermediary between the View and the Model; it usually includes presentation logic, that is, those methods that allow the data received from the Model to be transformed to be presented in the View.

Architecture Patterns

We have just seen that Software Architecture helps us to give structure to our project. However, not all projects are the same or have the same purpose, so, logically, the architectures used are different and appropriate to each project.

Developers have been finding different solutions when facing their projects. The fact that the requirements and functionalities of a project, its components, or the way of communicating between them vary from one project to another has given rise to different architectural solutions and architecture patterns.

Keep in mind that an architecture pattern is like a template that offers us some rules or guidelines on how to develop and structure the different components of the application. Each architectural pattern has its advantages and disadvantages, as we will see later.

Why Do We Need an Architecture Pattern for Our Applications?

The selection and use of an architecture pattern when developing our applications will allow us to avoid a series of problems that applications that have been developed without using these patterns can present.

Some of these problems are as follows:

- These are applications that are difficult to maintain. This problem increases if new developers are involved, as it is more costly for them to understand the software they are working on.

- It usually increases the development time and, therefore, increases its cost.

- As it is not a structured code, it is more complicated to add new features or scale it.

- They are very likely to have duplicate, unused, and messy code. All this makes it more prone to errors.

Therefore, the use of a good architecture pattern will allow us to reduce these problems:

- We will work with a code that is simpler, more organized, and easier to understand (and following good development practices, such as the SOLID principles) for all developers since they will act according to the same rules.

- The written code will be easily testable and less prone to errors.

- A correct distribution of the components and their responsibilities will lead to a structure that is easy to maintain, modify, and extend.

- All of this will result in reduced development time and, by extension, reduced costs.

Design from High Level to Low Level

In this book, we are going to study and apply different architectural patterns in iOS applications, so we will also see the code with which we implement them and the best way to implement it.

As we have seen, an architecture pattern gives us guidelines to build an application that is efficient, scalable, and easy to maintain, among other advantages.

But we can think of an architecture pattern as the high-level design of the application, and then we have to go down to the code (Figure 1-1).

This is where the design patterns and their implementation through the programming language come in, trying to follow some principles (SOLID), which will make the code flexible, stable, maintainable, and reusable.

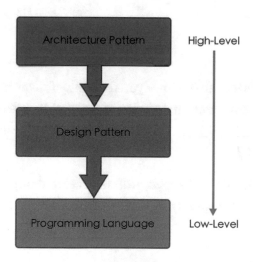

Figure 1-1. *Levels of design and implementation in an application*

Let's see briefly what design patterns are (some of which we will apply) and how to work following the SOLID principles.

Design Patterns

In the same way that an architecture pattern is a generic solution to a certain problem when it comes to the structure of our software (i.e., it will affect the entire project), design patterns give us solutions to recurring problems that affect a project component.

There are 23 design patterns, which are described in the book *Design Patterns: Elements of Reusable Object-Oriented Software.*[1] They described the 23 design patterns and classified them into three groups: structural patterns, creational patterns, and behavioral patterns.

Creational Patterns

Creational patterns are those that allow us to create objects. These patterns encapsulate the procedure for creating an object and generally work through interfaces.

Factory Method

It provides an interface that allows you to create objects in a superclass, but delegates the implementation and alteration of objects to subclasses.

Abstract Factory

It provides an interface that allows groups of related objects to be generated, but without specifying their specific classes or implementation.

---

[1] *Design Patterns: Elements of Reusable Object-Oriented Software* by E. Gamma, R. Helm, E. Johnson, and J. Vlissides. Addison Wesley, 1st Ed, 1994.

Builder

It allows building complex objects step by step, separating the creation of the object from its structure. In this way, we can use the same construction process to obtain different types and representations of an object.

Singleton

This pattern ensures that a class has only one possible instance, which is globally accessible.

Prototype

It allows you to copy or clone an object without requiring our code to depend on its classes.

Structural Patterns

Structural patterns specify how objects and classes relate to each other to form more complex structures so that they are flexible and efficient. They rely on inheritance to define interfaces and obtain new functionality.

Adapter

It is a structural pattern that allows two objects with incompatible interfaces to collaborate, through an intermediary with which they communicate and interact.

Bridge

In this pattern, an abstraction is decoupled from its implementation, so it can evolve independently.

Composite

It allows you to create objects with a tree-like structure and then work with these structures as if they were individual objects. In this case, all the elements of the structure use the same interface.

Decorator

This pattern allows you to add new features to an object (including this object in a container that contains the new features) without changing the behavior of objects of the same type.

Façade

It provides a simplified interface to a complex structure (such as a library or set of classes).

Flyweight

It is a pattern that allows you to save RAM by having many objects share common properties on the same object, instead of maintaining these properties on every object.

Proxy

It is an object that acts as a simplified version of the original. A proxy controls access to the original object, allowing it to perform some tasks before or after accessing that object. This pattern is often used for Internet connections, device file access, etc.

Behavioral Patterns

They are the most numerous, and they focus on communication between objects and are responsible for managing algorithms, relationships, and responsibilities between these objects.

Chain of Responsibility

It allows requests to be passed through a chain of handlers. Each of these handlers can either process the request or pass it on to the next. In this way, the transmitter and the final receiver are decoupled.

Command

It transforms a request into an object that encapsulates the action and information you need to execute it.

Interpreter

It is a pattern that, given a language, defines a representation for its grammar and the mechanism for evaluating it.

Iterator

It allows to cycle through the elements of a collection without exposing its representation (list, stack, tree...).

Mediator

It restricts direct communications between objects and forces communication through a single object, which acts as a mediator.

Memento

It allows you to save and restore an object to a previous state without revealing the details of its implementation.

Observe

It allows establishing a subscription mechanism to notify different objects of the events that occur in the object that they observe.

State

It allows an object to change its behavior when its internal state changes.

Strategy

It allows defining that, from a family of algorithms, we can select one of them at execution time to perform a certain action.

Template Method

This pattern defines the skeleton of an algorithm in a superclass but allows subclasses to override some methods without changing their structure.

Visitor

It allows algorithms to be separated from the objects with which they operate.

SOLID Principles

These are five principles that will allow us to create reusable components, easy to maintain, and with higher quality code.

SOLID is an acronym that comes from the first letter of the five principles.

Single-Responsibility Principle (SRP)

A class should have one reason, and one reason only, to change. That is, a class should only have one responsibility.

Open–Closed Principle (OCP)

We must be able to extend a class without changing its behavior. This is achieved by abstraction.

Liskov Substitution Principle (LSP)

In a program, any class should be able to be replaced by one of its subclasses without affecting its operation.

Interface Segregation Principle (ISP)

It is better to have different interfaces (protocols) that are specific to each client than to have a general interface. Also, a client would not have to implement methods that it does not use.

Dependency Inversion Principle (DIP)

High-level classes should not depend on low-level classes. Both should depend on abstractions. Abstractions should not depend on details. The details should depend on the abstractions. What is sought is to reduce dependencies between modules and thus achieve less coupling between classes.

How to Choose the Right Architectural Pattern

We have just seen the advantages that our applications have a good architecture offers us. But how do we choose the right architecture pattern for our project?

In the first place, we have to know some information about our project and the technology that we are going to use since we have seen that some architecture patterns are better adapted to some projects and other patterns to others.

Therefore, we must take into account, for example:

- The type of project

- The technologies used to develop it

- Support infrastructure (servers, clouds, databases...)

- User interface (usability, content, navigation...)

- Budget and development time

- Future scalability and the addition of new functionalities

If we take into account everything seen so far, the choice of a good architecture pattern (along with the use of design patterns and SOLID principles) will allow us to have the following:

- **A scalable application**: A good architecture pattern should allow us to add new features and even change some of the technologies used, without having to modify the entire application.

- **Separation of interests**: Each component should be independent of the code point of view. That is, to function correctly, a component should only be aware of those around it and nothing else. This will allow us, for example, to reuse these components or simply change them for others.

- **A code easy to maintain**: Well-written, structured code without repetition makes it easier to understand, review, or modify. Also, any new developer joining the project will require less time to get hold of.

- **A testable code**: The previous points result in the fact that it is easier to test a code if the functionalities are correctly separated than if they are not.

- **A solid, stable, reliable, and durable code over time**.

Most Used Architecture Patterns

From a generic point of view of software development, there are numerous architecture patterns, but we will focus on the most used for the development of iOS applications:

- Model–View–Controller (MVC)

- Model–View–Presenter (MVP)

- Model–View–ViewModel (MVVM)

- View–Interactor–Presenter–Entity–Router (VIPER)

- View–Interactor–Presenter (VIP)

We will start with the best-known model and the one that every developer usually starts working with, the MVC. From here we will work on models that derive from it, such as the MVP and the MVVM, to end up with much more elaborate models of higher complexity, such as the VIPER and the VIP.

After these architectural patterns, we will see, in a more summarized way, some more patterns, perhaps not so used or known, but that can give us a better perspective of how to structure an application. Examples of these types of patterns are RIBs (developed by Uber) and Redux (based on an initial idea of Facebook for a one-way architecture).

In Search of a "Clean Architecture"

The "Clean Architecture" concept was introduced by Robert C. Martin in 2012,[2] and it is not an architecture, but a series of rules that, together with the SOLID principles, will allow us to develop software with responsibilities separate, robust, easy to understand, and testable.

Clean Architecture Layers

According to this philosophy, for an architecture to be considered "clean" it must have at least the following three layers: Domain Layer, Presentation Layer, and Data Layer (Figure 1-2).

---

[2] https://blog.cleancoder.com/uncle-bob/2012/08/13/the-clean-architecture.html

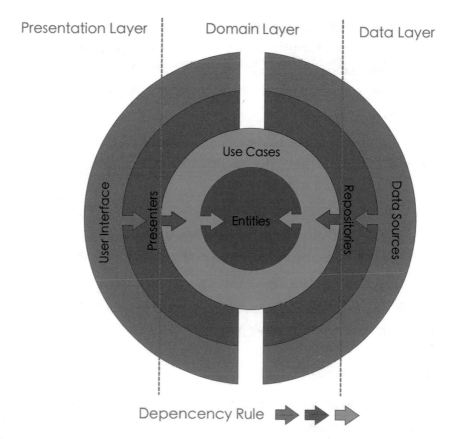

Presentation Layer   Domain Layer   Data Layer

Figure 1-2. *Scheme of the layer structure in Clean Architecture. Dependency rule arrows show how the outermost layers depend on the innermost ones and not the other way around*

Domain Layer

It is the core of this architecture and contains the application logic and business logic. In this layer we find the Use Cases or Interactors, the Entities, and the Interfaces of the Repositories:

- **Use Cases or interactors**: They are in charge of defining and implementing the business logic. They control the flow of information to and from the Entities. They can work with one or more entities and access their methods.

- **Entities**: These are simple objects (which can be simple data structures or can also contain methods) that contain the business rules.

- **Repository interfaces**: They contain the definition of the methods that will be implemented in the Repositories. Repositories are responsible for obtaining and passing data from databases, servers, etc.

This layer has no external dependencies, so it is easily testable (Use Cases) and can be reused in other projects.

Presentation Layer

This layer contains all those elements that show information to the user or that receive their interaction.

The Presentation layer also includes those components, such as ViewModels or Presenters, that help prepare the data to be displayed on the screen.

The ViewModels or Presenters are also in charge of executing the Use Cases. The Presentation Layer only depends on the Domain Layer.

Data Layer

It contains the implementation classes of the Repositories and the data sources such as databases, user preferences, or access to servers. In the same way as the Presentation Layer, the Data Layer only depends on the Domain Layer.

The Dependency Rule

For this type of architecture to work correctly, we must apply the so-called Dependency Rule. According to this rule, the inner layers must not know the outer layers (i.e., no variable, method, etc., of an outer layer is mentioned in a more inner layer).

Advantages of Applying a Clean Architecture

The application of a Clean Architecture in our projects will give us a series of advantages (some of which we have already seen in the introduction to Software Architecture):

- **Testable**: The fact that the business logic is isolated in its layer, and that it does not depend on the rest of the layers, makes it easily testable.

  In addition, this same separation by layers allows them to be tested separately and more easily locate any possible error.

- **Independent of frameworks**: The code must be independent of specific libraries.

  In other words, we can change one library for another without the need for major changes in the code and without the internal layers stopping working because of it. This is achieved by preventing our code from having direct dependencies on these libraries.

- **Independent of the user interface**: The user interface is the outermost layer and only displays the data supplied by the presenter.

Therefore, we must be able to modify it without affecting the most internal part, the business logic. In other words, the user interface must adapt to changes in business logic and not the other way around.

- **Independent of data sources**: In a similar way to what was explained for the independence of the user interface, we must be able to change the data sources (local, external databases…) without affecting the business logic, since it is these sources that fit the business logic.

- **Independent of external elements**: The business logic must be independent of everything that surrounds it, which must allow us to change any part of the rest of the system without affecting it.

MyToDos: A Simple App to Test Architectures

To work with the different architectures that we have mentioned before (MVC, MVP, MVVM, VIPER, and VIP), we are going to create a simple task management application, which is, usually, one of the first applications that a developer usually does.

App Screens

Our MyToDos app will allow us to work the navigation between different screens (create lists, create tasks…); use a database to save, update, or delete tasks; and, finally, manage user interactions on the different screens.

Launch Screen

It is the screen that appears when loading the application (Figure 1-3).

Figure 1-3. *Launch screen*

Home Screen

This screen shows the lists we have created. If we haven't created any list, an "Empty State" will appear to tell us to create our first list.

For each created list, we will be able to see the icon that we have associated with the list, the title of the list, and the number of tasks that compose it (Figure 1-4).

Figure 1-4. *Empty state on Home screen*

The user can interact on this screen at three points:

- Using the *Add List* button, which will allow us to create a new list

- Selecting one of the lists to access its content (Figure 1-5)

Figure 1-5. *Access tasks list on select cell*

- Deleting lists by a swipe gesture on the list (Figure 1-6)

Figure 1-6. *Delete list on swipe cell*

Add List Screen

This screen is navigated through the *Add List* button on the Home screen. Here, the user has to indicate the title that will be given to the list and select an icon from those that are shown (Figure 1-7).

When you select the *Add List* button, the entered information is saved in the database (Core Data) and you return to Home.

If the user wants to return to Home without creating any list, they simply have to select the button with the return arrow located at the top left of the screen.

Figure 1-7. *Add List screen*

Tasks List Screen

This screen is navigated by selecting one of the lists that appear in the Home. If we do not have any task created, an "Empty State" will appear indicating how to create a task (Figure 1-8).

Figure 1-8. *Tasks List empty state*

The user can interact on this screen at three points:

- Using the *Add Task* button, which will allow us to create a new task (Figure 1-9).

Figure 1-9. *Tasks List screen with an added task*

- Selecting the circle to the right of each task will allow us to mark it as done (Figure 1-10).

Figure 1-10. *Task checked as done*

- Deleting tasks using a swipe gesture in the list
  (Figure 1-11).

Figure 1-11. *Delete task*

Any modification on this screen (change the status of a task or delete it) is automatically saved in the database.

If the user wants to return to Home without creating any task, they simply have to select the button with the return arrow located at the top left of the screen.

Add Task Screen

This screen is navigated through the *Add Task* button on the Tasks List screen and is displayed as a modal. Here, the user has to indicate the title that will be given to the task and select an icon from those that are displayed.

When you select the *Add Task* button, the entered information is saved in the database (Core Data) and you are returned to the Tasks List screen.

If the user wants to return to the Tasks List screen without creating any tasks, they simply have to drag the screen down (Figure 1-12).

Figure 1-12. *Add Task screen*

App Development

Before we start working with the different architectures in the next chapters, let's first see how to prepare the application for it.

Technologies Used

For the development of this application with each of the architectures, Xcode 13.3 and Swift 5.6 have been used.

The database used is Apple's own Core Data, and the views and navigation between them have been developed directly with code, without using .xib or .storyboard files.

How to Remove Storyboard Dependence

To develop the application (with the different architectures) without using a storyboard, we have to do the following:

- First of all, we open Xcode and select the Create a new *Xcode project* option (Figure 1-13).

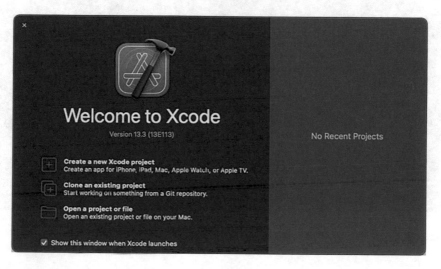

Figure 1-13. *Welcome to Xcode screen*

- Next, we select the App template in iOS (Figure 1-14).

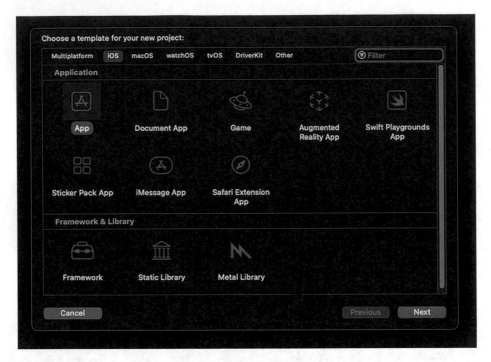

Figure 1-14. *App template selection screen*

- The next step is to indicate the name of the application (*Product Name*), select the development team and the organization identifier, and choose *Storyboard* as the interface, *Swift* as the language, and *Include Tests* (Figure 1-15).

Figure 1-15. *Choose project options screen*

- After creating the project, its configuration screen will appear. On this screen we must remove the "Main" option in the *Deployment Info* ➤ *Main Interface* section (Figure 1-16).

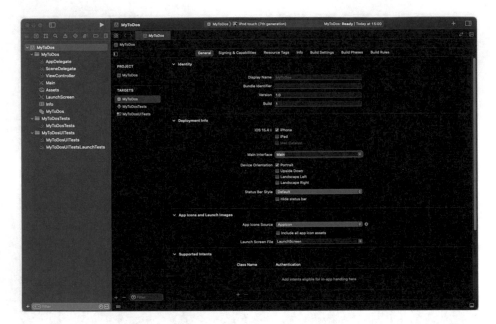

Figure 1-16. *Project configuration screen*

- Then we delete the Main.storyboard file (Figure 1-17).

Figure 1-17. *Remove Main.storyboard*

- Finally, we access the `Info.plist` file, display its content, and remove the Storyboard Name line: *Information Property List* ➤ *Application Scene Manifest* ➤ *Scene Configuration* ➤ *Application Session Role* ➤ *Item 0* ➤ *Storyboard Name* (Figure 1-18).

Figure 1-18. *Remove storyboard reference from Info.plist*

- When working with a storyboard, the window property
  is automatically initialized and the root view controller
  is set as the initial view controller in the storyboard.
  When removing the storyboard, we will have to do it
  ourselves.

  This is done in the SceneDelegate.swift file,
  modifying the content of the function

```
func scene(_ scene: UIScene, willConnectTo
session: UISceneSession, options
connectionOptions: UIScene.ConnectionOptions) {
    guard let _ = (scene as? UIWindowScene) else {
        return
    }
}
```

by this code (this part of the code can be modified depending on the needs of our application):

```
func scene(_ scene: UIScene, willConnectTo
session: UISceneSession, options
connectionOptions: UIScene.ConnectionOptions) {
    if let windowScene = scene as?
    UIWindowScene {
        let window = UIWindow(windowScene:
        windowScene)
        window.rootViewController =
        ViewController()
        window.makeKeyAndVisible()
        self.window = window
    }
}
```

Core Data Configuration

In this application we will use Apple's database, Core Data, but we have not selected it when setting up the project so that we can use our own database management class.

How to Create Database and Entities

To do this we will start by creating the database model and its entities:

- In the main menu of Xcode, we select *File* ➤ *New* ➤ *File....* In the templates menu that appears, descend to the *Core Data* section and select *Data Model* (Figure 1-19).

Figure 1-19. *Select Data Model file template*

- Next, we give the file a name (in this case *ToDoList*) and create it (Figure 1-20).

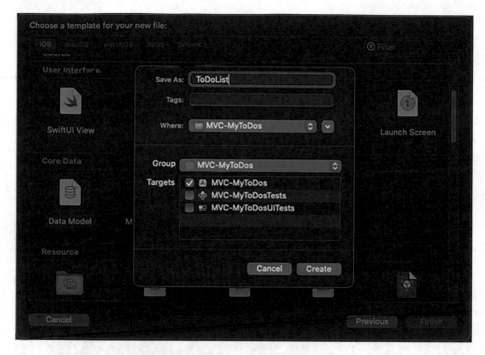

Figure 1-20. *Create a Data Model file*

- Now we are going to create the entities that we will use
  in the application, *TasksList,* and *Task.* To do this, we
  select the ToDoList.xcdatamodeld file and add the
  two entities mentioned with the properties shown in
  Figure 1-21 and Figure 1-22.

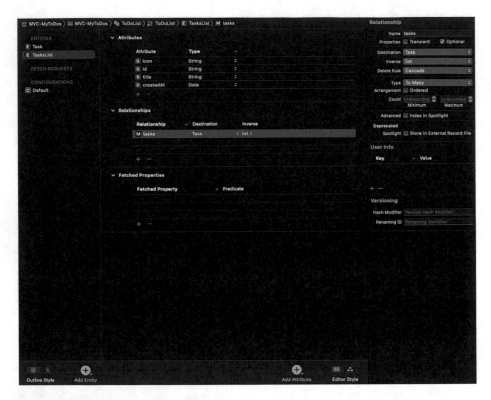

Figure 1-21. *Creation of the TasksList entity*

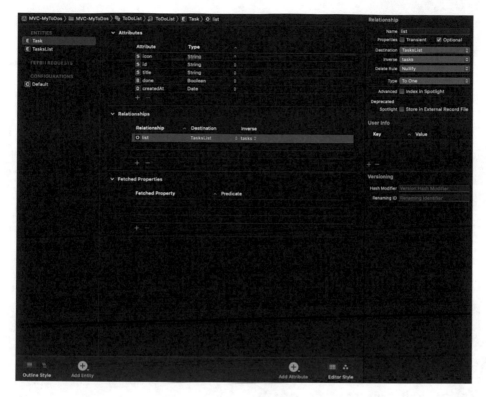

Figure 1-22. *Creation of the Task entity*

- By creating the entities, we have also created a 1-*n*
  relationship between them. That is, a list can be related
  to multiple tasks, but a task can only be related to
  one list.

Once the entities are created, we can use Xcode to generate the code that manages these entities (as NSManagedObject subclasses). To do this, we select the ToDoList.xcdatamodeld file and, in the main Xcode menu, select *Editor* ➤ *Create NSManagedObject Subclass...* (Figure 1-23).

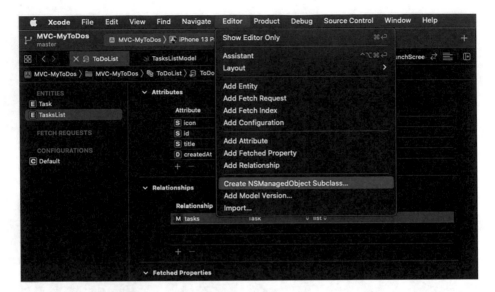

Figure 1-23. *Create NSManagedObject subclasses for our entities*

In this way, four files are generated (two for each of the entities):

```
Task+CoreDataClass.swift
Task+CoreDataProperties.swift
TasksList+CoreDataClass.swift
TasksList+CoreDataProperties.swift
```

Once these files have been generated, we can now use the entities in our project.

Create CoreDataManager

Now, we just need to create our class (`CoreDataManager.swift`) to manage the Core Data stack of our application. As shown in the following code, this class allows us to access the main context and to be able to save it:

```swift
import Foundation
import CoreData

class CoreDataManager {

    static let shared = CoreDataManager()

    init() {}

    lazy var persistentContainer: NSPersistentContainer = {
        let container = NSPersistentContainer(name: "ToDoList")
        container.loadPersistentStores { _, error in
            if let error = error {
                fatalError("Unable to load persistent stores:
                \(error)")
            }
        }
        return container
    }()

    lazy var mainContext: NSManagedObjectContext = {
        return persistentContainer.viewContext
    }()

    func saveContext() {
        saveContext(mainContext)
    }

    func saveContext(_ context: NSManagedObjectContext) {
        if context.parent == mainContext {
            saveDerivedContext(context)
            return
        }
```

41

```
    context.perform {
        do {
            try context.save()
        } catch let error as NSError {
            fatalError("Error: \(error.
            localizedDescription)")
        }
    }
}

func saveDerivedContext(_ context:
NSManagedObjectContext) {
    context.perform { [self] in
        do {
            try context.save()
        } catch let error as NSError {
            fatalError("Error: \(error.
            localizedDescription)")
        }

        saveContext(mainContext)
    }
}
}
```

Summary

For this chapter, we are going to make a summary of what we have worked on, and that we can divide into two blocks:

- In the first part, we have focused on how to structure and build an application efficiently, so we have studied

  - What is Software Architecture, what are architecture patterns, and why is it convenient to use them when developing an application

  - What is considered Clean Architecture and the advantages of its use

- In the second part of the chapter, we have focused on the example application that we will use to work with different architecture patterns:

  - We have seen a general description of what the application will be like, the different screens that make it up, and its functionality.

  - We have seen how we can develop an application that works without a storyboard.

  - We have created a database with Core Data, we have created the entities that we will use for our data, and, finally, we have established a class to handle the stack of the Core Data.

CHAPTER 2

MVC: Model–View– Controller

What Is MVC?

A Little History

The Model–View–Controller (MVC) pattern was introduced by Trygve Reenskaug for the Smalltalk-76 programming language in the late 1970s. As Reenskaug wrote: https://folk.universitetetioslo.no/trygver/.

> *I created the Model-View-Controller pattern as an obvious solution to the general problem of giving users control over their information as seen from multiple perspectives.*

In this first version, the user interacted through the View, which sent the actions to the Controller, and this, in turn, updated the Model (data) and redrew the View. The Model notified the View when it was updated and received the new state of the View (Figure 2-1).

© Raúl Ferrer García 2023
R. Ferrer García, *iOS Architecture Patterns*, https://doi.org/10.1007/978-1-4842-9069-9_2

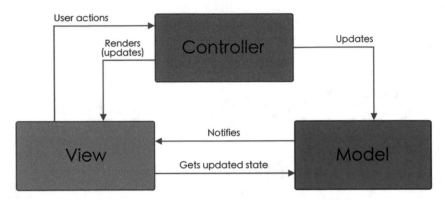

Figure 2-1. *Original Model–View–Controller schema*

Apple Model–View–Controller

Currently, the MVC pattern used is an updated version adapted to current software and devices. It is one of the best-known and used patterns today in the development of mobile applications, as well as the one recommended by Apple for such development (Figure 2-2).

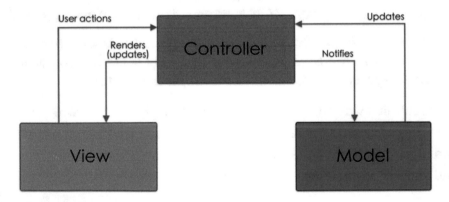

Figure 2-2. *Apple Model–View–Controller schema*

As in the development of mobile applications it is usual to reuse components, such as views, the original MVC pattern was modified so that the Model and the View are not linked.

With this new scheme, the View receives the user's actions and communicates them to the Controller. This, if necessary, updates the Model (data) and, once done, updates the View.

In its documentation,[1] Apple indicates that MVC is based on three design patterns (which we already saw in Chapter 1 in a generic way):

- **Composite**: Views are made up of other views following a tree-like structure. For example, imagine a view that was made up of more views (buttons, labels, images…).

- **Strategy**: Controllers can manage one or more views (which have no internal logic and are therefore reusable), and these delegate to Controllers how they should be displayed.

- **Observer**: A Controller that needs to know when the state of the application (i.e., the data in the Model) changes must be subscribed to these changes.

Components in MVC

We have just seen that there are three components in this architecture: View, Model, and Controller. Let us study each component's functions in more detail.

Model

The Model is the component (or components) that holds the business logic and is in charge of accessing, manipulating, or storing the data of the application.

---

[1]https://developer.apple.com/library/archive/documentation/General/ Conceptual/CocoaEncyclopedia/Model-View-Controller/Model-View- Controller.html

- It contains classes related to data persistence, for example, through the use of databases (Core Data, SQLite, Realm…) or the use of user preferences (UserDefaults).

- It contains the classes that manage the application's communications (Networking) and that allow us to receive and send data.

- It contains the classes that parse the information received from outside the application and convert it into model objects.

- It contains extensions, constants, and helper classes.

- A model object can communicate with other model objects.

- The Model must not communicate directly with the View. The communication between the Model and the View is done through the Controller.

View

The View is made up of those components that the user can see:

- They are the classes that derive from the UIKit, AppKit, Core Animation, and Core Graphics libraries.

- They show the data that comes from the Model, although they are not directly connected to it (they do it through the Controller).

- These components can receive user interactions.

Controller

The Controller acts as an intermediary between the Model and the View:

- It is the main component of the MVC model and communicates with both the View and the Model.

- It receives and interprets the actions that the user performs on the View and updates the Model accordingly.

- If the data in the Model changes, it updates the View according to these changes.

- It takes care of the life cycle of the application.

Advantages and Disadvantages of MVC

The MVC architecture pattern is the one recommended by Apple for application development; it is the first one that is usually learned and the most commonly used. Using the Model-View–Controller architecture has advantages and disadvantages.

Advantages of the MVC Pattern

The use of the MVC pattern has some advantages:

- Its design is simple.

- It uses less code compared to other architecture patterns.

- It presents a clear separation of responsibilities; each component has clearly defined responsibilities.

- It allows you to develop simple applications in a short time.

Disadvantages of the MVC Pattern

The main disadvantage of the MVC pattern is located in the Controller for several reasons:

- The Controller is very coupled to the View and the Model, so it is not very reusable.

- The Controller derives from the UIViewController class, where the View is closely tied to the Controller. This means that the separation of responsibilities is usually lost, giving rise to a scheme such as the following (Figure 2-3).

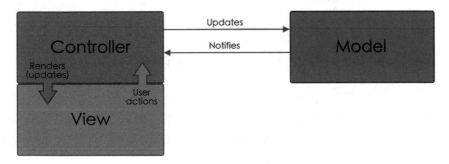

Figure 2-3. *Coupling between View and Controller*

Having this coupling between View and Controller, it becomes more complicated to test the Controller independently without the intervention of the View.

- There is a great tendency to "overload" the Controller, adding a series of responsibilities that do not correspond to it, such as part of the business logic, the delegates and the data sources of tables and collections, navigation, etc. This results in what is known as a "Massive View Controller."

To solve this problem, we can take some actions, such as moving the view code to other classes, separating the navigation between view controllers to a coordinator, or passing the *UITableViewControllers* or *UICollectionView* delegates and data sources out of the view controllers.

MVC Application

Once we have seen the characteristics of the MVC architecture, we are going to apply it in the development of our application.

Note   The entire project can be downloaded from the repository of this book. During the explanation of the implementation of the MVC architecture in our project, we will only show the most relevant parts of the code.

MVC Layers

To continue with the logic of the applied architecture pattern (Model–View–Controller), we will create a folder structure that simulates the layers of this architecture (Figure 2-4).

Figure 2-4. *MVC project folder structure*

Model

In this folder, we will have everything related to business logic, data access and manipulation, extensions, constants, etc. In addition, we can create subfolders to group files with similar functions (Figure 2-5): Core Data, Extensions, Services, etc.

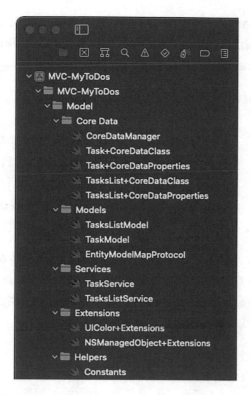

Figure 2-5. *Model layer files*

We have seen in the MVC model schema that the Model notifies the Controller (using the Observer design pattern).

In this way, the Controller should subscribe to the changes that occur in the model.

As the changes that occur in the model are basically those of adding, updating, or deleting data in the database, what we will do is use Core Data's own capabilities to be informed of the changes. Core Data is capable of issuing notifications based on the changes produced.

In our case, what we want to know is when a change occurs in the database, either by adding a new object, deleting it, or updating it, so we will use the following notification:

```
NSManagedObjectContextObjectsDidChangeNotification
```

To do this, we will simply have to add an observer for this notification in the *viewDidLoad* method of the controller that we want to be aware of the changes produced in the model:

```
NotificationCenter.default.addObserver(self,
                            selector:
                            #selector(methodToExecute),
                            name: NSNotification.Name.
                            NSManagedObjectContext
                            ObjectsDidChange,
                            object: context)
```

NSNotification.Name.NSManagedObjectContextObjectsDidChange is the name of the notification the controller subscribes to, *context* is the object we're looking at, and *methodToExecute* is the method to run when a change is detected, for example:

```
@objc func methodToExecute() {
    view.updateView()
}
```

Core Data

In this folder, we will have the `CoreDataManager.swift` file (which we created in Chapter 1), along with the four files created by Xcode automatically for the database entities.

Models

Here we have the models into which we can transform the database entities. In addition, we will create a protocol that the models must comply with, to transform from model to entity and vice versa (Listing 2-1).

Listing 2-1. EntityModelMapProtocol code

```
protocol EntityModelMapProtocol {
    associatedtype EntityType: NSManagedObject
    func mapToEntityInContext(_ context:
    NSManagedObjectContext) -> EntityType
    static func mapFromEntity(_ entity: EntityType) -> Self
}
```

In our application, we will define two models (*TaskModel* and *TasksListModel*), one for each entity in the database.

Each of these models will also conform to the *EntityModelMapProtocol* protocol so that we can go from model to entity (*NSManagedObject subclass*) and vice versa (Listing 2-2 and Listing 2-3).

Listing 2-2. TasksListModel.swift file content

```
struct TasksListModel {
    var id: String!
    var title: String!
    var icon: String!
    var tasks: [TaskModel]!
    var createdAt: Date!
}
```

Listing 2-3. TaskModel.swift file content

```
struct TaskModel {
    var id: String!
    var title: String!
    var icon: String!
    var done: Bool!
    var createdAt: Date!
}
```

Services

Here we will have the classes that allow us to send information to the database (create, update, or delete it) or retrieve information from the database and transform it into models.

In the case of the class that will manage the task lists, we will find the necessary methods to add, retrieve, or delete task lists. We will define these methods in the *TasksListServiceProtocol* protocol that we will then implement in the *TasksListService* class (Listing 2-4).

Listing 2-4. TasksListServiceProtocol and TasksListService structure and methods

```
protocol TasksListServiceProtocol: AnyObject {
    init(coreDataManager: CoreDataManager)
    func saveTasksList(_ list: TasksListModel)
    func fetchLists() -> [TasksListModel]
    func fetchListWithId(_ id: String) -> TasksListModel?
    func deleteList(_ list: TasksListModel)
}

class TasksListService: TasksListServiceProtocol {

    let context: NSManagedObjectContext
    let coreDataManager: CoreDataManager

    required init(coreDataManager: CoreDataManager =
    CoreDataManager.shared) {
        self.context = coreDataManager.mainContext
        self.coreDataManager = coreDataManager
    }
    func saveTasksList(_ list: TasksListModel) {
        _ = list.mapToEntityInContext(context)
        coreDataManager.saveContext(context)
    }
```

```swift
func fetchLists() -> [TasksListModel] {
    var lists = [TasksListModel]()
    do {
        let fetchRequest: NSFetchRequest<TasksList> =
        TasksList.fetchRequest()
        let value = try context.fetch(fetchRequest)
        lists = value.map({ TasksListModel.
        mapFromEntity($0) })
        lists = lists.sorted(by: { $0.createdAt.compare($1.
        createdAt) == .orderedDescending })
    } catch {
        debugPrint("CoreData Error")
    }

    return lists
}

func fetchListWithId(_ id: String) -> TasksListModel? {
    do {
        let fetchRequest: NSFetchRequest<TasksList> =
        TasksList.fetchRequest()
        fetchRequest.predicate = NSPredicate(format: "id =
        %@", id)
        let listEntities = try context.fetch(fetchRequest)
        guard let list = listEntities.first else {
            return nil
        }
        return TasksListModel.mapFromEntity(list)
    } catch {
        debugPrint("CoreData Error")
        return nil
    }
}
```

```
func deleteList(_ list: TasksListModel) {
    do {
        let fetchRequest: NSFetchRequest<TasksList> =
        TasksList.fetchRequest()
        fetchRequest.predicate = NSPredicate(format:
        "id = %@", list.id)
        let listEntities = try context.fetch(fetchRequest)
        for listEntity in listEntities {
            context.delete(listEntity)
        }
        coreDataManager.saveContext(context)
    } catch {
        debugPrint("CoreData Error")
    }
}
}
```

In the case of the class that will manage the tasks, *TaskService*, we will find the necessary methods to add, retrieve, update, or delete tasks (Listing 2-5). In this case, as in the previous ones, we will define the methods to be implemented in a protocol.

Listing 2-5. TaskServiceProtocol and TaskService structure and methods

```
protocol TaskServiceProtocol: AnyObject {
    init(coreDataManager: CoreDataManager)
    func saveTask(_ task: TaskModel, in taskList:
    TasksListModel)
    func fetchTasksForList(_ taskList: TasksListModel) ->
    [TaskModel]
    func updateTask(_ task: TaskModel)
    func deleteTask(_ task: TaskModel)
}
```

```swift
class TaskService: TaskServiceProtocol {

    let context: NSManagedObjectContext
    let coreDataManager: CoreDataManager

    required init(coreDataManager: CoreDataManager =
    CoreDataManager.shared) {
        self.context = coreDataManager.mainContext
        self.coreDataManager = coreDataManager
    }

    func saveTask(_ task: TaskModel, in taskList:
    TasksListModel) {
        do {
            let fetchRequest: NSFetchRequest<TasksList> =
            TasksList.fetchRequest()
            fetchRequest.predicate = NSPredicate(format:
            "id = %@", taskList.id)
            guard let list  = try context.fetch(fetchRequest).
            first else {
                return
            }

            let taskEntity = task.mapToEntityInContext(context)
            list.addToTasks(taskEntity)
            coreDataManager.saveContext(context)
        } catch {
            debugPrint("CoreData Error")
        }
    }
}
```

```swift
func fetchTasksForList(_ taskList: TasksListModel) ->
[TaskModel] {
    var tasks = [TaskModel]()
    do {
        let fetchRequest: NSFetchRequest<TasksList> =
        TasksList.fetchRequest()
        fetchRequest.predicate = NSPredicate(format: "id =
        %@", taskList.id)
        guard let list  = try context.
        fetch(fetchRequest).first,
            let taskEntities = list.tasks else {
            return tasks
        }

        tasks = taskEntities.map({ TaskModel.
        mapFromEntity($0 as! Task) })
    } catch {
        debugPrint("CoreData Error")
    }

    return tasks
}

func updateTask(_ task: TaskModel) {
    do {
        let fetchRequest: NSFetchRequest<Task> = Task.
        fetchRequest()
        fetchRequest.predicate = NSPredicate(format:
        "id = %@", task.id)
        guard let taskEntity = try context.
        fetch(fetchRequest).first else {
            return
        }
```

```
        taskEntity.done = task.done
        coreDataManager.saveContext(context)
    } catch {
        debugPrint("CoreData Error")
    }
}

func deleteTask(_ task: TaskModel) {
    do {
        let fetchRequest: NSFetchRequest<Task> = Task.
        fetchRequest()
        fetchRequest.predicate = NSPredicate(format: "id =
        %@", task.id)
        let taskEntities = try context.fetch(fetchRequest)
        for taskEntity in taskEntities {
            context.delete(taskEntity)
        }
        coreDataManager.saveContext(context)
    } catch {
        debugPrint("CoreData Error")
    }
}
}
```

Extensions

In this case, we have created a *UIColor* extension to be able to easily access the colors created especially for this application, which are found in the *Assets* file.

We will also add an extension to the *NSManagedObject* class that will prevent us from conflicting with the contexts when we do the testing part.

Constants

They contain the constant parameters that we will use in the application. In this case, it is a list with the names of the icons that the user can choose when creating tasks and task lists.

View

This layer contains all those elements that the user can see and that make up the graphical interface and those with which the user can interact (Figure 2-6).

These views can be simple, like a button or a label, or complex like the entire view of a page that contains buttons, labels, images, etc.

In the case of simple views, they are usually graphic elements that are reused throughout the application, such as a button, for example.

The most complex views are formed by the composition of simpler views. Since we are not working with *storyboards* or *xib* files, we will define the characteristics of each component, such as its position or size, using constraints.

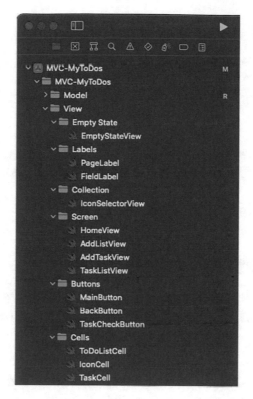

Figure 2-6. *View layer files*

Controller

The controllers (subclasses of *UIViewController*) are the main part of the application and the ones in charge of connecting the model with the view. Each of the screens in our application is a view controller (Figure 2-7).

Figure 2-7.   Controller layer files

MyToDos Application Screens

In Chapter 1, we described how the application that we would use to implement each of the architecture patterns that we will work on in this book would be.

As you may remember, this application has four screens, each one represented by a *UIViewController*, which will be related to the view and the model, managing the passage of information from one to the other.

Information Flow

But how will we pass this information?

The controller is the central part of the MVC model, and it will be the one that contains references (instances) to the view and the model. Therefore, the controller will be able to pass information by directly calling public methods of both the view and the model.

For example, if we have an instance of the *TasksListService* class (model) in our controller, we can retrieve the task lists by calling its *fetchList* method:

```
let tasksLists = tasksListService.fetchLists()
```

And then pass this information to the view:

```
let view = HomeView()
view.setLists(taskLists)
```

Delegate Pattern

And, the user interactions in the view, how do we pass them to the controller?

Since the view doesn't have a controller instance to call its methods, we can do that by using the *Delegate pattern.*

This design pattern allows a class to delegate some of its responsibilities to an instance of another class. In our case, the behavior against user interactions in the view will be implemented by the controller.

How to Implement Delegate Pattern

To implement the *Delegate pattern,* first, we create a protocol that will contain the methods we want to delegate. For example, let's create an example protocol with two methods:

```
protocol ExampleDelegate: AnyObject {
    func methodA()
    func methodB(value: String)
}
```

The next step is to create a property of the type of the protocol that we have created, which we will call *delegate*, in the class that delegates (which in our case would be the view):

```
class ExampleView {

    ...

    weak var delegate: ExampleDelegate?

    ...

}
```

Now, depending on what happens in the view (pressing a button, writing in a text field, etc.), we can call the different methods of the protocol:

```
delegate?.methodA()
delegate?.methodB(value: "Input text")
```

Now, in the controller, so that it can implement the protocol methods, we must configure the delegate property of the *exampleView* instance to "*self*," indicating that it will be the controller that implements the protocol methods:

```
class ExampleViewController {

    ...

    exampleView.delegate = self

    ...

}
```

And, finally, we have to make the controller adopt the protocol and its methods (we can do this in an extension to improve code readability):

```
extension ExampleViewController: ExampleDelegate {

    func methodA() { ... }

    func methodB(value: String) { ... }

}
```

Now we are going to see how to implement all this in the development of our application. At the beginning of each screen, we will show a diagram of how the different components (the main ones) communicate with each other.

AppDelegate and SceneDelegate

Since the release of iOS 13, some of the responsibilities that the *AppDelegate* had in previous versions were transferred to the *SceneDelegate*. Thus, now, while the *AppDelegate* is in charge of the life cycle of the application and its setup, the *SceneDelegate* is responsible for what is displayed on the screen and how it is displayed.

In the example application that we are going to develop, we will not modify the *AppDelegate* that Xcode generates when creating the application. What we will do is modify the *SceneDelegate*, specifically the *scene(_:willConnectTo:options:)* method, which is the first one called in the *UISceneSession* life cycle (Listing 2-6).

Listing 2-6. Modification in the SceneDelegate to call HomeViewController

```
func scene(_ scene: UIScene, willConnectTo session:
UISceneSession, options connectionOptions: UIScene.
ConnectionOptions) {

    if let windowScene = scene as? UIWindowScene {
        let window = UIWindow(windowScene: windowScene)
        let navigationController = UINavigationController(root
        ViewController: HomeViewController(tasksListService:
        TasksListService(), taskService: TaskService()))
        navigationController.interactivePopGestureRecognizer?.
        isEnabled = false
        window.backgroundColor = .white
```

```
window.rootViewController = navigationController
self.window = window
window.makeKeyAndVisible()
    }
}
```

As you can see, what we do in this method is create a new
UIWindow, we set the application's root view controller (which is a
UINavigationController component, whose first controller will be the
HomeViewController class), and finally, we make the window we have
created be the key window that should be displayed.

Home Screen

On the Home screen, the main component is the *HomeViewController*
class and we can see how it communicates with the rest of the components
in Figure 2-8.

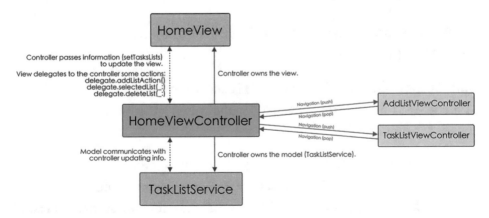

Figure 2-8. Home screen components communication schema

HomeViewController

The Controller (*HomeViewController*) is the core of the MVC model
and must have references to both the view (*HomeView*) and the model
(*TasksListServiceProtocol* and *TaskServiceProtocol*), as seen in Listing 2-7.

The fact of passing instances of the classes that we need in the
initializer (this is what is known as *dependency injection*) allows us a
greater decoupling of the components and facilitates the implementation
of unit tests (using, for example, mock objects).

Listing 2-7. HomeViewController initialization

```
class HomeViewController: UIViewController {

    private var homeView = HomeView()
    private var tasksListService: TasksListServiceProtocol!
    private var taskService: TaskServiceProtocol!

    init(tasksListService: TasksListServiceProtocol,
         taskService: TaskServiceProtocol) {
        super.init(nibName: nil, bundle: nil)
        self.tasksListService = tasksListService
        self.taskService = taskService
    }
    ...
}
```

As we have seen for the MVC architecture, the Controller will pass the
information to the View for display. We do this with the *fetchTasksLists*
method, whose function is to retrieve the information from the database
and pass it to the view (Listing 2-8).

Listing 2-8. The *fetchTasksLists* method calls the Model to fetch the lists and then passes them to the View

```
func fetchTasksLists() {
    let lists = tasksListService.fetchLists()
    homeView.setTasksLists(lists)
}
```

On the other hand, the Controller will receive user interactions (through the *Delegate pattern*) and act accordingly.

These interactions are as follows:

- Access a tasks list.

- Add a tasks list.

- Delete a tasks list.

To do this, we first define a protocol with the methods related to these interactions (Listing 2-9).

Listing 2-9. HomeViewDelegate protocol

```
protocol HomeViewDelegate: AnyObject {
    func addListAction()
    func selectedList(_ list: TasksListModel)
    func deleteList(_ list: TasksListModel)
}
```

And then, we make the *HomeViewController* adopt this protocol and implement its methods (Listing 2-10).

Listing 2-10. HomeViewController extension that implements the HomeViewDelegate protocol methods

```
extension HomeViewController: HomeViewDelegate {

    func addListAction() {
        let addListViewController = AddListViewController
        (tasksListModel: list, taskService: taskService,
        tasksListService: tasksListService)
        navigationController?.pushViewController(addListView
        Controller, animated: true)
    }

    func selectedList(_ list: TasksListModel) {
        let taskViewController = TaskListViewController(tasks
        ListModel: list)
                        navigationController?.pushViewController
                        (taskViewController, animated: true)
    }

    func deleteList(_ list: TasksListModel) {
        tasksListService.deleteList(list)
    }
}
```

The *addListAction* method is executed when the user clicks the "*Add list*" button and navigates the application to the *AddListViewController* screen.

The *selectedList* method navigates the application to the *TaskListViewController* screen (passing it the selected list information).

Finally, the *deleteList* method is in charge of communicating to the model that it must delete the selected list from the database and then reloads the view.

In addition, we have to implement the observation of the model to know when task lists are added or deleted and thus update the view (Listing 2-11).

Listing 2-11. Model observer implementation

```
override func viewDidLoad() {
    super.viewDidLoad()
    NotificationCenter.default.addObserver(self,
                                    selector: #selector
                                    (contextObjects
                                    DidChange),
                                    name: NSNotification.
                                    Name.NSManagedObject
                                    ContextObjects
                                    DidChange,
                                    object: CoreDataManager.
                                    shared.mainContext)
}

@objc func contextObjectsDidChange() {
    fetchTasksLists()
}
```

HomeView

Basically, the *HomeView* is made up of a *UITableView* element (to display the information) and a *UIButton* element (to be able to add a new list). We have seen how the Controller will pass the information that the View should display through the *setTasksList* method of the View (Listing 2-12).

Listing 2-12. Upon receiving the information from
HomeViewController, the HomeView is updated with the new data

```
func setTasksLists(_ lists: [TasksListModel]) {
    tasksList = lists
    tableView.reloadData()
    emptyState.isHidden = tasksList.count > 0
}
```

What we do in this function is take the "lists" parameter and assign it
to the *taskList* variable of our class (which is the one we will use to fill the
table), reload the table, and hide or show an "*Empty state*" depending on
whether or not the list contains values.

On the other hand, the View will also need to pass user interactions to
the controller via delegation.

We will do this by adding a delegate property of the type
HomeViewDelegate to the top of our *HomeView*:

```
class HomeView: UIView {

    ...
    weak var delegate: HomeViewDelegate?
    ...
}
```

Also, in the *HomeViewController*, we must configure the delegate
property of the *HomeView* instance to "*self*," indicating that it will be the
HomeViewController that implements the protocol methods (Listing 2-13).

Listing 2-13. Setting HomeView delegate on HomeViewController

```
class HomeViewController: UIViewController {
    ...
    override func loadView() {
        super.loadView()
```

```
        setupHomeView()
    }

    private func setupHomeView() {
        homeView.delegate = self
        self.view = homeView
    }

    ...
}
```

Once the delegate is defined, we can use it to implement it in our code and call each of the protocol functions.

Thus, the *addListAction* method will be called from the function associated with the add list button (Listing 2-14).

Listing 2-14. Configure the addListButton target

```
extension HomeView {
    ...

    func configureAddListButton() {
        addListButton.addTarget(self, action:
        #selector(addListAction), for: .touchUpInside)
        ...
    }

    @objc func addListAction() {
        delegate?.addListAction()
    }
    ...
}
```

The *selectList* method will be called when the user selects a cell in the table (Listing 2-15).

Listing 2-15. HomeView delegates the *selectedList* method implementation to the HomeViewController

```
func tableView(_ tableView: UITableView, didSelectRowAt
indexPath: IndexPath) {
    delegate?.selectedList(tasksList[indexPath.row])
}
```

And the method *deleteList* will be called on swipe a cell (Listing 2-16).

Listing 2-16. On swipe a cell, the delete method is called (removing cell from the table, and delegating the deletion from the Model to the HomeViewController)

```
func tableView(_ tableView: UITableView, commit editingStyle:
UITableViewCell.EditingStyle, forRowAt indexPath: IndexPath) {
    if editingStyle == .delete {
        let list = tasksList[indexPath.row]
        tasksList.remove(at: indexPath.row)
        tableView.deleteRows(at: [indexPath], with: .automatic)
        delegate?.deleteList(list)
    }
}
```

Add List Screen

This screen is responsible for adding task lists and the communication between its components is shown in Figure 2-9.

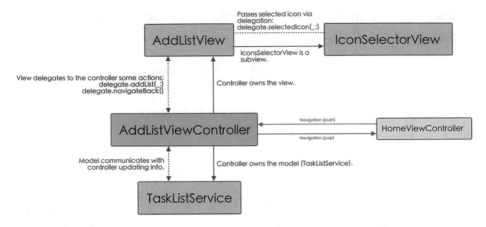

Figure 2-9. *Add list screen components communication schema*

AddListViewController

In the *AddListViewController* (the screen where we can add task lists),
we have a reference to the View (*AddListView*) and another to the Model
(TasksListService); although in this case, we will not pass information
from the Controller to the View, we will only receive user interactions via
delegation (Listing 2-17).

Listing 2-17. AddListViewController implementation

```
class AddListViewController: UIViewController {

    private var tasksListService: TasksListService!

    init(tasksListService: TasksListService) {
        super.init(nibName: nil, bundle: nil)
        self.tasksListService = tasksListService
    }

    ...
```

```swift
    private func setupAddListView() {
        addListView.delegate = self
        self.view = addListView
    }

    private func backToHome() {
        navigationController?.popViewController(animated: true)
    }
}

extension AddListViewController: AddListViewDelegate {
    func addList(_ list: TasksListModel) {
        tasksListService.saveTasksList(list)
        backToHome()
    }
}

extension AddListViewController: BackButtonDelegate {
    func navigateBack() {
        backToHome()
    }
}
```

As you can see, we have set a single delegate parameter on the *AddListView* class, but the *AddListViewController* is adopting two protocols: *AddListViewDelegate* and *BackButtonDelegate*. This is because, as we will now see, we can set multiple types for the delegate.

AddListView

AddListView contains a *UITextField* element to enter the name of the task list, a *UICollectionView* element to choose an icon for the list, a button to create the list, and another button to return to the *Home* screen.

In this view, we can see both sides of the Delegate pattern at the same time.

On the one hand, it delegates the implementation of a series of methods to the controller that references it.

Thus, *AddListView* delegates to *AddListViewController* the implementation of the methods referring to the *BackButtonDelegate* and *AddListViewDelegate* protocols (Listing 2-18).

Listing 2-18. BackButtonDelegate and AddListViewDelegate implementation

```
protocol BackButtonDelegate: AnyObject {
    func navigateBack()
}

protocol AddListViewDelegate: AnyObject {
    func addList(_ list: TasksListModel)
}
```

The first serves to indicate that the user has selected the button to navigate back without having created any list. The second allows us to pass the data of the created list to the Controller (which will be in charge of asking the Model to save it in the database).

Since we want to implement all these protocols in our controller, in the View we can create a delegate that conforms to all of them (in case we don't want to implement any of them, we should create independent delegates with different names):

```
weak var delegate: (AddListViewDelegate & BackButtonDelegate)?
```

Now we can call the different methods via the delegate (Listing 2-19).

Listing 2-19. Calling methods on AddListViewController via delegate

```
@objc func backAction() {
    delegate?.navigateBack()
}

@objc func addListAction() {
    guard titleTextfield.hasText else { return }

    listModel.title = titleTextfield.text
    listModel.id = ProcessInfo().globallyUniqueString
    listModel.icon = listModel.icon ?? "checkmark.seal.fill"
    listModel.createdAt = Date()
    delegate?.addList(listModel)
}
```

But *AddListView* not only delegates the implementation of methods but also implements others. Thus, the icon selector of icons that we have incorporated in this view, *IconSelectorView*, introduces the *IconSelectorViewDelegate* protocol.

This protocol makes us implement the method that returns the icon selected by the user (Listing 2-20).

Listing 2-20. IconSelectorViewDelegate implementation

```
protocol IconSelectorViewDelegate: AnyObject {
    func selectedIcon(_ icon: String)
}

func configureCollectionView() {
    ...
    iconSelectorView.delegate = self
    ...
}
```

```
extension AddListView: IconSelectorViewDelegate {

    func selectedIcon(_ icon: String) {
        listModel.icon = icon
    }
}
```

Tasks List Screen

This screen is responsible for displaying the tasks that make up a list, marking them as done, deleting them, and adding new ones. The communication between its components is shown in Figure 2-10.

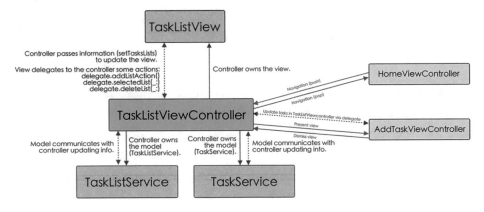

Figure 2-10. *Tasks list screen components communication schema*

TaskListViewController

The *TaskListViewController*, which controls the screen in which we are shown the tasks that make up a list, has a reference to the view (*TaskListView*) and the model (*TaskServiceProtocol* and *TasksListServiceProtocol*).

Also, as this screen will show the tasks that make up a list, when we start it by calling it from the *HomeViewController*, we will have to pass it an object with the list we want to show (*TaskListModel*), as shown in Listing 2-21.

Listing 2-21. TaskListViewController initialization

```
class TaskListViewController: UIViewController {

    private var taskListView = TaskListView()
    private var tasksListModel: TasksListModel!
    private var taskService: TaskServiceProtocol!
    private var tasksListService: TasksListServiceProtocol!

    init(tasksListModel: TasksListModel,
        taskService: TaskServiceProtocol,
        tasksListService: TasksListServiceProtocol) {
        super.init(nibName: nil, bundle: nil)
        self.tasksListModel = tasksListModel
        self.taskService = taskService
        self.tasksListService = tasksListService
    }   ...
}
```

As the view is the one that shows the tasks, we have to pass our object of type *TaskListModel* and also establish the delegate of the view to be able to receive the interactions of the user (along with the methods associated with the delegate protocols: *TaskListViewDelegate* and *BackButtonDelegate*), as shown in Listing 2-22.

Listing 2-22. TaskListViewController implementation

```
class TaskListViewController: UIViewController {
    ...
    override func loadView() {
        super.loadView()
        navigationController?.navigationBar.isHidden = true
        setupTaskListView()
    }
```

81

```
    override func viewDidLoad() {
        super.viewDidLoad()
        NotificationCenter.default.addObserver(self,
                            selector: #selector(contextObjects
                            DidChange),
                            name: NSNotification.Name.
                            NSManagedObjectContextObjectsDid
                            Change,
                            object: CoreDataManager.shared.
                            mainContext)
        taskListView.setTasksList(tasksListModel)
    }

    private func setupTaskListView() {
        taskListView.delegate = self
        self.view = taskListView
    }

    private func updateTasksList() {
        guard let list = tasksListService.
        fetchListWithId(tasksListModel.id) else { return }
        tasksListModel = list
        taskListView.setTasksList(tasksListModel)
    }

    @objc func contextObjectsDidChange() {
        updateTasksList()
    }
}

extension TaskListViewController: TaskListViewDelegate {

    func addTaskAction() {
        let addTaskViewController = AddTaskViewController(tasks
        ListModel: tasksListModel, taskService: taskService)
```

```
    addTaskViewController.modalPresentationStyle =
    .pageSheet
    present(addTaskViewController, animated: true)
}

func updateTask(_ task: TaskModel) {
    taskService.updateTask(task)
}

func deleteTask(_ task: TaskModel) {
    taskService.deleteTask(task)
}
}

extension TaskListViewController: BackButtonDelegate {
    func navigateBack() {
        navigationController?.popViewController(animated: true)
    }
}
```

If you notice, in the *addTaskAction* function, which is executed when we select the "*Add Task*" button, we show as a modal the screen of creating a new task.

TaskListView

This view will show us the tasks that make up a list, which, as we have just seen, we pass from the controller with the *setTasksLists* method (Listing 2-23).

Listing 2-23. Upon receiving the information from
TaskListViewController, the TaskListView is updated with the
new data

```
func setTasksLists(_ tasksList: TasksListModel) {
    tasks = tasksList.tasks.sorted(by: { $0.createdAt.
    compare($1.createdAt) == .orderedDescending })
    pageTitle.setTitle(tasksList.title)
    tableView.reloadData()
    emptyState.isHidden = tasks.count > 0
}
```

This View contains as user interaction elements a *UITableView*
element that shows the tasks in the list and two buttons: the one to go back
(to the Home screen) and the "*Add Task*" button (Listing 2-24).

As we have seen in previous cases, the actions on these elements are
delegated to the controller.

Listing 2-24. TaskListView implementation

```
class TaskListView: UIView {
...
    weak var delegate: (TaskListViewDelegate &
    BackButtonDelegate)?
...
}

private extension TaskListView {
...
    @objc func backAction() {
        delegate?.navigateBack()
    }
    ...
    @objc func addTaskAction() {
```

```swift
        delegate?.addTaskAction()
    }
}

TaskListView extension: UITableViewDelegate,
UITableViewDataSource {
    ...
    func tableView(_ tableView: UITableView, cellForRowAt
    indexPath: IndexPath) -> UITableViewCell {
        let cell = tableView.dequeueReusableCell(withIdentifier:
        TaskCell.reuseId, for: indexPath) as! TaskCell
        cell.setParametersForTask(tasksList[indexPath.row])
        cell.delegate = self
        return cell
    }
...
    func tableView(_ tableView: UITableView, commit
    editingStyle: UITableViewCell.EditingStyle, forRowAt
    indexPath: IndexPath) {
        if editingStyle == .delete {
            let task = tasksList[indexPath.row]
            list.remove(at: indexPath.row tasks)
            tableView.deleteRows(at: [indexPath], with:
            .automatic)
            delegate?.deleteTask(task)
        }
    }
}

extension TaskListView: TaskCellDelegate {
    func updateTask(_ task: TaskModel) {
        delegate?.updateTask(task)
    }
}
```

But, as we can see in that code, the cells that are displayed in the table delegate (*TaskCellDelegate*) to it to implement the update of the cells when they are made to go to the Done state by pressing the circle to the right of each cell.

Since the fact of updating the database is called from the Controller, we will have to pass the update call of the tasks from this View (*TaskListView*) to the Controller (*TaskListViewController*).

Add Task Screen

This screen is responsible for adding tasks to a given list and the communication between its components is shown in Figure 2-11.

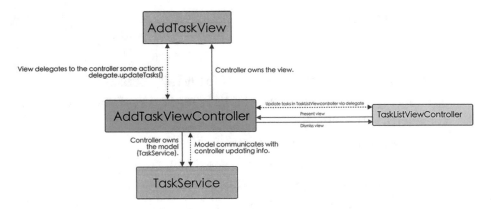

Figure 2-11. *Add task screen components communication schema*

AddTaskViewController

The last screen, controlled by *AddTaskViewController*, is the one that will allow us to add new tasks to a list. This Controller presents references to the View, *AddTaskView*, and the model. The information entered by the user in the View will reach the Controller (as in the previous cases) by delegation (Listing 2-25).

Listing 2-25. AddTaskViewController initialization

```
class AddTaskViewController: UIViewController {

    private var taskService: TaskServiceProtocol!

    init(tasksListModel: TasksListModel,
        taskService: TaskServiceProtocol) {
        super.init(nibName: nil, bundle: nil)
        self.tasksListModel = tasksListModel
        self.taskService = taskService
    }
    ...
    private func setupAddTaskView() {
        addTaskView.delegate = self
        self.view = addTaskView
    }
}

extension AddTaskViewController: AddTaskViewDelegate {
    func addTask(_ task: TaskModel) {
        taskService.saveTask(task, in: tasksListModel)
        dismiss(animated: true)
    }
}
```

AddTaskView

This View has a structure similar to the one we use to create task lists, with a *UITextField* element, an *IconSelectorView* element, and a *UIButton* element.

This View will both delegate task creation to the Controller via the protocol, as well as implement the method associated with the icon selector (Listing 2-26).

Listing 2-26. AddTaskViewDelegate and AddTaskView
implementation

```
protocol AddTaskViewDelegate: AnyObject {
    func addTask(_ task: TaskModel)
}

class AddTaskView: UIView {

    ...

    weak var delegate: AddTaskViewDelegate?

    ...

}

private extension AddTaskView {

    ...

    @objc func addTaskAction() {
        guard titleTextfield.hasText else { return }

        taskModel.title = titleTextfield.text
        taskModel.icon = taskModel.icon ?? "checkmark.
        seal.fill"
        taskModel.done = false
        taskModel.id = ProcessInfo().globallyUniqueString
        taskModel.createdAt = Date()
        delegate?.addTask(taskModel)
    }

    func configureCollectionView() {
        ...
        iconSelectorView.delegate = self
        ...
    }
}
```

```
extension AddTaskView: IconSelectorViewDelegate {

    func selectedIcon(_ icon: String) {
        taskModel.icon = icon
    }
}
```

Testing

In Chapter 1 we saw that one of the important points of a good architecture is that it is testable. Now we are going to write a few tests for the application that we have developed with the MVC architecture.

For this, we will use Apple's framework, XCTest, to write our tests. As an introduction to the development of tests, and that will serve us for the next chapters, what we will do is test the main functionalities, such as the services that work with the database, the user interactions, and the main navigation flows.

How Should the Tests Be?

In addition, when writing the tests, we have to take into account a series of criteria, known by the acronym FIRST:

- **Fast**: The tests must be fast.

- **Independent**: The tests must be independent of each other and not pass information so that they can be executed in any order.

- **Repeatable**: The result of the tests must be the same each time they are executed and in any environment.

- **Self-validating**: The tests must be self-validating, that is, whether they pass or fail must not depend on any external intervention (such as having to check a log).

- **Timely**: Tests should be written before the production code is written. This is what is known as *test-driven development.*

Let's Create the First Test

In Chapter 1, we saw how to create our application project and how to activate the "Include Tests" option when creating it. In this way, Xcode creates our test target, so that we only have to add our tests.

When initially creating our project, for the MVC architecture, with the name *MVC-MyToDos*, we will see that two folders have been created, *MVC-MyToDosTests* and *MVC-MyToDosUITests*, although we will only focus on the first one, which will be the one that contains the unit tests that we have mentioned before (Figure 2-12).

Figure 2-12. MVC-MyToDos test files

Now, let's create our first test. Suppose we first create the Home view, `HomeView.swift`. We select the *MVC-MyToDosTests* folder and add a new file. From the different file options, we choose the *"Unit Test Case Class"* and give it the name *HomeViewTest* (Figure 2-13 and Figure 2-14).

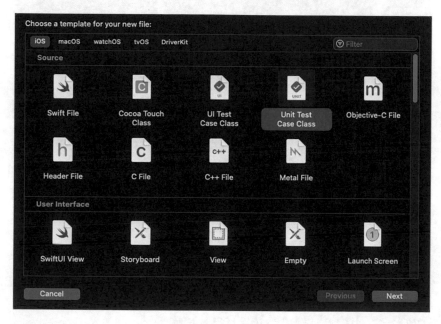

Figure 2-13. *Unit Test Case Class template selection*

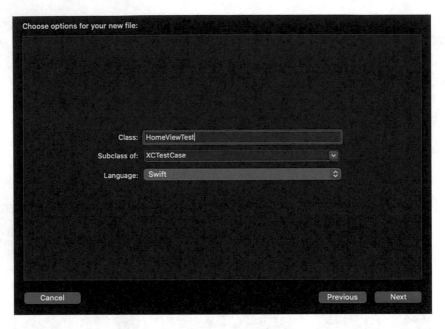

Figure 2-14. *HomeViewTest class creation*

Doing this, Xcode will create a file with some initial code (Listing 2-27).

Listing 2-27. Initial HomeViewTest code

```
import XCTest

class HomeViewTestd: XCTestCase {
    override func setUpWithError() throws {}
    override func tearDownWithError() throws {}
    func testExample() throws {}
    func testPerformanceExample() throws {}
}
```

In the *setUpWithError()* function, we will put the code that is executed before each test and in *tearDownWithError()*, the one that should be executed after each test.

The other two functions are examples, which tell us that all the tests we write (the functions) must start with the word "*test*."

Once we know this, we are going to write the first test (Listing 2-28).

Listing 2-28. Test code for checking HomeView components

```
import XCTest

@testable import MVC_MyToDos

class HomeViewTest: XCTestCase {

    var sut: HomeView!

    override func setUpWithError() throws {
        sut = HomeView()
    }

    func testViewLoaded_whenViewIsInstantiated_
    shouldBeComponents() {
        XCTAssertNotNil(sut.pageTitle)
        XCTAssertNotNil(sut.addListButton)
        XCTAssertNotNil(sut.tableView)
        XCTAssertNotNil(sut.emptyState)
    }
}
```

In order to test the *HomeView*, we must first make it visible to our *MVC_MyTodosTests* target. To do this, we have imported our project using the command:

```
@testable import MVC_MyToDos
```

The next step has been to create a variable of type *HomeView*:

```
var sut: HomeView!
```

The name of the parameter, *sut*, comes from "*system under test.*" By this, we mean which class we are testing.

Finally, we have created the test:

```
testViewLoaded_whenViewIsInstantiated_shouldBeComponents
```

For the Apple framework to detect that it is a test to run, the function must begin with the word "*test.*" Also, it is a good practice to define in the name of the function that you want to test (*ViewLoaded*), when (*whenViewIsInstantiated*), and what we should get as a result (*shouldBeComponents*).

When creating the different components of the HomeView, we have defined them as *private(set)*, which allows us to access them from outside the class to read them but not modify them (Figure 2-15).

```
     func testViewLoaded_whenViewIsInstantiated_shouldBeComponents() {
32       XCTAssertNotNil(sut.pageTitle)
33       XCTAssertNotNil(sut.addListButton)
34       XCTAssertNotNil(sut.tableView)
35       XCTAssertNotNil(sut.emptyState)
36   }
```

Figure 2-15. *First test passed*

In this case, we have used a type of *XCAssert* function, *XCTAssertNotNil*; what it does is to validate that what is inside the parentheses is not nil (different functions depend on what we want to test: *XCAssertEqual, XCAssertTrue*, etc.).

Helper Classes

To facilitate the testing of our code, it is necessary to create some classes that will help us.

The first of them, *InMemoryCoreDataManager*, has the same functionalities as the application's CoreDataManager file, but the database is generated in memory and does not persist when the tests are finished (Listing 2-29).

Listing 2-29. InMemoryCoreDataManager help class

```
class InMemoryCoreDataManager: CoreDataManager {
        override init() {
        super.init()

        let persistentStoreDescription =
        NSPersistentStoreDescription()
        persistentStoreDescription.type = NSInMemoryStoreType

        let container = NSPersistentContainer(name: "ToDoList")
        container.persistentStoreDescriptions =
        [persistentStoreDescription]
        container.loadPersistentStores { _, error in
            if let error = error as NSError? {
                fatalError("Unresolved error \(error), \(error.
                userInfo)")
            }
        }

        persistentContainer = container
    }
}
```

The second file, *MockNavigationController*, allows us to identify when navigation calls (push and pop) have been made in the application. This is achieved by making a *mock* of the *UINavigationController* class in which some variables are introduced that allow us to know if a push call or a pop call has occurred (Listing 2-30).

Listing 2-30. MockNavigationController to test navigation in app

```
class MockNavigationController: UINavigationController {
    var vcIsPushed: Bool = false
    var vcIsPopped: Bool = false

    override func pushViewController(_ viewController:
    UIViewController,
                                        animated: Bool) {
        super.pushViewController(viewController,
                                     animated: animated)
        vcIsPushed = true
    }

    override func popViewController(animated: Bool) ->
    UIViewController? {
        vcIsPopped = true
        return viewControllers.first
    }
}
```

MVC-MyToDos Testing

With all this in mind, we continue to develop our tests and code. We have a test file for each of the services (access to the database), two files per screen (for each controller and each view), and two more files that will help when performing the tests.

We are not going to show on these pages all the tests carried out for the *MVC-MyToDos* project since you can find them in its repository. However, we are going to show those that may be more relevant.

Note   From the pedagogical point of view when working with the different architectures of an application, we will first see how the code is structured, and then, with ease or difficulty from the point of view of its testing, it is recommended that in our day-to-day work as developers, we work with the TDD (test-driven development) methodology. This methodology is based on first writing the tests (generally unit tests), then writing the code that allows the tests to pass, and, finally, refactoring said code.[2]

TasksListServiceTest

This class contains the tests for the *TasksListService* class (we won't put the tests for the *TaskService* class because they are very similar), as shown in Listing 2-31.

Listing 2-31. TaskListServiceTest file code tests

```
class TasksListServiceTest: XCTestCase {
    var sut:TasksListServiceProtocol!
    var list: TasksListModel!

    override func setUpWithError() throws {
        sut = TasksListService(coreDataManager:
        InMemoryCoreDataManager())
        list = TasksListModel(id: "12345-67890",
                              title: "Test List",
                              icon: "test.icon",
                              tasks: [TaskModel](),
                              createdAt: Date())
    }
```

---

[2] *Test-Driven Development in Swift* (https://link.springer.com/book/10.1007/978-1-4842-7002-8)

```
override func tearDownWithError() throws { ... }

func testSaveOnDB_whenSavesAList_shouldBeOneOnDatabase() {
sut.saveTasksList(list)
XCTAssertEqual(sut.fetchLists().count, 1)
}

func testSaveOnDB_whenSavesAList_
shouldBeOneWithGivenIdOnDatabase() { ... }

func testDeleteOnDB_whenSavesAListAndThenDeleted_
shouldBeNoneOnDatabase() {
sut.saveTasksList(list)
XCTAssertNotNil(sut.fetchListWithId("12345-67890"))
sut.deleteList(list)
XCTAssertEqual(sut.fetchLists().count, 0)
}
}
```

In the test

testSaveOnDB_whenSavesAList_shouldBeOneOnDatabase

we first save a list to the database and then check that a list exists in the database (we use the *XCTAssertEqual* function to do this).

In the test

```
testDeleteOnDB_whenSavesAListAndThenDeleted_
shouldBeNoneOnDatabase
```

we first save a list to the database, check that the list exists, then delete it, and finally check that it no longer exists in the database. In this case, we have combined two *XCTAssert* functions (*XCTAssertNotNil* and *XCTAssertEqual*).

Mocking Services

To facilitate the testing of those classes that depend on access to the Model layer, we can use "mocks" of said model, which will allow us to simulate the behavior of real classes and, at the same time, more easily verify the results.

In our case, we will set two such classes to "impersonate" the services: *MockTaskListService* and *MockTaskService* (Listing 2-32 and Listing 2-33).

Listing 2-32. MockTaskListService code

```
class MockTaskListService: TasksListServiceProtocol {

    private var lists: [TasksListModel] = [TasksListModel]()

    required init(coreDataManager: CoreDataManager) {}

    convenience init(lists: [TasksListModel]) {
        self.init(coreDataManager: CoreDataManager.shared)
        self.lists = lists
    }

    override func saveTasksList(_ list: TasksListModel) {
        lists.append(list)
    }

    override func fetchLists() -> [TasksListModel] {
        return lists
    }

    override func fetchListWithId(_ id: String) ->
    TasksListModel? {
        return lists.filter({ $0.id == id }).first
    }

    override func deleteList(_ list: TasksListModel) {
```

99

```
        lists = lists.filter({ $0.id != list.id })
    }
}
```

Listing 2-33. MockTaskService code

```
class MockTaskService: TaskServiceProtocol {

    private var list: TasksListModel!

    required init(coreDataManager: CoreDataManager) {}

    convenience init(list: TasksListModel) {
        self.init(coreDataManager: CoreDataManager.shared)
        self.list = list
    }

    override func saveTask(_ task: TaskModel, in taskList:
    TasksListModel) {
        list = taskList
        list.tasks.append(task)
    }

    override func fetchTasksForList(_ taskList: TasksListModel)
    -> [TaskModel] {
        return list.tasks
    }

    override func updateTask(_ task: TaskModel) {
        guard let tasks = list.tasks else { return }
        var updatedTasks = [TaskModel]()
        tasks.forEach({
            var updatedTask = $0
            if $0.id == task.id {
                updatedTask.done.toggle()
            }
```

```
        updatedTasks.append(updatedTask)
    })
    list.tasks = updatedTasks
}

override func deleteTask(_ task: TaskModel) {
    list.tasks = list.tasks.filter({ $0.id != task.id })
}
}
```

As we can see, these classes override the methods of the original classes, but they work with the data that we pass to them and without accessing the database.

Controllers Testing

The Controllers are the heart of the MVC and are the ones that act as intermediaries between the View and the Model, apart from managing the navigation between screens. For this reason, the tests that we will carry out in the Controllers will be focused on the interaction with the Model and on the navigation from one screen to another.

For example, in the HomeViewControllerTest.swift file we have a test that allows us to verify that when the *deleteList* method is executed, the selected list of tasks will be deleted from the database (Listing 2-34).

Listing 2-34. HomeViewControllerTest code tests

```
class HomeViewControllerTest: XCTestCase {

    var sut: HomeViewController!
    var navigationController: MockNavigationController!
    var tasksListService: MockTaskListService!
    var taskService: MockTaskService!
    let list = TasksListModel(id: ProcessInfo().
    globallyUniqueString,
```

```
                            title: "Test title",
                            icon: "test.icon",
                            tasks: [TaskModel](),
                            createdAt: Date())

override func setUpWithError() throws {
    tasksListService = MockTaskListService(lists: [list])
    taskService = MockTaskService()
    sut = HomeViewController(tasksListService:
    tasksListService, taskService: taskService)
    navigationController = MockNavigationController(root
    ViewController: UIViewController())
    navigationController.pushViewController(sut,
    animated: false)
    navigationController.vcIsPushed = false
}

override func tearDownWithError() throws {
    sut = nil
    navigationController = nil
    taskService = nil
    super.tearDown()
}

func testDeleteList_whenDeletedActionIsCalled_
shouldBeNoneOnDatabase() {
    sut.deleteList(list)
    XCTAssertEqual(tasksListService.fetchLists().count, 0)
}

func testPushVC_whenAddListIsCalled_
thenPushAddListVCCalled() {
    sut.addListAction()
```

```
        XCTAssertTrue(navigationController.vcIsPushed)
    }

    func testPushVC_whenTaskListIsCalled_
    thenPushTaskListVCCalled() {
        sut.selectedList(TasksListModel())
        XCTAssertTrue(navigationController.vcIsPushed)
    }
}
```

Here, we can see how the fact of injecting the dependencies of the *MockTasksListService* and *MockTaskService* classes when initializing the controller allows us to use those "*mock*" classes with controlled results (which speeds up testing).

What we have done in the *testDeleteList_whenDeletedActionIsCalled_ shouldBeNoneOnDatabase* test is, first, create a list of tasks and save it in the database, and then execute the *deleteList* method and check that it has been deleted from the database.

In the *testPushVC_whenAddListIsCalled_thenPushAddListVCCalled,* what we do is execute the *addListAction* method and check that the *vcIsPushed* parameter is true, as we have defined in the *MockNavigationController.*

The rest of the controllers in the application have similar unit tests, as you can see in the project code.

Views Testing

In the Views, what we will test is that the different components display the correct information and that the user interactions produce the expected result.

For example, for the *HomeView* we have a button to go to the add tasks list screen. So, we will test that this button has the *addListAction* method as its target (Listing 2-35).

Listing 2-35. HomeView addListButton test code

```
func testButtonAction_whenAddListButtonIsTapped_
shouldBeCalledAddListAction() {
    let addListButton = sut.addListButton
    XCTAssertNotNil(addListButton, "UIButton does not exist")

    guard let addListButtonAction = addListButton.
    actions(forTarget: sut, forControlEvent:
    .touchUpInside) else {
        XCTFail("Not actions assigned for .touchUpInside")
            return
    }

    XCTAssertTrue(addListButtonAction.
    contains("addListAction"))
}
```

What we do in the test is, first, check that the button exists, then that it has an associated method, and that this is *addListAction*.

In the *HomeView* there is also a table that shows the lists of tasks created by the user. A table carries different methods, which we will have to test. Thus, for example, if in the *setUpWithError* method we have created a list in our database, we must verify that the list has a row, that this row shows a cell, or that, if we delete the list, the number of lists is not zero (Listing 2-36).

Listing 2-36. Tests for the UITableView methods

```
// UITableView has one row
func testTableView_whenModelHasAList_shouldBeOneRow() {
    XCTAssertEqual(sut.tableView.numberOfRows(inSection: 0), 1)
}
```

```
// UITableView at IndexPath(row: 0, section: 0) has a
UITableViewCell
func testTableView_whenModelHasAList_
shoulBeACellAtIndexPath() {
    let indexPath = IndexPath(row: 0, section: 0)
    let cell = sut.tableView.dataSource?.tableView(sut.
    tableView, cellForRowAt: indexPath)
    XCTAssertNotNil(cell)
}

// After TasksList object has been deleted, taksList contains 0
elements
func testTableView_whenListIsDeleted_shouldBeNoneOnModel() {
    let indexPath = IndexPath(row: 0, section: 0)
    sut.tableView.dataSource?.tableView?(sut.tableView, commit:
    .delete, forRowAt: indexPath)
    XCTAssertEqual(sut.tasksList.count, 0)
}
```

Summary

The Model–View–Controller architecture is perhaps the most used and the first one that is usually used when starting to develop applications since it is the simplest.

MVC has a clear separation of responsibilities (Model, View, and Controller), although many times the View is very tied to the Controller, which reduces its usability. This makes it more difficult to test the Controller without the View intervening.

On the other hand, you have to be careful not to overload the controller since, being the central part of the MVC, responsibilities are usually added to it as part of the business logic, navigation to other screens, the view itself, and its components.

In the example of the application that we have worked on, being a fairly simple application, the controllers are small but think about what could happen if we start adding additional functionality. For this reason, it is better to take some actions that help us reduce its size (some of which we have already applied):

- Move the View code to its own class, with a reference in the Controller itself.

- Pass everything related to the data to the model (such as obtaining and processing data, or its ordering).

- Manage navigation between screens through Coordinators.

From now on, we will see more elaborate architectures that seek to solve the problems that MVC may present, and in which some of the solutions that will be shown could be transferred to this architecture.

CHAPTER 3

MVP: Model–View–Presenter

What Is MVP?

A Little History

The Model–View–Presenter pattern derives from the Model–View–Controller pattern that we have seen in the previous chapter. It was developed in the early 1990s, at the software company Taligent (which was owned by Apple, IBM, and Hewlett-Packard).[1]

How It Works

The MVP pattern is made up of three components: Model, View, and Presenter, where the Presenter acts as an intermediary between the Model and the View (UIViewController + View), connected as shown in Figure 3-1.

---

[1] https://en.wikipedia.org/wiki/Model-view-presenter

© Raúl Ferrer García 2023
R. Ferrer García, *iOS Architecture Patterns*, https://doi.org/10.1007/978-1-4842-9069-9_3

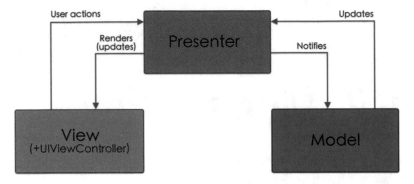

Figure 3-1. *Model–View–Presenter schema*

Components in MVP

We are now going to see in more detail the characteristics of these three components in the MVP pattern.

Model

In the same way as in the MVC pattern, the Model is the component (or components) in charge of the business logic and of storing, manipulating, and accessing the application data:

- It contains classes related to data persistence.

- It contains the classes that control the communications of the application.

- It is responsible for transforming the information it receives from the outside into model objects.

- It contains extensions, constants…

- In MVP, the Model layer can only communicate with the Presenter layer (i.e., the Model is unaware of the existence of a View).

So, for example, when the user interacts with the
View, this interaction is transmitted to the Model
through the Presenter. In the same way, if the Model
is updated and the View needs to be updated, the
Presenter will be in charge of updating it.

View

In the MVP model, the View layer contains both the View (*UIView*) and
the Controller (*UIViewController*) components, unlike the MVC pattern,
where we put them on different layers.

Also, in the MVP pattern, both the View and the Controller store much
less logic than in the MVC model, which makes them lighter.

Now, the Controller only has coordination/routing functions, handling
navigation between screens and, if necessary, passing information via a
Delegation pattern.

In MVP, the Controller is in charge of instantiating the View and
passing it to the Presenter (Listing 3-1).

Listing 3-1. Presenter and View instantiation; passing View to the
Presenter

```
class ExampleController: UIViewController {

    private var exampleView = ExampleView()
    ...
    override func loadView() {
        super.loadView()
        setupExampleView()
    }

    private func setupExampleView() {
```

```
    let presenter = ExamplePresenter(exampleView:
    ExampleView)
    exampleView.presenter = presenter
    exampleView.setupView()
    self.view = exampleView
  }
}
```

Presenter

The Presenter is in charge of receiving the events that occur in the View and passing them to the Model. On the other hand, the Presenter is also in charge of updating the View when the data changes.

For further decoupling, rather than passing the View to the Presenter, we will create a protocol with the methods that the Presenter will execute to update the View (Listing 3-2).

Listing 3-2. Passing View to the Presenter in the init method

```
protocol ExampleViewDelegate: AnyObject {
    func updateView()
}

class ExamplePresenter {

    private weak var exampleView: ExampleViewDelegate?

    init(exampleView: ExampleViewDelegate? = nil) {
        self.exampleView = exampleView
    }
    ...
}
```

110

Advantages and Disadvantages of the MVP

The MVP model is somewhat more complex than the MVC model as a new element comes into play, the Presenter, and therefore requires a little more experience.

In the following, you can see what are the most important advantages and disadvantages of this architecture.

Advantages

The main advantages of the MVP architecture are as follows:

- Although it is somewhat more complex than MVC, it derives from it, so in a short time we can get used to working with it.

- It presents a better separation of responsibilities than the MVC pattern.

- Business logic can be tested better.

Disadvantages

The main disadvantages are as follows:

- Being more complex than MVC, it is not usually recommended for use in small and simple applications.

- Although we have further modularized the architecture, there are still some issues, such as the fact that the Controller still handles navigation between screens. This can be solved by introducing a Router or Coordinator to take care of that task.

- In the same way that in the MVC the Controller could become a massive component, in the MVP the same can happen with the Presenter.

111

MVP Application

Once we have seen the characteristics of the MVP architecture, we are going to apply it in the development of our application.

Note   The entire project can be downloaded from the repository of this book. During the explanation of the implementation of the MVP architecture in our project, we will only show the most relevant parts of the code.

MVP Layers

To continue with the logic of the applied architecture pattern (Model–View–Presenter), we will create a folder structure that simulates its layers (Figure 3-2).

Figure 3-2. *MVP project folder structure*

Model

In the same way as in the MVC architecture, this folder contains everything related to business logic, data access, and its manipulation. It contains the same files as in the case of MVC (Figure 3-3).

Figure 3-3. *Model layer files*

However, while in the MVC architecture the changes produced in the model were notified to the Controller (using the Observe pattern), in the MVP architecture these changes are notified to the Presenter (i.e., the Presenter must be subscribed to these changes).

Unlike in the MVC architecture, where we added the observer in the Controller's *viewDidLoad* method, in the MVP architecture, we will add it in the Presenter's *init* method (Listing 3-3).

Listing 3-3. Setting the observer on Presenter initialization

```
init() {
    NotificationCenter.default.addObserver(self,
                    selector:
                    #selector(contextObjectsDidChange),
```

```
                          name: NSNotification.Name.
                          NSManagedObjectContextObjectsDidChange,
                          object: CoreDataManager.shared.
                          mainContext)
}

@objc func contextObjectsDidChange() {
    updateView()
}
```

Core Data

In this folder, we will have the CoreDataManager.swift file (which
we created in Chapter 1), along with the four files created by Xcode
automatically for the database entities.

Models

As described in Chapter 2, here we have the models into which we can
transform the database entities. In addition, we will create a protocol that the
models must comply with, to transform from model to entity and vice versa.

Services

Here we will have the classes that allow us to send information to the
database (create, update, or delete it) or retrieve information from the
database and transform it into models.

Extensions

In this case, we have created a *UIColor* extension to be able to easily access
the colors created especially for this application and an extension to the
NSManagedObject class that will prevent us from conflicting with the
contexts when we do the testing part.

Constants

They contain the constant parameters that we will use in the application.

View

In the View folder, we will not only have the View files and the components that form them (as in MVC), but also the Controller files (subclasses of *UIViewController*), as shown in Figure 3-4.

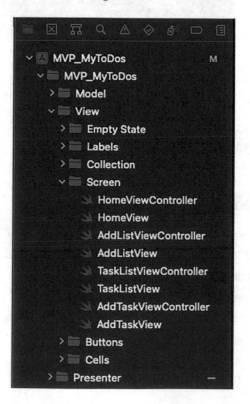

Figure 3-4. *View layer files*

Remember that in MVP, Controllers usually only have coordination/ routing functions (to navigate between screens) and, in some cases, pass information (via a Delegate pattern, for example).

Presenter

This folder only contains the Presenters, which, as we have seen, connect the Model to the View (Figure 3-5).

Figure 3-5. *Presenter layer files*

MyToDos Application Screens

As we have just commented, in the MVP architecture, unlike the MVC, it is the Presenter that is in charge of the business logic (leaving the navigation tasks to the Controller).

Next, we will see, for each of the different screens of our app, how we connect the different layers with each other: Model, View(+*UIViewController*), and Presenter.

AppDelegate and SceneDelegate

As we saw in Chapter 2, the *AppDelegate* and the *SceneDelegate* are in charge of managing the life cycle of the application and what is displayed and how it is displayed on the screen.

In our case, we will only modify the *SceneDelegate*, which will be in charge of creating a new *UIWindow*, configuring the root view controller of the application, and, finally, that the created *UIWindow* is the key window.

Unlike when we studied the MVC, in which we passed an instance of the *HomeViewController* to the *UINavigationController* component, which in its initialization required that the dependencies be passed to the *TasksListService* and *TaskService* services, now the *HomeViewController* does not require them, since as we will see in a moment, these dependencies will be held by the *HomePresenter* component.

```
func scene(_ scene: UIScene, willConnectTo session:
UISceneSession, options connectionOptions: UIScene.
ConnectionOptions) {
    if let windowScene = scene as? UIWindowScene {
        let window = UIWindow(windowScene: windowScene)
        let navigationController = UINavigationController(root
        ViewController: HomeViewController())
        navigationController.navigationBar.isHidden = true
        navigationController.interactivePopGestureRecognizer?.
        isEnabled = false
        window.backgroundColor = .white
        window.rootViewController = navigationController
        self.window = window
        window.makeKeyAndVisible()
    }
}
```

Home Screen

On the Home screen, the main component is the Presenter, which is in charge of passing information to the Model and subscribing to notifications of its changes. In addition, it is also responsible for receiving user interactions in the View and updating it with the information it receives from the Model.

The View is separate from the Controller, and some of its actions, such as navigating to another screen, are delegated to the Controller (Figure 3-6).

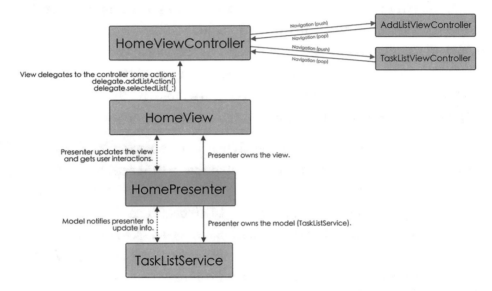

Figure 3-6. *Home screen components communication schema*

HomeController

Regarding the MVC architecture, in the MVP architecture, the *HomeController* has lost its relationship with the Model layer. Now, it is in charge, on the one hand, of instantiating the *HomeView* and passing it to the *HomePresenter* (which, as we have seen, we will pass as a protocol with the methods it must use) (Listing 3-4).

Listing 3-4. HomePresenter instantiation in HomeViewController

```
class HomeViewController: UIViewController {

    private var homeView = HomeView()
    ...
```

```
override func loadView() {
    super.loadView()
    setupHomeView()
}

private func setupHomeView() {
    let presenter = HomePresenter(homeView: homeView,
    tasksListService: TasksListService())
    homeView.delegate = self
    homeView.presenter = presenter
    homeView.setupView()
    self.view = homeView
}
}
```

On the other hand, *HomeViewController* also takes care of the routing between screens (in the *HomeView*, the user can select to access a list or create a new one, and this delegates the navigation to the *HomeViewController*), as shown in Listing 3-5.

Listing 3-5. Implementation of the methods of the HomeViewControllerDelegate

```
extension HomeViewController: HomeViewControllerDelegate {

    func addList() {
        navigationController?.pushViewController(AddListView
        Controller(), animated: true)
    }

    func selectedList(_ list: TasksListModel) {
        let taskViewController = TaskListViewController(tasks
        ListModel: list)
```

```
        navigationController?.pushViewController(taskView
        Controller, animated: true)
    }
}
```

HomeView

Now the *HomeView* receives from the *HomePresenter* the information it should display. This is seen when filling the table with the task lists that are created or the *HomeViewDelegate* implementation (Listing 3-6).

Listing 3-6. Setup of the tasks lists table in the HomeView

```
extension HomeView: UITableViewDataSource {
    ...
    func tableView(_ tableView: UITableView,
    numberOfRowsInSection section: Int) -> Int {
                    return presenter.numberOfTaskLists
    }

    func tableView(_ tableView: UITableView, cellForRowAt
    indexPath: IndexPath) -> UITableViewCell {
        let cell = tableView.dequeueReusableCell(withIdentifier:
        ToDoListCell.reuseId, for: indexPath) as! ToDoListCell
                    cell.setCellParametersForList(presenter.
                    listAtIndex(indexPath.row))
        return cell
    }

    func tableView(_ tableView: UITableView, commit
    editingStyle: UITableViewCell.EditingStyle, forRowAt
    indexPath: IndexPath) {
        if editingStyle == .delete {
```

```
                        presenter.removeList
                        AtIndex(indexPath.row)
        tableView.deleteRows(at: [indexPath], with:
        .automatic)
    }
  }
}

extension HomeView: HomeViewDelegate {

  func reloadData() {
    tableView.reloadData()
              emptyState.isHidden = presenter.
              numberOfTaskLists > 0
  }
}
```

On the other hand, it delegates to the Controller those actions that require navigation within the application, such as when selecting and accessing a list of tasks or creating a new one (Listing 3-7).

Listing 3-7. HomeView delegates navigation methods to HomeViewController

```
extension HomeView: UITableViewDelegate {
    ...
    func tableView(_ tableView: UITableView, didSelectRowAt
    indexPath: IndexPath) {
        delegate?.selectedList(presenter.
        listAtIndex(indexPath.row))
    }
}

private extension HomeView {
```

```
    ...

    @objc func addListAction() {
        delegate?.addList()
    }
    ...
}
```

HomePresenter

The Presenter is in charge of acting as an intermediary between the View and the Model. For this reason, in the initialization of the *HomePresenter*, we pass references to both the View (*HomeView*, in protocol form) and the Model (*TaskListService*). Access to the Model through the *TaskListService* will allow us both to retrieve the information that we want to show (task lists) and to delete those lists that we select.

To know when there was a change in the database and, thus, update the view, we also introduce an observer in the initialization of the *HomePresenter*, as shown in Listing 3-8.

Listing 3-8. HomePresenter initialization

```
class HomePresenter {

    private weak var homeView: HomeViewDelegate?
    private var tasksListService: TasksListService!
    private var lists: [TasksListModel] = [TasksListModel]()

    init(homeView: HomeViewDelegate? = nil,
         tasksListService: TasksListService) {
        self.homeView = homeView
        self.tasksListService = tasksListService

        NotificationCenter.default.addObserver(self,
                        selector: #selector(contextObjects
                        DidChange),
```

```
        name: NSNotification.Name.
        NSManagedObjectContextObjectsDidChange,
        object: CoreDataManager.shared.
        mainContext)
    }

    @objc func contextObjectsDidChange() {
        fetchTasksLists()
    }

    func fetchTasksLists() {
        lists = tasksListService.fetchLists()
        homeView?.reloadData()
    }

    var numberOfTaskLists: Int {
        return lists.count
    }

    func listAtIndex(_ index: Int) -> TasksListModel {
        return lists[index]
    }

    ...
}
```

When the observer receives a notification that the database has changed, the *contextObjectsDidChange* event is fired (which calls the *fetchTasksLists* event), with which the information that the *HomePresenter* has about the task lists to be displayed is updated, to then call to the *reloadData* method of the *HomeView*.

If the user wants to delete a task list, the *HomeView* will pass the action to the *HomePresenter* and this will be in charge of communicating it to the Model (Listing 3-9).

Listing 3-9. HomePresenter communicates with Model to delete lists

```
class HomePresenter {
    ...
    func removeListAtIndex(_ index: Int) {
        let list = listAtIndex(index)
        tasksListService.deleteList(list)
        lists.remove(at: index)
    }
}
```

Add List Screen

This screen is responsible for adding task lists and the communication between its components. The connection between the different components is shown in Figure 3-7.

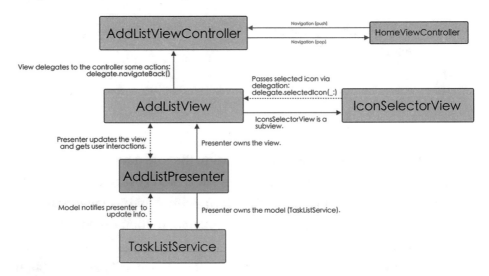

Figure 3-7. *Add list screen components communication schema*

AddListViewController

In the same way that we did in the *HomeViewController*, the
AddListViewController class is in charge of initializing the Presenter and
passing it to the view (Listing 3-10).

Listing 3-10. AddListPresenter instantiation in
AddListViewController

```
private func setupAddListView() {
    let presenter = AddListPresenter(addListView:
    addListView, tasksListService: TasksListService())
    addListView.delegate = self
    addListView.presenter = presenter
    self.view = addListView
}
```

Once the list is created, or also by user action on the back button, it
navigates back to the Home screen (which the *AddListView* has delegated,
as shown in Listing 3-11).

Listing 3-11. BackButtonDelegate implementation in
AddListViewController

```
extension AddListViewController: BackButtonDelegate {

    func navigateBack() {
        backToHome()
    }
}
```

AddListView

In *AddListView* the user can create a task list by selecting an icon and adding a title. All this information is passed to the *AddListPresenter* through the reference that the view maintains with it (Listing 3-12).

Listing 3-12. Presenter gets info from the view

```
extension AddListView {

    @objc func addListAction() {
        guard titleTextfield.hasText else { return }
        presenter.addListWithTitle(titleTextfield.text!)
    }
}

extension AddListView: IconSelectorViewDelegate {

    func selectedIcon(_ icon: String) {
        presenter.setListIcon(icon)
    }
}
```

The user can also exit this screen without creating any task lists. Simply select the navigate back button (the *HomePresenter* can call this method because when instantiating it we have passed it to the *AddListViewDelegate* protocol that it must comply with). In this case, the View delegates to the Controller to implement this action (Listing 3-13).

Listing 3-13. AddListView implements the AddListViewDelegate protocol

```
extension AddListView: AddListViewDelegate {

    func backToHome() {
```

```
        delegate?.navigateBack()
    }
}
```

AddListPresenter

The *AddListPresenter* is in charge of managing the creation of lists on this screen. In its initialization, we will pass both the *AddListView* (as a protocol) and the *TaskListService* that allows it to connect to the Model.

In addition, we will initialize a list that will be completed with the information of the title and the icon that comes from the View (Listing 3-14).

Listing 3-14. AddListPresenter code

```
class AddListPresenter {

    private weak var addListView: AddListViewDelegate?
    private var tasksListService: TasksListService!
    private var list: TasksListModel!

    init(addListView: AddListViewDelegate? = nil,
         tasksListService: TasksListService) {
        self.addListView = addListView
        self.tasksListService = tasksListService
        self.list = TasksListModel(id: ProcessInfo().
        globallyUniqueString,
                        icon: "checkmark.seal.fill",
                        createdAt: Date())
    }

    func setListIcon(_ icon: String) {
        list.icon = icon
    }
```

```
    func addListWithTitle(_ title: String) {
        list.title = title
        tasksListService.saveTasksList(list)
        addListView?.backToHome()
    }
}
```

As you can see at the end of the *addListWithTitle* method, once the order to create the list has been sent to the service, the Presenter tells the view to execute the *backToHome* method to return to the Home screen (which, as we just saw, it does by delegation).

Tasks List Screen

This screen is responsible for displaying the tasks that make up a list, marking them as done, deleting them, and adding new ones. The communication between its components is shown in Figure 3-8.

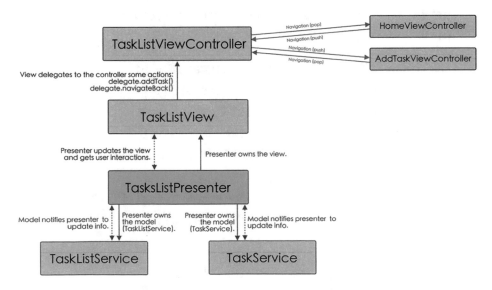

Figure 3-8. *Tasks list screen components communication schema*

TaskListViewController

Unlike the MVC architecture, in which the *TaskListViewController* had communication functions with the Model, here it is only in charge of instantiating the *TaskListPresenter* (Listing 3-15).

Listing 3-15. TaskListPresenter instantiation in TaskListViewController

```
private func setupTaskListView() {
    let presenter = TasksListPresenter(taskListView: taskListView,
                                       tasksListModel:
                                       tasksListModel,
                                       taskService: TaskService(),
                                       tasksListService:
                                       TasksListService())
    taskListView.delegate = self
    taskListView.presenter = presenter
    taskListView.setupView()
        self.view = taskListView
}
```

And to manage navigation, either to the add tasks screen (*AddTaskViewController*) or to return to the Home screen, we'll implement the methods associated with the *TaskListViewControllerDelegate* and *BackButtonDelegate* protocols (Listing 3-16).

Listing 3-16. Implementation of TaskListViewControllerDelegate and BackButtonDelegate methods

```
extension TaskListViewController:
TaskListViewControllerDelegate {
    func addTask() {
```

```
        let addTaskViewController = AddTaskViewController(tasks
        ListModel: tasksListModel)
        addTaskViewController.modalPresentationStyle =
        .pageSheet
        present(addTaskViewController, animated: true)
    }
}

extension TaskListViewController: BackButtonDelegate {
    func navigateBack() {
        navigationController?.popViewController(animated: true)
    }
}
```

TaskListView

In the *TaskListView,* similar to what we did in the *HomeView,* we have
a *UITableView* element that shows us the information it gets from the
TaskListPresenter (Listing 3-17).

Listing 3-17. UITableViewDelegate and UITableViewDatasource
implementation in TaskListView

```
extension TaskListView: UITableViewDelegate,
UITableViewDataSource {
    ...
    func tableView(_ tableView: UITableView,
    numberOfRowsInSection section: Int) -> Int {
        return presenter.numberOfTasks
    }
```

```
func tableView(_ tableView: UITableView, cellForRowAt
indexPath: IndexPath) -> UITableViewCell {
    let cell = tableView.dequeueReusableCell(withIdentifier:
    TaskCell.reuseId, for: indexPath) as! TaskCell
    cell.setParametersForTask(presenter.
    taskAtIndex(indexPath.row))
    cell.delegate = self
    return cell
}

func tableView(_ tableView: UITableView, commit
editingStyle: UITableViewCell.EditingStyle, forRowAt
indexPath: IndexPath) {
    if editingStyle == .delete {
        presenter.removeTaskAtIndex(indexPath.row)
        tableView.deleteRows(at: [indexPath], with:
        .automatic)
    }
}
}
```

On the other hand, you have to implement the methods of the
TaskListViewDelegate protocol that will allow the *TaskListPresenter* to
update the view (Listing 3-18).

Listing 3-18. TaskListViewDelegate methods implementation in
TaskListView

```
extension TaskListView: TaskListViewDelegate {

    func setPageTitle(_ title: String) {
        pageTitle.text = title
    }
```

```
    func reloadData() {
        tableView.reloadData()
        emptyState.isHidden = presenter.numberOfTasks > 0
    }
}
```

Finally, we must also implement the *TaskCellDelegate* protocol method associated with the *TaskCell* component, and that is the one that will allow us to modify the state of a task in the database via the *TaskListPresenter* (Listing 3-19).

Listing 3-19. TaskCellDelegate method implementation in TaskListView

```
extension TaskListView: TaskCellDelegate {

    func updateTask(_ task: TaskModel) {
        presenter.updateTask(task)
    }
}
```

TaskListPresenter

The *TaskListPresenter* is the most complex of the four since it has to display the tasks that make up a list, manage the deletion or update of a task, as well as observe the addition of new tasks.

Therefore, in the initialization of this class, we must pass not only the view but also the *TaskListModel* object with the tasks to be displayed, and instances to the *TaskListService* and *TaskService* services, which will allow us to interact with the Model.

We'll use the *TaskListService* to retrieve the list of tasks we're working with from the database and the *TaskService* to update or delete a given task.

In addition, we will need to add an observer for changes in the database (Listing 3-20).

Listing 3-20. TaskListPresenter initialization code

```
class TasksListPresenter {
    ...
    init(taskListView: TaskListViewDelegate? = nil,
        tasksListModel: TasksListModel,
        taskService: TaskService,
        tasksListService: TasksListService) {
        self.taskListView = taskListView
        self.tasksListModel = tasksListModel
        self.taskService = taskService
        self.tasksListService = tasksListService

        NotificationCenter.default.addObserver(self,
                    selector: #selector(contextObjectsD
                    idChange),
                    name: NSNotification.Name.
                    NSManagedObjectContextObjectsDidChange,
                    object: CoreDataManager.shared.
                    mainContext)
    }

    @objc func contextObjectsDidChange() {
        fetchTasks()
    }

    func fetchTasks() {
        guard let list = tasksListService.
        fetchListWithId(tasksListModel.id) else { return }
        tasksListModel = list
```

```
        tasks = tasksListModel.tasks.sorted(by: { $0.createdAt.
        compare($1.createdAt) == .orderedDescending })
        taskListView?.reloadData()
    }

    ...
}
```

In Listing 3-21, you can also see the code for the interaction of the *TaskListPresenter* with the Model. In this case, *TaskListView* will pass the delete task action to the *TaskListPresenter*, which will be in charge of communicating it to the Model.

Listing 3-21. TaskListPresenter code for interaction with TaskService

```
extension TasksListPresenter {

    func updateTask(_ task: TaskModel) {
        taskService.updateTask(task)
    }

    func removeTaskAtIndex(_ index: Int) {
        let task = taskAtIndex(index)
        taskService.deleteTask(task)
        tasks.remove(at: index)
    }
}
```

Add Task Screen

This screen is responsible for adding tasks to a given list and the communication between its components is shown in Figure 3-9.

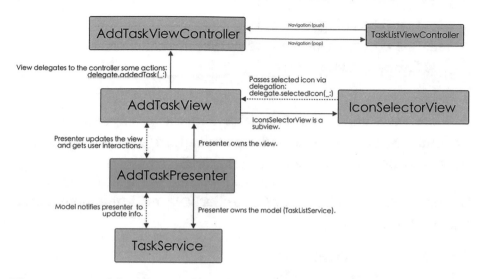

Figure 3-9. *Add task screen components communication schema*

AddTaskViewController

As in the case of the previous controllers, in the *AddTaskViewController* the *AddTaskPresenter* is initialized, to which the view is passed, the object of the list of tasks to which we want to add a new task, and the service with which to access the Model (*TaskService*) (Listing 3-22).

Listing 3-22. AddTaskPresenter instantiation in AddTaskViewController

```
private func setupAddTaskView() {
    let presenter = AddTaskPresenter(addTaskView: addTaskView,
                                 tasksListModel:
                                 tasksListModel,
                                 taskService:
                                 TaskService())
```

```
    addTaskView.delegate = self
    addTaskView.presenter = presenter
    self.view = addTaskView
}
```

From a navigation point of view, this Controller is only responsible for dismissing the View once a task has been added (since this screen is presented as a modal), as shown in Listing 3-23.

Listing 3-23. AddedTaskViewControllerDelegate implementation in AddTaskViewController

```
extension AddTaskViewController:
AddedTaskViewControllerDelegate {

    func addedTask() {
        dismiss(animated: true)
    }
}
```

AddTaskView

In *AddTaskView*, the user can create a task by selecting an icon and adding a title. All of this information is passed to the *AddTaskPresenter* through the reference the View maintains to it (Listing 3-24).

Listing 3-24. Presenter gets info from the view

```
private extension AddTaskView {
    @objc func addTaskAction() {
        guard titleTextfield.hasText else { return }
        presenter.addTaskWithTitle(titleTextfield.text!)
    }
}
```

```
extension AddTaskView: IconSelectorViewDelegate {

    func selectedIcon(_ icon: String) {
        presenter.setTaskIcon(icon)
    }
}
```

On the other hand, once the user performs the action of adding the task, the *AddTaskPresenter* will call the *addedTask* method (defined in the *AddTaskViewDelegate* protocol, and which *AddTaskView* should implement) (Listing 3-25).

Listing 3-25. AddTaskViewDelegate implementation in AddTaskView

```
extension AddTaskView: AddTaskViewDelegate {

    func addedTask() {
        delegate?.addedTask()
    }
}
```

In turn, the action related to the *addedTask* method is delegated to the *AddTaskViewController* which, as we just saw, will remove the screen.

AddTaskPresenter

The *AddTaskPresenter* is in charge of creating and adding tasks to a list. In its initialization, we will pass the *AddTaskView* (as a protocol), the object (*TaskListModel*) that contains the list to which we will add the new task, and the *TaskService*, which will be the connection with the Model layer, and that will allow us to add the task in the database.

Also, similar to how we did when adding a new task list, we will initialize a task that we only have to complete later with the title and the selected icon (Listing 3-26).

Listing 3-26. AddTaskPresenter code

```
class AddTaskPresenter {

    private var addTaskView: AddTaskViewDelegate?
    private var tasksListModel: TasksListModel!
    private var taskService: TaskService!
    private var task: TaskModel!

    init(addTaskView: AddTaskViewDelegate? = nil,
        tasksListModel: TasksListModel,
        taskService: TaskService) {
      self.addTaskView = addTaskView
      self.tasksListModel = tasksListModel
      self.taskService = taskService
      self.task = TaskModel(id: ProcessInfo().
      globallyUniqueString,
                            icon: "checkmark.seal.fill",
                            done: false,
                            createdAt: Date())
    }

    func setTaskIcon(_ icon:  String) {
      task.icon = icon
    }

    func addTaskWithTitle(_ title: String) {
      task.title = title
      taskService.saveTask(task, in: tasksListModel)
      addTaskView?.addedTask()
    }
}
```

MVP-MyToDos Testing

If we compare the MVC architecture with the MVP, we can see that in the MVP the business logic has passed from the Controller to the Presenter, leaving only the navigation in the Controller. Therefore, all the testing of the business logic will have to be transferred to the Presenter.

We are now going to see how the testing of the components belonging to the screen that allows the user to add a new list would be.

Note   Remember, as we indicated in Chapter 2, that although we show the code and the tests separately for pedagogical reasons, it is recommended that when developing our applications, we work according to the TDD (test-driven development) methodology.

AddListViewController

As we just discussed, the Controller only handles navigation. In this case, we will have the navigation back to the Home screen (Listing 3-27).

Listing 3-27. AddListViewControllerTest code

```
class AddListViewControllerTest: XCTestCase {

    var sut: AddListViewController!
    var navigationController: MockNavigationController!

    override func setUpWithError() throws {
        sut = AddListViewController()
        navigationController = MockNavigationController(root
        ViewController: UIViewController())
        navigationController.pushViewController(sut,
        animated: false)
```

```
        navigationController.vcIsPushed = false
    }

    override func tearDownWithError() throws {
        sut = nil
        navigationController = nil
        super.tearDown()
    }

    func testPopVC_whenBackActionIsCalled_thenPopHomeCalled() {
        sut.navigateBack()
        XCTAssertTrue(navigationController.vcIsPopped)
    }
}
```

AddListView

Most of the tests of *AddListView* are the same as in the case of the MVC architecture (such as the instantiation of the different components).

But now the view interacts with the Presenter to communicate the user's actions to it (instead of with the Controller), so we'll need to introduce them in the tests (Listing 3-28).

Listing 3-28. AddListViewTest code

```
class AddListViewTest: XCTestCase {

    var sut: AddListView!
    var presenter: AddListPresenter!

    override func setUpWithError() throws {
        sut = AddListView()
    }

    override func tearDownWithError() throws {
```

```swift
    sut = nil
    super.tearDown()
}

func testViewLoaded_whenViewIsInstantiated_
shouldBeComponents() {
    XCTAssertNotNil(sut.pageTitle)
    XCTAssertNotNil(sut.backButton)
    XCTAssertNotNil(sut.titleTextfield)
    XCTAssertNotNil(sut.iconLabel)
    XCTAssertNotNil(sut.iconSelectorView)
    XCTAssertNotNil(sut.addListButton)
}

func testButtonAction_whenAddListButtonIsTapped_
shouldBeCalledAddListAction() {
    let addListButton = sut.addListButton
    XCTAssertNotNil(addListButton, "UIButton does not
    exists")

    guard let addListButtonAction = addListButton.
    actions(forTarget: sut, forControlEvent:
    .touchUpInside) else {
        XCTFail("Not actions assigned for .touchUpInside")
        return
    }

    XCTAssertTrue(addListButtonAction.
    contains("addListAction"))
}

func testButtonAction_whenBackButtonIsTapped_
shouldBeCalledBackAction() {
    let backButton = sut.backButton
    XCTAssertNotNil(backButton, "UIButton does not exists")
```

```
        guard let backButtonAction = backButton.actions
        (forTarget: sut, forControlEvent: .touchUpInside) else {
            XCTFail("Not actions assigned for .touchUpInside")
            return
        }

        XCTAssertTrue(backButtonAction.contains("backAction"))
}

func testTextField_whenTextfieldIsCreated_shouldBeEmpty() {
    XCTAssertEqual(sut.titleTextfield.text, "")
}

func testTextField_whenTextfiledhasText_
shouldBeCreatedList() {
    let mockTaskListService = MockTaskListService(lists:
    [TasksListModel]())
    presenter = AddListPresenter(addListView: sut,
    tasksListService: mockTaskListService)
    sut.presenter = presenter
    sut.titleTextfield.text = "Test title"
    sut.addListAction()
    XCTAssertEqual(presenter.list.title, "Test title")
}

func testIcon_whenIconIsSetted_shouldBeIconInList() {
    let mockTaskListService = MockTaskListService(lists:
    [TasksListModel]())
    presenter = AddListPresenter(addListView: sut,
    tasksListService: mockTaskListService)
    sut.presenter = presenter
    sut.selectedIcon("test.icon")
    XCTAssertEqual(presenter.list.icon, "test.icon")
}
}
```

AddListViewPresenter

From the Presenter, we are going to test that when selecting an icon, it is added to the *TaskListModel* object that we have initialized and that when we add a title it is added to the *TaskListModel* object and sent to the database (Listing 3-29).

Listing 3-29. AddListViewPresenterTest code

```
class AddListPresenterTest: XCTestCase {

    var sut: AddListPresenter!
    let mockTaskListService = MockTaskListService(lists:
    [TasksListModel]())
    override func setUpWithError() throws {
        sut = AddListPresenter(tasksListService:
        mockTaskListService)
    }

    override func tearDownWithError() throws {
        sut = nil
        super.tearDown()
    }

    func testAddIcon_whenAddedIcon_shouldContainObjectIcon() {
        sut.setListIcon("test.icon")
        XCTAssertEqual(sut.list.icon, "test.icon")
    }

    func testAddTitle_whenAddedTitle_
    shouldContainObjectTitle() {
        sut.addListWithTitle("Test List")
        XCTAssertEqual(sut.list.title, "Test List")
```

```
    XCTAssertEqual(mockTaskListService.fetchLists().first?.
    title, "Test List")
  }
}
```

As you can see, we use the *MockTaskListService* class, which, as we saw in Chapter 2, allows us to simulate the original behavior of the *TaskListService* class, but it returns the data that we indicate.

Summary

We can consider the MVP architecture as an evolution of the MVC architecture. What we have done is pass the business logic from the Controller to the Presenter. The Presenter will also receive the user's interactions from the View and will act accordingly.

We have seen some of the advantages that the use of the MVP architecture presents, such as a better separation of responsibilities is obtained than in the case of the MVC and the business logic can be better tested in the Presenter.

However, it is also necessary to take into account some of the problems that it can present, such as the fact that more code is required in development (and somewhat more complex than in MVC) or that, in the same way as with the Controller in the MVC, the Presenter can become massive by adding more responsibilities.

In the next chapter, we will see an architecture similar to MVP: MVVM, or Model–View–ViewModel. We will see how the view is linked to the model (for which we will use reactive functional programming with the *RxSwift* library), and, finally, we will make a variation of the MVVM with the addition of a Coordinate that manages the navigation between screens (MVVM-C).

CHAPTER 4

MVVM: Model–View–ViewModel

What Is MVVM?

A Little History

The MVVM architecture was developed by Ken Cooper and Ted Peters of Microsoft (and later announced by John Gossman on his blog in 2005), to simplify event-driven programming (in which events drive program flow) of web interfaces.[1]

How It Works

The MVVM architecture is an evolution of the MVP architecture, in which the Presenter layer is replaced by the ViewModel layer. In addition, it solves some of the problems presented by the MVP architecture. The main one is the coupling that exists in the MVP architecture between the View and the Presenter. In the case of the MVVM architecture, the ViewModel has no references to the view, that is, there is no coupling (Figure 4-1).

---

[1] https://docs.microsoft.com/en-us/archive/blogs/johngossman/introduction-to-modelviewviewmodel-pattern-for-building-wpf-apps

© Raúl Ferrer García 2023
R. Ferrer García, *iOS Architecture Patterns*, https://doi.org/10.1007/978-1-4842-9069-9_4

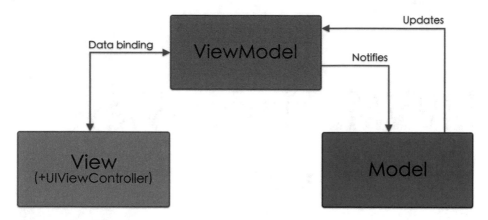

Figure 4-1. *Model–View–ViewModel schema*

Components in MVVM

We are now going to see in more detail the characteristics of these three components in the MVVM pattern.

Model

In the same way as in the MVC or MVP patterns, the Model is the component (or components) in charge of the business logic and of storing, manipulating, and accessing the application data:

- It contains classes related to data persistence.

- It contains the classes that control the communications of the application.

- It is responsible for transforming the information it receives from the outside into model objects.

- It contains extensions, constants...

- The Model layer can only communicate with the ViewModel layer (i.e., the Model is unaware of the existence of a View).

View

The View layer contains both the *UIView* components and the *UIViewController* elements (which we keep in separate files, as we have seen in previous chapters):

- The View is responsible for showing the user updated information at all times (which comes from the ViewModel).

- The View does not contain any logic.

- The View can have multiple references to the ViewModel.

The Controller only has coordination/routing functions, handling navigation between screens and, if necessary, passing information through a Delegation pattern. At the end of this chapter, we will see how we can pass all this coordination/routing to a new class, a Coordinator, giving rise to the MVVM-C architecture.

ViewModel

The ViewModel is the core of the MVVM architecture (as is the Controller in MVC or the Presenter in MVP) and sits between the View and the Model:

- The ViewModel must present the current state of the View at all times.

- The ViewModel is in charge of processing the Input/Output information that controls the View.

- The ViewModel is owned by the View, and the Model is owned by the ViewModel.

The ViewModel is bound to the View through what is known as Data Binding.[2] This process allows you to connect the View with the ViewModel so that if the state of the information managed by the ViewModel changes, the View is updated automatically.

Data Binding

There are different methodologies to apply the Data Binding between the View and the ViewModel, such as follows:

- By using libraries like RxSwift, Bond, or Combine. It is the most used system, and for the development of our application with MVVM, we will use the RxSwift library.[3]

- With the KVO (key-value observing) pattern, by which we can notify certain objects about the changes produced in the properties of other objects.[4]

- By using the Delegated Pattern, using closures...

Advantages and Disadvantages of MVVM

The MVVM architecture pattern is often used as a replacement for the MVC architecture, and as with other architectures, using the Model–View–ViewModel architecture has advantages and disadvantages.

---

[2] https://en.wikipedia.org/wiki/Data_binding
[3] https://github.com/ReactiveX/RxSwift
[4] https://developer.apple.com/documentation/swift/using-key-value-observing-in-swift

Advantages

The main advantages of the MVVM architecture are as follows:

- It presents a good separation of responsibilities since we have introduced a new component (ViewModel) that is responsible for transforming the Model data to display it in the View. In this way, we release the Controller from said work (as it did not happen in the MVC).

- By having a greater separation of responsibilities, its maintenance becomes easier.

- It improves testability since we can test the business logic of the ViewModel without having to take the View into account. It's also easier to test Controllers, since, unlike MVC, they don't depend on the Model.

- The MVVM architecture is widely used in application development when migrating from the MVC architecture.

Disadvantages

The main disadvantages are as follows:

- If we use third-party libraries to perform the Data Binding (such as RxSwift or Bond), we have to take several factors into account:

  - On the one hand, by adding an external library, we are increasing the size of our app.

  - On the other hand, the addition of these libraries usually affects the performance of the applications.

- Finally, we must also take into account the learning curve required to correctly use each of these libraries.

- Data Binding is a declarative paradigm, in which we tell the program what to do, and not how to do it (imperative paradigm), which can make debugging difficult. Also, this kind of paradigm makes a lot more sense in SwiftUI than in UIKit.

- In the same way as in other architectures, if it is not applied well, we can end up overloading the ViewModel with functions that do not correspond to it.

- It presents some complexity for developers just starting.

MVVM Application

Once we have seen the characteristics of the MVVM architecture, we are going to apply them in the development of our application.

Note The entire project can be downloaded from the repository of this book. During the explanation of the implementation of the MVVM architecture in our project, we will only show the most relevant parts of the code.

MVVM Layers

To continue with the logic of the applied architecture pattern (Model–View-ViewModel), we will create a folder structure that simulates its layers (Figure 4-2).

Figure 4-2. *MVVM project folder structure*

Model

In the same way as in the previous cases, this folder contains everything related to business logic, data access, and its manipulation (Figure 4-3).

Figure 4-3. *Model layer files*

In the MVVM architecture, the changes produced in the Model are notified to the ViewModel (in the same way that they were communicated to the Controller in the MVC and the Presenter in the MVP).

In this case, we add the observer in the ViewModel's *init* method (Listing 4-1).

Listing 4-1. Setting the observer on ViewModel initialization

```
init() {
    NotificationCenter.default.addObserver(self,
                                selector: #selector
                                (contextObjects
                                DidChange),
                                name:
NSNotification.Name.NSManagedObjectContextObjectsDidChange,
                                object:
                                CoreDataManager.
                                shared.mainContext)
}
```

```
@objc func contextObjectsDidChange() {
    updateView()
}
```

Core Data

In this folder, we will have the CoreDataManager.swift file, along with the four files created by Xcode automatically for the database entities.

Models

Here we have the models into which we can transform the database entities. In addition, we will create a protocol that the models must comply with, to transform from model to entity and vice versa.

Services

Here we will have the classes that allow us to send information to the database (create, update, or delete it) or retrieve information from the database and transform it into models.

Extensions

In this case, we have created a *UIColor* extension to be able to easily access the colors created especially for this application and an extension to the *NSManagedObject* class that will prevent us from conflicting with the contexts when we do the testing part.

Constants

They contain the constant parameters that we will use in the application.

View

In the View folder, we will not only have the View files and the components that form them (as in MVC), but also the Controller files (subclasses of *UIViewController*), as shown in Figure 4-4.

Figure 4-4. *View layer files*

Remember that in MVVM, Controllers usually only have coordination/routing functions (to navigate between screens) and, in some cases, pass information (via a Delegate pattern, for example).

ViewModel

This folder only contains the ViewModels, which, as we have seen, connect the Model to the View (Figure 4-5).

Figure 4-5. *ViewModel layer files*

MyToDos Data Binding

Before starting to see how the different screens of our application are configured, as we have done in the case of MVC and MVP, we are going to see how we will carry out the Data Binding process between the ViewModel and the View.

As we have seen before, there are different ways to carry out this procedure, but in our case, we will use RxSwift.

What Is RxSwift?

RxSwift is a reactive programming library for iOS application development.

RxSwift is a library that allows us to develop asynchronous code in our applications, simplifying the way our code will act in front of the new data that arrives, treating them in a sequential and isolated way.

In this book, we will not delve into the study of RxSwift and reactive programming, suffice it to say that reactive programming allows you to dynamically respond to changes in data and user events.

RxSwift works with what we call *Observables*, which are wrapper objects for any type of data, to which we can subscribe or link so that any change that occurs in said *Observables* triggers a series of previously programmed operations.

Observables and Observers

When using this library, we will have two types of elements:

- **Observable**: Issue notifications when a change occurs.

- **Observer**: An Observer subscribe to an Observable to receive its notifications. An Observable can have one or more observers.

Installing RxSwift

The installation of RxSwift, as it is an external library, can be done in different ways (*Swift Package Manager, Carthage, CocoaPods*). In our case, we will use the Swift Package Manager (SPM), which is the system integrated with Xcode to introduce third-party libraries in our applications.

To install RxSwift in our project, we will follow these steps:

First of all, we access the Xcode main menu and select *File ➤ Add Packages...* (Figure 4-6).

Figure 4-6. *Add Packages... menu selection*

The Xcode Swift Package manager will appear on the screen (Figure 4-7).

Figure 4-7. *Swift Package Manager screen*

At this point, what we do is copy the address of the RxSwift git repository (which we will find on their website), and we will place it in the search field that appears in the upper right (Figure 4-8).

```
https://github.com/ReactiveX/RxSwift.git
```

By doing this, Xcode takes care of searching for this library and tells us if we want to install it.

Figure 4-8. *Search for the RxSwift package*

Before adding RxSwift, what we will do is change the *"Dependency Rule"* option from *"Branch"* to *"Up To Next Major Version."* Once this change is made, select *"Add Package."*

Next, a screen will appear in which we can select which components or products of the RxSwift library we want to install. For our application, we will select RxCocoa, RxRelay, and RxSwift (for main code), along with RxTest (for testing purposes), and select *"Add Package"* again (Figure 4-9).

Choose Package Products for RxSwift

Package Product	Kind	Add to Target	
☐ RxBlocking	Library	MVVM_MyToDos	⬍
☐ RxBlocking-Dynamic	Library	MVVM_MyToDos	⬍
☑ RxCocoa	Library	MVVM_MyToDos	⬍
☐ RxCocoa-Dynamic	Library	MVVM_MyToDos	⬍
☑ RxRelay	Library	MVVM_MyToDos	⬍
☐ RxRelay-Dynamic	Library	MVVM_MyToDos	⬍
☑ RxSwift	Library	MVVM_MyToDos	⬍
☐ RxSwift-Dynamic	Library	MVVM_MyToDos	⬍
☑ RxTest	Library	MVVM_MyToDosTests	⬍
☐ RxTest-Dynamic	Library	MVVM_MyToDos	⬍

Cancel   Add Package

Figure 4-9. *Products selector for RxSwift*

Once the installation is finished, we can see that our project already presents RxSwift as a dependency (Figure 4-10).

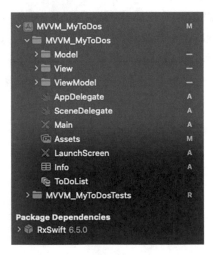

Figure 4-10. *Under Package Dependencies, all SPM dependencies installed are shown*

To use any of these products in our code, we simply have to import them (the ones we need at any given time):

```
import RxCocoa
import RxRelay
import RxSwift
```

Input/Output Approach

To work in a more organized way with RxSwift and the bind between the different components and events, we will use a simplified procedure based on a fairly widespread convention whose origin is the Kickstarter company.[5]

It is a functional approach in which the concept of Input/Output is used.

- **Input**: It refers to all the events and interactions that occur in the View and that affect the ViewModel (write a text, press a button…).

- **Output**: These are the changes that occur in the model and that must be reflected in the View.

Let's see a simple example of the application of this convention. We will start with the code of the ViewModel (Listing 4-2).

Listing 4-2. Example of RxSwift Input/Output approach in the ViewModel

```
class ExampleViewModel {

    var output: Output!
    var input: Input!
```

---

[5] https://github.com/kickstarter/ios-oss

```
struct Input {
    let text: PublishRelay<String>
}

struct Output {
    let title: Driver<String>
}

init() {
    let text = PublishRelay<String>()
    let capsTitle = text
        .map({
            return text.uppercased()
        })
        .asDriver(onErrorJustReturn: "")
    input = Input(text: text)
    output = Output(title: capsTitle)
}
}
```

Although, as we have said, we are not going to delve into a library as extensive and complex as RxSwift, we will explain the different elements used in our application and what their function is.

First, we can see the *PublishRelay<String>* and *Driver<String>* elements:

- *PublishRelay* is a component of RxSwift whose function is to broadcast the most recent item it has watched (and subsequent ones) to all those watchers that have subscribed. In this case, the passed item is of type String and is the text that we put in the *UITextField* element.

- *Driver* is an observable that runs on the main thread
  (so it's used to update the View). In this case, what it
  does is pass the value that comes from the *UITextField*
  element (through the *PublishRelay* created and that it
  is observing). Since we're passing it to a UI component,
  we have to do it on the main thread.

Now, let's see how we bind the ViewModel with the elements of the
View (Listing 4-3).

Listing 4-3. Element binding in the View

```
class ExampleView {

    func bind() {
        textfield.rx.text
            .bind(to: viewModel.input.text )
            .disposed(by: disposeBag)

        viewModel.output.title
            .drive(titleLabel.rx.text)
            .disposed(by: disposeBag)
    }
}
```

Here we can see two blocks of code:

- The first binds the text parameter of the *UITextField*
  element to the text variable (as *Input*) of the
  ViewModel. In this way, when we write in that field, the
  ViewModel will receive it.

- The second block binds the title variable (such as
  Output) of the ViewModel to the text parameter of the
  UILabel element. Therefore, as we type, the text in the
  ViewModel is converted to uppercase and forwarded to
  the View for display.

163

> **Note**   RxSwift provides several extensions for most of the objects and classes we use in Swift development. These extensions are accessed via the *rx* particle, as in *tableView.rx*.
>
> When we want to destroy an observable that we have created, we must call the *dispose*( ) method. To make this job easier, we have *DisposeBag* from RxSwift. Therefore, every time we create an observable, we must add it to the created *diposeBag* object using the *.disposed(by: disposeBag)* method.

MyToDos Application Screens

As we have just seen, the core of the MVVM architecture is the ViewModel, which is in charge of maintaining the state of the View and modifying it every time that state changes (thanks to the Data Binding).

Although the MVVM architecture is similar to the MVP architecture (which we have already seen in Chapter 3), where the ViewModel would have similar functions to the Presenter, MVVM solves the coupling problem between the View and Presenter of the MVP (in which the View has a reference to the Presenter and vice versa): in the MVVM this coupling does not exist thanks to the use of Data Binding.

Therefore, we are going to focus on how to program the ViewModel and the View (along with the Controller) and the binding between them.

AppDelegate and SceneDelegate

In our MVVM project, *AppDelegate* and *SceneDelegate* present the same code as in the case of the MVP, in which we add an instance of the *HomeViewController* to the *UINavigationController* component, without passing the dependencies to the *TasksListService* and *TaskService* services since these dependencies will be established in the *HomeViewModel* component (Listing 4-4).

Listing 4-4. SceneDelegate changes to load HomeViewController

```
func scene(_ scene: UIScene, willConnectTo session:
UISceneSession, options connectionOptions: UIScene.
ConnectionOptions) {
    if let windowScene = scene as? UIWindowScene {
        let window = UIWindow(windowScene: windowScene)
        let navigationController = UINavigationController(rootV
        iewController: HomeViewController())
        navigationController.navigationBar.isHidden = true
        navigationController.interactivePopGestureRecognizer?.
        isEnabled = false
        window.backgroundColor = .white
        window.rootViewController = navigationController
        self.window = window
        window.makeKeyAndVisible()
    }
}
```

Home Screen

On the Home screen, the main component is the *HomeViewModel*, which is bound to the *HomeView* (Data Binding) (Figure 4-11).

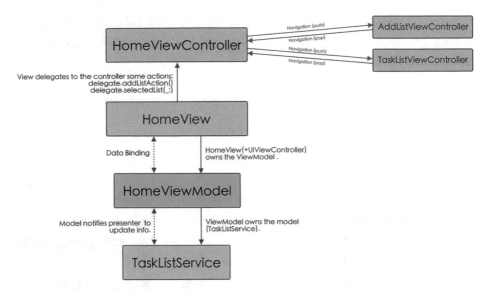

***Figure 4-11.** Home screen components communication schema*

HomeViewController

The Controller for this screen is similar to the one we saw in the MVP model: now it is in charge of instantiating the *HomeViewModel* and passing it to the View (Listing 4-5).

***Listing 4-5.** HomeViewModel instantiation in HomeViewController*

```
class HomeViewController: UIViewController {

    private var homeView: HomeView!

    ...

    override func loadView() {
        super.loadView()
        setupHomeView()
    }

    private func setupHomeView() {
```

```
let viewModel = HomeViewModel(tasksListService:
TasksListService())
homeView = HomeView(viewModel: viewModel)
homeView.delegate = self
self.view = homeView
    }
}
```

On the other hand, the *HomeViewController* also handles the routing between screens (in *HomeView*, the user can select to access a list or create a new one, and this delegates the navigation to the *HomeViewController*), as shown in Listing 4-6.

Listing 4-6. Implementation of the methods of the HomeViewControllerDelegate

```
extension HomeViewController: HomeViewControllerDelegate {

    func addList() {
        navigationController?.pushViewController(AddListView
        Controller(), animated: true)
    }

    func selectedList(_ list: TasksListModel) {
        let taskViewController = TaskListViewController(tasks
        ListModel: list)
        navigationController?.pushViewController(taskView
        Controller, animated: true)
    }
}
```

At the end of this chapter, we will see how to remove this navigation part of the *UIViewController* by using a Coordinator.

HomeView

HomeView changes quite a bit concerning the one we saw in the MVC or the MVP, not from the point of view of the components that form it, but from the point of view of how they are aware of the changes in the state of the ViewModel through Data Binding.

The fact of using a library like RxSwift allows us to easily link each of the components of the view (and its properties) to the model.

To establish all the links between the ViewModel and the components of the View, we will create a method that groups them (Listing 4-7).

Listing 4-7. Setting ViewModel in HomeView

```
class HomeView: UIView {
    ...
    private let viewModel: HomeViewModel!
    private let disposeBag = DisposeBag()

    init(frame: CGRect = .zero, viewModel: HomeViewModel) {
        self.viewModel = viewModel
        ...
        bindViewToModel(viewModel)
    }
}

private extension HomeView {
    ...
    func bindViewToModel(_ viewModel: HomeViewModel) {
        ...
    }
}
```

We are now going to see what is the code we will introduce in this method, and that will allow us to link the components of the View with the ViewModel.

We start with the *UITableView* component, which is the one that shows us which lists of tasks we have created.

First, we set the table's delegate (for the *UITableViewDelegate* protocol) and which we will only use to set the height of the row (Listing 4-8).

Listing 4-8. Setting tableView delegate with RxSwift

```
tableView.rx
        .setDelegate(self)
        .disposed(by: disposeBag)
```

Next, we need to pass information about the number of sections, rows, and items that make up the table to the table.

From the point of view of the Input/Output convention that we are going to use, the task lists will be an output of the ViewModel (*output. lists*). Linking this data to the *UITableView* element is done through the statement *tableView.rx.items(cellIdentifier: ...* (Listing 4-9).

Listing 4-9. Binding tasks lists data to tableView

```
viewModel.output.lists
    .drive(tableView.rx.items(cellIdentifier: ToDoListCell.
    reuseId, cellType: ToDoListCell.self)) { (_, list, cell) in
        cell.setCellParametersForList(list)
    }
.disposed(by: disposeBag)
```

Next, we set the instruction that allows us to subscribe to the user's cell selection action. This is done via the *input.selectRow* parameter. Every time the user selects a cell, the *IndexPath* information of the selected cell is sent to the *ViewModel* (Listing 4-10).

When we select a table cell and pass the corresponding *IndexPath* value to the *ViewModel*, it will take care of selecting the corresponding *TaskListModel* object and will emit it as output. Therefore, we must bind this output (*output.selectedList*) from the View.

Listing 4-10. Subscription to the itemSelected event

```
tableView.rx.itemSelected
    .bind(to: viewModel.input.selectRow)
    .disposed(by: disposeBag)

viewModel.output.selectedList
    .drive(onNext: { [self] list in
        delegate?.selectedList(list)
    })
    .disposed(by: disposeBag)
```

The last instruction related to the *UITableView* component is to delete a cell (Listing 4-11). Every time the user makes the gesture to delete a cell, the ViewModel will be asked to delete it in the Model. This event of deleting a list will correspond to an input of the ViewModel (*input.deleteRow*).

Listing 4-11. Subscription to the itemDeleted event

```
tableView.rx.itemDeleted
    .bind(to: viewModel.input.deleteRow)
    .disposed(by: disposeBag)
```

Once we have finished binding the *UITableView* component, we move on to binding the *EmptyState* component and the *AddListButton* component.

In the first case, what we want is to hide or show the *EmptyState* depending on whether or not there are task lists created. The ViewModel must communicate to the View if it should show the *EmptyState* or not, so this information will be an output (*output.hideEmptyState*), as shown in Listing 4-12.

Listing 4-12. Binding output.hideEmptyState property of the ViewModel to the EmptyState's isHidden property

```
viewModel.output.hideEmptyState
    .drive(emptyState.rx.isHidden)
    .disposed(by: disposeBag)
```

When in the ViewModel *hideEmptyState* takes a false value, the *EmptyState* will be visible, while if it takes a true value, it will be hidden.

Regarding the *AddListButton*, while in MVC or MVP, we assigned a target that called a method that we had created, with RxSwift we simply assigned the code to be executed to the *tap* method (Listing 4-13).

Listing 4-13. Setting tap event for AddListButton

```
addListButton.rx.tap
    .asDriver()
    .drive(onNext: { [self] in
        delegate?.addList()
    })
    .disposed(by: disposeBag)
```

At the end of the *bindToViewModel* method, what we do is make a call to reload the table which, as we will see now in the ViewModel, calls the database to obtain the created task lists.

```
viewModel.input.reload.accept(())
```

As we have commented in the introduction to RxSwift, we are not going to delve into the possibilities offered by this library (which are many). We simply show how to use some of them in our example project.

171

HomeViewModel

As we have seen at the beginning of this chapter, the ViewModel is responsible for obtaining the data from the Model and preparing it to be displayed by the View and also manages the business logic of this View.

As we have seen in the development of the *HomeView*, the *HomeViewModel* must have three inputs (reload, *deleteRow*, and *selectRow*) and three outputs (*lists*, *selectedList*, and *hideEmptyState*). Therefore, we will define the *struct Input* and the *struct Output* as follows (Listing 4-14).

Listing 4-14. Definition of Input and Output for the HomeViewModel

```
class HomeViewModel {

    var output: Output!
    var input: Input!

    struct Input {
        let reload: PublishRelay<Void>
        let deleteRow: PublishRelay<IndexPath>
        let selectRow: PublishRelay<IndexPath>
    }
    struct Output {
        let hideEmptyState: Driver<Bool>
        let lists: Driver<[TasksListModel]>
        let selectedList: Driver<TasksListModel>
    }
    ...
}
```

Once we have defined Input and Output, we set their behavior in the initialization of the *HomeViewModel* (Listing 4-15).

Listing 4-15. Establishment of the behavior of the parameters associated with the inputs and outputs

```
class HomeViewModel {

    ...

    private let lists = BehaviorRelay<[TasksListModel]>(
    value: [])
    private let taskList = BehaviorRelay<TasksListModel>(value:
    TasksListModel())
    private var tasksListService: TasksListServiceProtocol!

    init(tasksListService: TasksListServiceProtocol) {
        self.tasksListService = tasksListService
        // Inputs
        let reload = PublishRelay<Void>()
        _ = reload.subscribe(onNext: { [self] _ in
            fetchTasksLists()
        })
        let deleteRow = PublishRelay<IndexPath>()
        _ = deleteRow.subscribe(onNext: { [self] indexPath in
            tasksListService.deleteList(listAtIndexPath
            (indexPath))
        })
        let selectRow = PublishRelay<IndexPath>()
        _ = selectRow.subscribe(onNext: { [self]
            indexPath in
         taskList.accept(listAtIndexPath(indexPath))
        })
        self.input = Input(reload: reload,
        deleteRow: deleteRow, selectRow: selectRow)
```

```
    // Outputs
    let items = lists
        .asDriver(onErrorJustReturn: [])
    let hideEmptyState = lists
        .map({ items in
            return !items.isEmpty
        })
        .asDriver(onErrorJustReturn: false)
         let selectedList = taskList.asDriver()
    output = Output(hideEmptyState: hideEmptyState, lists:
    items, selectedList: selectedList)

    ...
}

...
}
```

The *input.reload* parameter will execute the method that fetches the lists recorded in the database.

The *input.deleteRow* parameter will receive the position in the table of the cell we want to delete (as *IndexPath*).

The *input.selectRow* parameter will receive the position in the table of the cell we have selected (as *IndexPath*).

The *output.lists* parameter will emit an array of *TasksListModel*, each time it receives it from the database.

The *output.selectedList* parameter will emit a *TasksListModel* object, corresponding to the cell selected by the user.

The *output.hideEmptyState* parameter will emit a boolean that will be *true* if there are task lists in the database and *false* if there aren't.

Finally, we set the methods related to accessing the Model, such as calls to the database, or setting a database change observer (Listing 4-16).

Listing 4-16. Relationship between the ViewModel and the Model

```
class HomeViewModel {

    ...

    init(tasksListService: TasksListServiceProtocol) {

        ...

        NotificationCenter.default.addObserver(self,
                                    selector: #selector
                                    (contextObjectsDidChange),
                                    name: NSNotification.Name
                                    .NSManagedObjectContext
                                    ObjectsDidChange,
                                    object: CoreDataManager
                                    .shared.mainContext)
    }

    @objc func contextObjectsDidChange() {
        fetchTasksLists()
    }

    func fetchTasksLists() {
        lists.accept(tasksListService.fetchLists())
    }

    func listAtIndexPath(_ indexPath: IndexPath) ->
    TasksListModel {
        lists.value[indexPath.row]
    }
}
```

Add List Screen

This screen is responsible for adding task lists and the communication between its components. The communication between these components according to an MVVM architecture is shown in Figure 4-12.

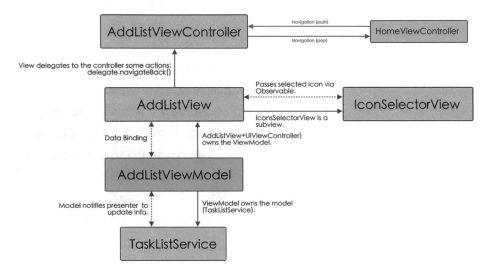

Figure 4-12. *Add list screen components communication schema*

AddListViewController

The *AddListViewController* only takes care of installing the *AddListViewModel* and passing it to the *AddListView*, and handling the navigation back to the home screen (Listing 4-17).

Listing 4-17. Setting AddListViewController code

```
class AddListViewController: UIViewController {

    private var addListView: AddListView!

    ...

    private function setupAddListView() {
```

```
        let viewModel = AddListViewModel(tasksListService:
        TasksListService())
        addListView = AddListView(viewmodel: viewmodel)
        addListView.delegate = self
        self.view = addListView
    }
}

AddListViewController extension: BackButtonDelegate {

    func navigateBack() {
        navigationController?.popViewController(animated: true)
    }
}
```

AddListView

As we have seen in previous chapters, *AddListView* has the following
elements that the user can interact with and that we must link to the
AddListViewModel: a *UITextField* element, two *UIButton* elements (one to
add the list and another to go back), and an IconSelector.

We are now going to see how we perform the Data Binding
with the *AddListViewModel* for each of these elements in the
bindViewToModel method.

The *titleTextField* element is where we will enter the title of the list.
We have to remember that to create a task this field cannot be empty;
otherwise, the *addListButton* button will be disabled.

Therefore, we must bind the content of *titleTextField* both to the
addListButton button to enable it (*addListButton.rx.isEnabled*) and to the
title input in the *AddListViewModel* (*input.title*) (Listing 4-18).

Listing 4-18. Binding of the content of titleTextField to the state of addListButton

```
titleTextfield
    .rx.text
    .map({ !($0?.isEmpty)! })
    .bind(to: addListButton.rx.isEnabled)
    .disposed(by: disposeBag)

titleTextfield.rx.text
    .map({ $0! })
    .bind(to: viewModel.input.title )
    .disposed(by: disposeBag)
```

With *rx.text*, we access the content of the UITextField; then through *map*, we evaluate whether or not it is empty and we pass the state to the *isEnabled* parameter of the *addListButton* (so that if it is empty, *isEnabled* is *false*, and if it contains text, *isEnabled* is *true*).

Next, we configure the behavior of the *addListButton* and *backButton* buttons in front of the *tap* event (Listing 4-19).

Listing 4-19. Bind addListButton and backButton to their corresponding tap events

```
addListButton.rx.tap
    .bind(to: viewModel.input.addList)
    .disposed(by: disposeBag)

backButton.rx.tap
    .bind(to: viewModel.input.dismiss)
    .disposed(by: disposeBag)

viewModel.output.dismiss
    .drive(onNext: { [self] _ in
```

```
        delegate?.navigateBack()
    })
    .disposed(by: disposeBag
```

The function of *addListButton* is to tell the *AddListViewModel* to save the new task list to the database (and then report that it's already added, so we're back on the *Home* screen). We communicate this to the *input.addList* parameter.

The *backButton's* function is to return to the *HomeScreen*, such as when finishing adding a new task list. For this reason, instead of associating a direct call to the *delegate.navigateBack* method, we will create an Output in the ViewModel that fulfills that call function (*output.dismiss*) and an Input that allows it to be called (*input.dismiss*).

For the case of the *iconSelectorView*, we will modify the *IconSelectorView* component to work with RxSwift instead of using the delegate pattern. To do this, what we do is eliminate the protocol of this component (which we use in the MVC and MVP architectures) and introduce a new variable of type *BehaviorRelay*, which will emit the name of the selected icon.

```
var selectedIcon = BehaviorRelay<String>(value: "checkmark.
seal.fill")
```

We will also modify the method by which when selecting one of the icons, its name was sent through the delegate. We simply pass that value to the created variable for it to pass:

```
func collectionView(_ collectionView: UICollectionView,
didSelectItemAt indexPath: IndexPath) {
    selectedIcon.accept(Constants.icons[indexPath.item])
}
```

Now we can bind the *iconSelectorView* to the *AddListViewModel* to pass the icon name to it as an input (*input.icon*) (Listing 4-20):

Listing 4-20. Binding of the name of the selected icon with the
AddListViewModel

```
iconSelectorView.selectedIcon
    .bind(to: viewModel.input.icon)
    .disposed(by: disposeBag)
```

Finally, we will bind to the *addedList* method of the *AddListViewModel*,
so that when this method is executed, the application navigates back to
the *Home*.

AddListViewModel

The *AddListModel* class is pretty straightforward. What is done in this
class when instantiating it is to pass a reference to the *TaskListService*
(as a protocol) so that it can interact with the Model, and in addition, we
initialize a *TaskListModel* object.

Following the Input/Output convention, we set the input and output
parameters of the *AddListViewModel*.

Definition of Input and Output for the AddListViewModel.

```
class AddListViewModel {

    var output: Output!
    var input: Input!

    struct Input {
        let icon: PublishRelay<String>
        let title: PublishRelay<String>
        let addList: PublishRelay<Void>
        let dismiss: PublishRelay<Void>
    }

    struct Output {
        let dismiss: Driver<Void>
```

```
    }

    ...
}
```

Now we only have to set the behavior of these parameters in the initialization of the *AddListViewModel* (Listing 4-21).

Listing 4-21. Establishment of the behavior of the parameters associated with the inputs and outputs

```
class AddListViewModel {

    ...

    private var tasksListService: TasksListServiceProtocol!
    private(set) var list: TasksListModel!

    private let dismiss = BehaviorRelay<Void>(value: ())

    init(tasksListService: TasksListServiceProtocol) {
        self.tasksListService = tasksListService
        self.list = TasksListModel(id: ProcessInfo().
        globallyUniqueString, icon: "checkmark.seal.fill",
        createdAt: Date())
        // Inputs
        let icon = PublishRelay<String>()
        _ = icon.subscribe(onNext: { [self] newIcon in
            list.icon = newIcon
        })
        let title = PublishRelay<String>()
        _ = title.subscribe(onNext: { [self] newTitle in
            list.title = newTitle
        })
```

```
    let addList = PublishRelay<Void>()
    _ = addList.subscribe(onNext: { [self] _ in
        tasksListService.saveTasksList(list)
        dismiss.accept(())
    })
    let dismissView = PublishRelay<Void>()
    _ = dismissView.subscribe(onNext: { [self] _ in
        dismiss.accept(())
    })
    input = Input(icon: icon, title: title, addList:
            addList, dismiss: dismissView)

    // Outputs
    let backNavigation = dismiss.asDriver()
    output = Output(dismiss: backNavigation)

    ...
  }
}
```

The input.icon and *input.title* parameters will receive the corresponding values for the selected icon and the entered title.

For the *input.addList* parameter, it will execute the method that adds the new list to the database and then call the *dismiss* method (which we've seen is bound to the delegate's *navigateBack* method on the *AddListView*).

The *dismiss* method will be the same method that we call via the *input.dismiss* parameter (which we have bound to the *backButton* in the *AddListView*).

Tasks List Screen

This screen is responsible for displaying the tasks that make up a list, marking them as done, deleting them, and adding new ones. The communication between its components is shown in Figure 4-13.

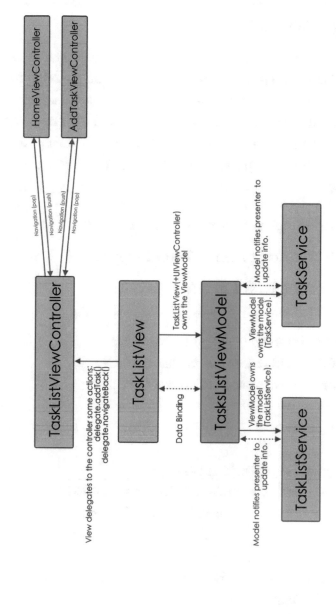

Figure 4-13. Tasks list screen components communication schema

TaskListViewController

This controller is responsible for, on the one hand, instantiating the *TaskListViewModel* and passing it to the View and, on the other hand, managing navigation to the add tasks screen or the *Home* screen.

On this screen we show the tasks that make up the list that we have selected in the *Home* screen, so in its initialization, we must pass the object *taskListModel*, which then passes it in turn to the *TaskListViewModel* (Listing 4-22).

Listing 4-22. Setting TaskListViewController code

```
class TaskListViewController: UIViewController {

    private var taskListView: TaskListView!
    private var tasksListModel: TasksListModel!

    init(tasksListModel: TasksListModel) {
        self.tasksListModel = tasksListModel
        super.init(nibName: nil, bundle: nil)
    }

    ...

    private func setupTaskListView() {
        let viewModel = TaskListViewModel(tasksListModel:
                        tasksListModel, taskService:
                        TaskService(), tasksListService:
                        TasksListService())
        taskListView = TaskListView(viewModel: viewModel)
        taskListView.delegate = self
        self.view = taskListView
    }
}
```

```
extension TaskListViewController:
TaskListViewControllerDelegate {

    func addTask() {
        let addTaskViewController = AddTaskViewController(tasks
        ListModel: tasksListModel)
        addTaskViewController.modalPresentationStyle =
        .pageSheet
        present(addTaskViewController, animated: true)
    }
}

extension TaskListViewController: BackButtonDelegate {

    func navigateBack() {
        navigationController?.popViewController(animated: true)
    }
}
```

TaskListView

TaskListView has, from the point of view of the components that make it up, functionality similar to *HomeView*: it presents a *UITableView* component that must be filled with the tasks that make up a list, a button to be able to add a new task, and we can delete tasks. But, in addition, it includes the title of the task list, a button to return to *HomeView*, and the possibility of updating a task, employing a button that allows it to go from undone to done, and vice versa.

So, let's start by seeing what code we have to introduce in the *TaskListView's bindToModel* method to bind the *UITableView* element with the *TaskListViewModel*, keeping in mind that we are working with inputs and outputs (Listing 4-23).

Listing 4-23. Binding between the UITableView component and the TaskListViewModel

```
tableView.rx
    .setDelegate(self)
    .disposed(by: disposeBag)

tableView.rx.itemDeleted
    .bind(to: viewModel.input.deleteRow)
    .disposed(by: disposeBag)

viewModel.output.tasks
    .drive(tableView.rx.items(cellIdentifier: TaskCell.reuseId,
    cellType: TaskCell.self)) { (index, task, cell) in
        cell.setParametersForTask(task, at: index)
        cell.checkButton.rx.tap
            .map({ IndexPath(row: cell.cellIndex,
            section: 0) })
            .bind(to: viewModel.input.updateRow)
            .disposed(by: cell.disposeBag)
    }
    .disposed(by: disposeBag)
```

Surely all this code is familiar to you. The only addition is the button that allows us to update the status of the task (*checkButton*), and that we configure for each of the cells of the table.

Next, we have the code that allows us to associate a target to each of the two buttons on this screen (Listing 4-24).

Listing 4-24. Configuration of the targets of the addTaskButton and backButton buttons

```
addTaskButton.rx.tap
    .asDriver()
```

```
    .drive(onNext: { [self] in
        delegate?.addTask()
    })
    .disposed(by: disposeBag)

backButton.rx.tap
    .asDriver()
    .drive(onNext: { [self] in
        delegate?.navigateBack()
    })
    .disposed(by: disposeBag)
```

Pressing these buttons will call the corresponding methods of the
TaskListViewController via the *delegate*.

Finally, we have the link with two parameters of type output of the
TaskListViewModel, and that will allow us, on the one hand, to show
the title of the task list and, on the other, to hide or show the *EmptyState*
depending on whether or not there are tasks in the list (Listing 4-25).

Listing 4-25. Binding of the pageTitle and emptyState elements to
the pageTitle and hideEmptyState outputs of the TaskListViewModel

```
viewModel.output.pageTitle
    .drive(pageTitle.rx.text)
    .disposed(by: disposeBag)

viewModel.output.hideEmptyState
    .drive(emptyState.rx.isHidden)
    .disposed(by: disposeBag)
```

As we have done in the *HomeView*, at the end of the *bindToViewModel*
method, what we do is make a call to reload the table which, as we will see
now in the ViewModel, calls the database to obtain the created task lists.

```
viewModel.input.reload.accept(())
```

TasksListViewModel

In the *TasksListViewModel*, we will have the logic that will manage this screen of the application and in which we will establish the inputs and outputs to which we will bind from the *TaskListView* (Listing 4-26).

Listing 4-26. Setting the inputs and outputs of the TaskListViewModel

```
class TaskListViewModel {

    var output: Output!
    var input: Input!

    struct Input {
        let reload: PublishRelay<Void>
        let deleteRow: PublishRelay<IndexPath>
        let updateRow: PublishRelay<IndexPath>
    }

    struct Output {
        let hideEmptyState: Driver<Bool>
        let tasks: Driver<[TaskModel]>
        let pageTitle: Driver<String>
    }
    ...
}
```

Now, as in the previous cases, we set them in the initialization of the *TaskListViewModel* (Listing 4-27).

Listing 4-27. Establishment of the behavior of the parameters associated with the inputs and outputs

```
class TaskListViewModel {

    ...

    init(tasksListModel: TasksListModel,
        taskService: TaskServiceProtocol,
        tasksListService: TasksListServiceProtocol) {
        self.tasksListModel = tasksListModel
        self.taskService = taskService
        self.tasksListService = tasksListService

        // Inputs
        let reload = PublishRelay<Void>()
        _ = reload.subscribe(onNext: { [self] _ in
            fetchTasks()
        })
        let deleteRow = PublishRelay<IndexPath>()
        _ = deleteRow.subscribe(onNext: { [self] indexPath in
            deleteTaskAt(indexPath: indexPath)
        })
        let updateRow = PublishRelay<IndexPath>()
                _ = updateRow.subscribe(onNext: { [self]
                    indexPath in
                    updateTaskAt(indexPath: indexPath)
                })
                input = Input(reload: reload, deleteRow:
                    deleteRow, updateRow: updateRow)

        // Outputs
        let items = tasks
            .asDriver(onErrorJustReturn: [])
```

```
    let hideEmptyState = tasks
        .map({ items in
            return !items.isEmpty
        })
        .asDriver(onErrorJustReturn: false)
    let pageTitle = pageTitle
        .asDriver(onErrorJustReturn: "")
    output = Output(hideEmptyState: hideEmptyState, tasks:
    items, pageTitle: pageTitle)
        ...
    }

    ...
}
```

The *input.reload* parameter will execute the method that fetches the tasks recorded in the database.

The *input.deleteRow* parameter will receive the position in the table of the cell we want to delete (as *IndexPath*) and will execute the corresponding *TaskService* method.

The *input.updateRow* parameter will receive the position in the table of the cell that we want to update (as *IndexPath*) and will execute the corresponding *TaskService* method.

The parameter *output.hideEmptyState* will emit a boolean that will be true if there are tasks in the list and false if there are not.

The *output.tasks* parameter will emit an array with the tasks that form a list (as a *TaskModel*), each time it receives them from the database.

The *output.pageTitle* parameter is in charge of passing the title of the task list.

Finally, we establish the methods that allow us to access the model (the database), as shown in Listing 4-28.

Listing 4-28. Relationship between the ViewModel and the Model

```swift
class TaskListViewModel {

    ...
    private var tasksListModel: TasksListModel!
    private var taskService: TaskServiceProtocol!
    private var tasksListService: TasksListServiceProtocol!

    let tasks = BehaviorRelay<[TaskModel]>(value: [])
    let pageTitle = BehaviorRelay<String>(value: "")

    init(tasksListModel: TasksListModel,
        taskService: TaskServiceProtocol,
        tasksListService: TasksListServiceProtocol) {
        ...

        NotificationCenter.default.addObserver(self,
                        selector: #selector(contextObjects
                        DidChange),
                        name: NSNotification.Name.NSManaged
                        ObjectContextObjectsDidChange,
                        object: CoreDataManager.shared
                        .mainContext)
    }

    @objc func contextObjectsDidChange() {
        fetchTasks()
    }

    func fetchTasks() {
        guard let list = tasksListService.
        fetchListWithId(tasksListModel.id) else { return }
```

```
    let orderedTasks = list.tasks.sorted(by:
    { $0.createdAt.compare($1.createdAt) ==
    .orderedDescending })
    tasks.accept(orderedTasks)
    pageTitle.accept(list.title)
}

func deleteTaskAt(indexPath: IndexPath) {
    taskService.deleteTask(tasks.value[indexPath.row])
}

func updateTaskAt(indexPath: IndexPath) {
    var taskToUpdate = tasks.value[indexPath.row]
    taskToUpdate.done.toggle()
    taskService.updateTask(taskToUpdate)
}
}
```

As you can see, by initializing this class we set the database change watcher. In this way, every time there is a change, the *fetchTasks* function will be called, which will be in charge of calling the database (through the *TaskListService*), it will order the tasks by creation date, and then, it will pass the corresponding values to the Observables that we have created so that the View is updated according to the new data.

Add Task Screen

This screen is responsible for adding tasks to a given list and the communication between its components is shown in Figure 4-14.

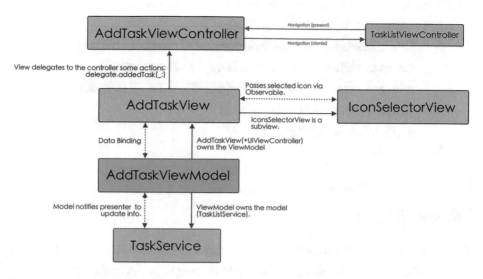

Figure 4-14. *Add task screen components communication schema*

AddTaskViewController

In this case, *AddTaskViewController* is in charge of receiving the
taskListModel object in its initialization (with the list of tasks in which
we want to add new tasks) and of instantiating the *AddTaskViewModel*
(passing it the list of tasks and an instance of the *TaskService*), and later
passing it to the view (Listing 4-29).

Listing 4-29. Setting AddTaskViewController code

```swift
class AddTaskViewController: UIViewController {
    private var addTaskView: AddTaskView!
    private var tasksListModel: TasksListModel!
    init(tasksListModel: TasksListModel) {
        super.init(nibName: nil, bundle: nil)
        self.tasksListModel = tasksListModel
    }

    ...
```

```
private func setupAddTaskView() {
    let viewModel = AddTaskViewModel(tasksListModel:
    tasksListModel, taskService: TaskService())
    addTaskView = AddTaskView(viewModel: viewModel)
    addTaskView.delegate = self
    self.view = addTaskView
}
}
```

AddTaskView

The code for the *AddTaskView* is very similar to what we developed for the *AddListView*, as it contains a *UITextField* element, an *IconsSelectorView* element, and a *UIButton* element. Therefore, the code of the *bindViewToModel* method will be familiar to you (Listing 4-30).

Listing 4-30. Binding elements between AddTaskView and AddTaskViewModel

```
func bindViewToModel(_ viewModel: AddTaskViewModel) {

    titleTextfield.rx.text
        .map({!($0?.isEmpty)!})
        .bind(to: addTaskButton.rx.isEnabled)
        .disposed(by: disposeBag)

    titleTextfield.rx.text
        .map({ $0! })
        .bind(to: viewModel.input.title )
        .disposed(by: disposeBag)

    addTaskButton.rx.tap
        .bind(to: viewModel.input.addTask)
```

```
    .disposed(by: disposeBag)

iconSelectorView.selectedIcon
    .bind(to: viewModel.input.icon)
    .disposed(by: disposeBag)

viewModel.output.dismiss
    .skip(1)
    .drive(onNext: { [self] in
        delegate?.addedTask()
    })
    .disposed(by: disposeBag)
}
```

AddTaskViewModel

The *AddTaskViewModel* class will be in charge of creating and recording a task in the database. In the same way as in the ViewModel earlier, we start by setting the inputs and outputs (Listing 4-31).

Listing 4-31. Setting the inputs and outputs of the AddTaskViewModel

```
class AddTaskViewModel {

    var output: Output!
    var input: Input!

    struct Input {
        let icon: PublishRelay<String>
        let title: PublishRelay<String>
        let addTask: PublishRelay<Void>
    }

    struct Output {
```

```
    let dismiss: Driver<Void>
  }
  ...
}
```

In this case, we only have three inputs (the icon, the task title, and the action to register the task) and one output (the action to dismiss the view).

Then we just have to set them in the initialization of the *AddTaskViewModel* (Listing 4-32).

Listing 4-32. Establishment of the behavior of the parameters associated with the inputs and outputs

```
class AddTaskViewModel {

    ...

    private var tasksListModel: TasksListModel!
    private var taskService: TaskServiceProtocol!
    private(set) var task: TaskModel!

    let dismiss = BehaviorRelay<Void>(value: ())

    init(tasksListModel: TasksListModel,
         taskService: TaskServiceProtocol) {
        self.tasksListModel = tasksListModel
        self.taskService = taskService
        self.task = TaskModel(id: ProcessInfo().
        globallyUniqueString, icon: "checkmark.seal.fill",
        done: false,
        createdAt: Date())

        // Inputs
```

```
    let icon = PublishRelay<String>()
    _ = icon.subscribe(onNext: { [self] newIcon in
        task.icon = newIcon
    })
    let title = PublishRelay<String>()
    _ = title.subscribe(onNext: { [self] newTitle in
        task.title = newTitle
    })
    let addTask = PublishRelay<Void>()
    _ = addTask.subscribe(onNext: { [self] _ in
        taskService.saveTask(task, in: tasksListModel)
        dismiss.accept(())
    })
    input = Input(icon: icon, title: title, addTask:
            addTask)

    // Outputs
    let dismissView = dismiss.asDriver()
    output = Output(dismiss: dismissView)
    }
}
```

The *input.icon* and *input.title* parameters will receive the corresponding values for the selected icon and the entered title.

For the *input.addTask* parameter, it will execute the method that adds the new task to the database and then call the dismiss method (which we've seen is bound to the delegate's *navigateBack* method on the *AddTaskView*).

MVVM–MyToDos Testing

In the MVVM architecture that we have just studied, the link between the View and the Model has been done through a new component, the ViewModel. But, in addition to the link between the View and the ViewModel, we have done it through a process called Data Binding, for which we have used a specific library: RxSWift. In this way, we get the View to be aware of the changes that occur in the ViewModel, and update accordingly.

Therefore, the question that arises is, how can we test a system that works with events and data streams (i.e., values that change over time)? How do we test code developed with RxSwift? For this, we will use a library that accompanies RxSwift: RxTest.

Note   As you will remember, at the beginning of this chapter, when we installed RxSwift with the Swift Package Manager, together with RxSwift, RxCocoa, and RxRelay, we also included RxTest (which we added to the MVVM_MyToDosTests target).

RxTest Introduction

As we have seen, using RxSwift, we go from working with individual values to working with streams that emit values over time. And RxTest is going to help us test these streams.

For this, we will use the main component of RxTest: *TestScheduler*.

This component allows us to create Observables and Observers that we can bind and intercept so that we can see what goes in and what goes out of our ViewModel. We can do this in certain "virtual times"; therefore, we can create events at specific times.

Therefore, to carry out a test, we must first create an instance of *TestScheduler* (with an initial argument "*initialClock*", which will define the start of the transmission), an instance of DisposeBag to have the subscriptions of previous tests, and also an instance of the ViewModel (Listing 4-33).

Listing 4-33. Creating instances of TestScheduler, DisposeBag, and ViewModel for our tests

```
class ExampleTests: XCTestCase {

    var testScheduler: TestScheduler!
    var disposeBag: DisposeBag!
    var viewModel: ViewModel!

    override func setUpWithError() throws {
        testScheduler = TestScheduler(initialClock: 0)
        disposeBag = DisposeBag()
        vieModel = ViewModel()
    }

    override func tearDownWithError() throws {
        testScheduler = nil
        disposeBag = nil
        viewModel = nil
        super.tearDown()
    }
}
```

Now we just have to apply these elements to a test. For example, suppose we want to test if the data has been loaded from a server after activating the redial button (Listing 4-34).

Listing 4-34. Test example with TestScheduler

```
func testLoading_whenThereIsNoList_shouldShowEmptyState() {
```

    // We create an observer that will be what we want
to observe and that will be the result of the
ViewModel output.
```
let isLoaded = testScheduler.createObserver(Bool.self)
```

    // We link the output we want to test to the observable.
```
viewModel.output.isLoadedData
    .drive(isLoaded)
    .disposed(by: disposeBag)
```

    // We send to the ViewModel the action of calling the
server through a *next* event at time 10.
```
testScheduler.createColdObservable([.next(10, ())])
    .bind(to: viewModel.input.callServer)
    .disposed(by: disposeBag)
```
    // Start the scheduler
```
testScheduler.start()
```

    // Finally, we test using XCAssert.
```
XCTAssertEqual(isLoaded.events, [.next(0, false),
.next(10, true)])
}
```

HomeViewModel Tests

Now we are going to apply what we have just seen about RxTest and the testing of RxSwift-based ViewModels in the *HomeViewModel* component.

Note   Remember that you can find the complete project code, including the tests, in the repository associated with this book.

First, we create instances of *TestScheduler*, *DisposeBag*, and *HomeViewModel*. Also, since to instantiate the *HomeViewModel* we have to pass a reference to the *TaskListService*, we also create an instance of it and an additional *TaskList* object (Listing 4-35).

Listing 4-35. Instantiation of the different components of the HomeViewModelTests

```
import XCTest
import RxSwift
import RxTest

@testable import MVVM_MyToDos

var disposeBag: DisposeBag!
    var viewModel: HomeViewModel!
    var testScheduler: TestScheduler!

    let tasksListService = TasksListService(coreDataManager:
    InMemoryCoreDataManager.shared)
    let taskList = TasksListModel(id: "12345-67890",
                                 title: "Test List",
                                 icon: "test.icon",
                                 tasks: [TaskModel](),
                                 createdAt: Date())

    override func setUpWithError() throws {
        disposeBag = DisposeBag()
        testScheduler = TestScheduler(initialClock: 0)
        tasksListService.fetchLists().forEach {
        tasksListService.deleteList($0) }
        viewModel = HomeViewModel(tasksListService:
        tasksListService)
    }
```

```
    override func tearDownWithError() throws {
        disposeBag = nil
        viewModel = nil
        testScheduler = nil
        tasksListService.fetchLists().forEach {
        tasksListService.deleteList($0) }
        super.tearDown()
    }
    ...
}
```

Unlike what we did in the MVC and MVP architectures, in which we used *TasksListSevice* and *TaskService* mocks, here we will use the application's database (Core Data), but we will configure it to work its persistence in memory and not in the memory of the device (*InMemoryCoreDataManager*).

To work with a clean database, we have introduced some calls that allow us to delete all the lists created in each test, both before and after performing the test:

```
tasksListService.fetchLists().forEach { tasksListService.
deleteList($0) }
```

Now we just have to create the different tests for the *HomeViewModel*.

EmptyState Test

As we can see in Listing 4-36, in the first test we check that, with the database empty, the *EmptyState* will be displayed. For this reason, the last event (after reloading the table) must return false (*.next(10, false)*), since according to the *HomeViewModel*, the *output.hideEmptyState* returns the boolean *!items.isEmpty*.

In the second test, since we first added a list, now the value of *!items. isEmpty* will be true, so the last event is *.next(10, true)*.

Listing 4-36. EmptyState test methods

```
func testEmptyState_whenThereIsNoList_shouldShowEmptyState() {
    let hideEmptyState = testScheduler.
    createObserver(Bool.self)

    viewModel.output.hideEmptyState
        .drive(hideEmptyState)
        .disposed(by: disposeBag)

    testScheduler.createColdObservable([.next(10, ())])
        .bind(to: viewModel.input.reload)
        .disposed(by: disposeBag)
    testScheduler.start()

    XCTAssertEqual(hideEmptyState.events, [.next(0, false),
    .next(10, false)])
}

func testEmptyState_whenAddOneList_shouldHideEmptyState() {
    let hideEmptyState = testScheduler.
    createObserver(Bool.self)
    tasksListService.saveTasksList(taskList)

    viewModel.output.hideEmptyState
        .drive(hideEmptyState)
        .disposed(by: disposeBag)

    testScheduler.createColdObservable([.next(10, ())])
        .bind(to: viewModel.input.reload)
        .disposed(by: disposeBag)
    testScheduler.start()
```

```
    XCTAssertEqual(hideEmptyState.events, [.next(0, false),
    .next(10, true)])
}
```

Note   Note that every time the *HomeViewModel* has a change in the *output.hideEmptyState*, we'll have to handle it in the *XCTAssertEqual*.

Testing the Deletion of Lists

In this test, we will prove that after the action of deleting a cell from the table, the table is empty (Listing 4-37). The steps to follow will be to add a list to the database, reload the table, launch the delete action of the cell, reload the list again, and verify that there are no lists in the database.

Listing 4-37. Method for testing cell deletion

```
func testRemoveListAtIndex_whenAddedOneList_
shouldBeEmptyModelOnDeleteList() {
    let lists = testScheduler.
    createObserver([TasksListModel].self)
    tasksListService.saveTasksList(taskList)

    viewModel.output.lists
        .drive(lists)
        .disposed(by: disposeBag)

    testScheduler.createColdObservable([.next(10, ())])
        .bind(to: viewModel.input.reload)
        .disposed(by: disposeBag)
    testScheduler.createColdObservable([.next(20,
    IndexPath(row: 0, section: 0))])
        .bind(to: viewModel.input.deleteRow)
```

```
        .disposed(by: disposeBag)
    testScheduler.createColdObservable([.next(30, ())])
        .bind(to: viewModel.input.reload)
        .disposed(by: disposeBag)
    testScheduler.start()

    XCTAssertEqual(lists.events, [.next(0, []), .next(10,
    [taskList]), .next(30, []), .next(30, [])])
}
```

List Selection Testing

In the last test, we will verify that after adding a list to the database, we can select it in the table and that the model returns that list (Listing 4-38).

Listing 4-38. Method for testing the selection of lists

```
func testSelectListAtIndex_whenSelectAList_
shouldBeReturnOneList() {
    let selectedList = testScheduler.
    createObserver(TasksListModel.self)
    tasksListService.saveTasksList(taskList)

    viewModel.output.selectedList
        .drive(selectedList)
        .disposed(by: disposeBag)

    testScheduler.createColdObservable([.next(10, ())])
        .bind(to: viewModel.input.reload)
        .disposed(by: disposeBag)
    testScheduler.createColdObservable([.next(20,
    IndexPath(row: 0, section: 0))])
        .bind(to: viewModel.input.selectRow)
        .disposed(by: disposeBag)
```

```
testScheduler.start()

XCTAssertEqual(selectedList.events, [.next(0,
TasksListModel()), .next(20, taskList)])
}
```

MVVM-C: Model–View–ViewModel–Coordinator

Until now, in the different architectures studied, we have seen how the navigation between the different screens, or what is the same between the different view controllers, occurred within said controllers.

This made it difficult, on the one hand, to test them and, on the other, that they could be reused in other parts of the application.

To solve this situation, we are going to use the Coordinator pattern.

What Is a Coordinator?

A *Coordinator* is a class that handles navigation outside of view controllers. This way we extract the navigation code from the view controllers, making them simpler and more reusable. Therefore, a Coordinator will have the tasks of loading the view controller that we are going to access and managing the navigation flow from that view controller to others (Figure 4-15).

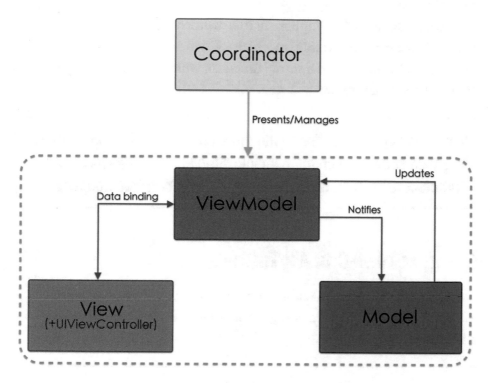

Figure 4-15. *Model–View–ViewModel–Coordinator schema*

The first thing we will do is create a protocol for all of our coordinators to adhere to. Since the application is simple, this protocol will also be simple (Listing 4-39).

Listing 4-39. Coordinator protocol

```
protocol Coordinator {

    var navigationController: UINavigationController {
    get set }

    func start()
}
```

All coordinators that implement this protocol must define a *navigationController* variable (to which we will assign the application's *navigationController*) and a *start()* function, which will be in charge of calling the view controller.

Note   In large applications, with more complex navigation flows, it is a good strategy to break them into simpler parts, managed by a *ParentCoordinator* on which an array of *ChildCoordinator* depends.

Using MVVM-C in MyToDos

As most of the application code is the same as when we have seen the MVVM architecture, we are going to see only those things that we have added new.

Note   Remember that all the code of the project can be found in the repository of this book.

SceneDelegate

In the *SceneDelegate,* what we do now is load the *HomeCoordinator,* passing it the *navigationController*. Next, we call *the start()* method.

```
class SceneDelegate: UIResponder, UIWindowSceneDelegate {

    var window: UIWindow?
    var homeCoordinator: HomeCoordinator?
```

```
func scene(_ scene: UIScene, willConnectTo session:
UISceneSession, options connectionOptions: UIScene.
ConnectionOptions) {
    if let windowScene = scene as? UIWindowScene {
        let window = UIWindow(windowScene: windowScene)
        let navigationController =
        UINavigationController.init()
        navigationController.navigationBar.isHidden = true
        navigationController.
        interactivePopGestureRecognizer?.isEnabled = false
        homeCoordinator = HomeCoordinator(navigation
        Controller: navigationController)
        homeCoordinator?.start()
        window.backgroundColor = .white
        window.rootViewController = navigationController
        self.window = window
        window.makeKeyAndVisible()
    }
}
...
}
```

Home Screen

The class that will manage the navigation, and which we have called from the *SceneDelegate*, is the *HomeCoordinator*. As shown in Listing 4-40, in addition to the start method, which is given by the protocol, it presents a couple of methods plus the *showSelectedList* method (which loads the Coordinator of the screen that shows the tasks of a list) and *addList* (which loads the Coordinator from the create a new list screen).

Listing 4-40. HomeCoordinatorProtocol and
HomeCoordinator class

```
protocol HomeCoordinatorProtocol {
    func showSelectedList(_ list: TasksListModel)
    func gotoAddList()
}

class HomeCoordinator: Coordinator, HomeCoordinatorProtocol {

    var navigationController: UINavigationController

    init(navigationController: UINavigationController) {
        self.navigationController = navigationController
    }

    func start() {
        let viewModel = HomeViewModel(tasksListService:
        TasksListService(), coordinator: self)
        navigationController.pushViewController(HomeView
        Controller(viewModel: viewModel), animated: true)
    }

    func showSelectedList(_ list: TasksListModel) {
        let taskListCoordinator = TaskListCoordinator(navigation
        Controller: navigationController, taskList: list)
        taskListCoordinator.start()
    }

    func gotoAddList() {
        let addListCoordinator = AddListCoordinator(navigation
        Controller: navigationController)
        addListCoordinator.start()
    }
}
```

As you can see, when passing the *HomeViewController* to the navigation controller, we are also passing an instance of the *HomeViewModel*, which includes a reference to the Coordinator itself to be able to manage navigation calls from said ViewModel, without the need for it to go through the View and the Controller.

Therefore, if we call, for example, the *gotAddList* method of the *HomeCoordinator*, it will take care of instantiating the *AddListCoordinator* and calling its *start()* method, which will load the navigation stack in the *AddListController* (and all this without going through the *HomeViewController*).

In this way, the *HomeViewController* only takes care of instantiating the View (which, as we already know, we have in a different class) and passing the ViewModel to it (Listing 4-41).

Listing 4-41. HomeViewController has reduced significantly its functions

```
class HomeViewController: UIViewController {

    private var homeView: HomeView!
    private var viewModel: HomeViewModel!

    init(viewModel: HomeViewModel) {
        super.init(nibName: nil, bundle: nil)
        self.viewModel = viewModel
    }

    required init?(coder: NSCoder) {
        fatalError("init(coder:) has not been implemented")
    }

    override func loadView() {
        super.loadView()
        setupHomeView()
    }
```

```
    private func setupHomeView() {
        homeView = HomeView(viewModel: viewModel)
        self.view = homeView
    }
}
```

By adding the coordinate in the initialization of the *HomeViewModel*, we have moved the *HomeViewModel* that we saw in the MVVM architecture as follows (Listing 4-42).

Listing 4-42. HomeViewModel adaptation for the use of a Coordinator

```
class HomeViewModel {

    var output: Output!
    var input: Input!
    let coordinator: HomeCoordinator

    struct Input {
        ...
        let addList: PublishRelay<Void>
    }
    ...

    init(tasksListService: TasksListServiceProtocol,
    coordinator: HomeCoordinator) {
        self.tasksListService = tasksListService
        self.coordinator = coordinator
        // Inputs
        ...
        let selectRow = PublishRelay<IndexPath>()
        _ = selectRow.subscribe(onNext: { [self] indexPath in
```

```
      coordinator.showSelectedList(listAtIndexPath(i
      ndexPath))
    })
    let addList = PublishRelay<Void>()
    _ = addList.subscribe(onNext: { _ in
      coordinator.gotoAddList()
    })
    self.input = Input(reload: reload, deleteRow: deleteRow,
                selectRow: selectRow, addList: addList)
    ...
  }
  ...
}
```

In this way, when we select a list or click the *addListButton*, instead of executing calls in the View and then passing it via delegate to the Controller, from the *HomeViewModel* itself, the *HomeCoordinator* will be called to execute the navigation flow.

Finally, in the *HomeView* class, we have changed in the *bindingToModel* method the link associated with the *addListButton* (Listing 4-43).

Listing 4-43. New bind for addListButton

```
addListButton.rx.tap
    .bind(to: viewModel.input.addList)
    .disposed(by: disposeBag)
```

And we have removed the link to the *viewModel.output.selectedList*, since its function of calling the *HomeViewController* (via *delegate*), so that it loads the *TasksListViewController*, is fulfilled by the *HomeViewModel* itself calling the *HomeCoordinator*.

Add List Screen

This screen is the one that allows us to create a new task list, and it only presents one possible navigation flow from it: return to Home. For this reason, the *AddListCoordinator* will only contain one method (in addition to *the start()* method), the *navigateBack* method, which will be called either on adding a new list or on selecting the back button (Listing 4-44).

Listing 4-44. AddListCoordinatorProtocol and AddListCoordinator code

```
protocol AddListCoordinatorProtocol {
    func navigateBack()
}

class AddListCoordinator: Coordinator,
AddListCoordinatorProtocol {

    var navigationController: UINavigationController

    init(navigationController: UINavigationController) {
        self.navigationController = navigationController
    }

    func start() {
        let viewModel = AddListViewModel(tasksListService:
        TasksListService(), coordinator: self)
        navigationController.pushViewController(AddListView
        Controller(viewModel: viewModel), animated: true)
    }

    func navigateBack() {
        navigationController.popViewController(animated: true)
    }
}
```

In this way, the code of the *AddListViewController* class is reduced to a minimum expression (Listing 4-45).

Listing 4-45. AddListViewController code

```
class AddListViewController: UIViewController {

    private var addListView: AddListView!
    private var viewModel: AddListViewModel!

    init(viewModel: AddListViewModel) {
        super.init(nibName: nil, bundle: nil)
        self.viewModel = viewModel
    }
    ...
    private func setupAddListView() {
        addListView = AddListView(viewModel: viewModel)
        self.view = addListView
    }
}
```

Now, as when creating the instance of *AddListViewModel*, we will pass the Coordinator, we will not need to add a dismiss event related to the View in the inputs to add list (*addList*) or return to *Home* (*dismiss*), we will simply call the *navigateBack* method of the Coordinator. Therefore, we can remove the output part of the ViewModel (Listing 4-46).

Listing 4-46. Use of the coordinator in the addList and dismiss inputs

```
class AddListViewModel {

    ...
    var coordinator: AddListCoordinator!

    struct Input {
```

```
    ...
    let addList: PublishRelay<Void>
    let dismiss: PublishRelay<Void>
}
...
init(tasksListService: TasksListServiceProtocol,
coordinator: AddListCoordinator) {
    self.tasksListService = tasksListService
    self.coordinator = coordinator
    ...
    let addList = PublishRelay<Void>()
    _ = addList.subscribe(onNext: { [self] _ in
        tasksListService.saveTasksList(list)
        coordinator.navigateBack()
    })
    let dismissView = PublishRelay<Void>()
    _ = dismissView.subscribe(onNext: { _ in
        coordinator.navigateBack()
    })
    ...
  }
}
```

By removing the output, we will also remove its binding on the View (*viewModel.output.dismiss*) that we had used in the MVVM architecture.

Tasks List Screen

This screen shows us the tasks in a list and presents two possible navigation flows: show the screen to add a new task or return to the *Home* screen. Thus, in the *TaskListCoordiantor*, we must have, together with the *start()* method, the *gotoAddTask* method and the *navigateBack* method (Listing 4-47).

Listing 4-47. TaskListCoordinatorProtocol and TaskListCoordinator code

```
protocol TaskListCoordinatorProtocol {
    func gotoAddTask()
    func navigateBack()
}

class TaskListCoordinator: Coordinator,
TaskListCoordinatorProtocol {

    var navigationController: UINavigationController
    var taskList: TasksListModel!

    init(navigationController: UINavigationController,
    taskList: TasksListModel) {
        self.navigationController = navigationController
        self.taskList = taskList
    }

    func start() {
        let viewModel = TaskListViewModel(tasksListModel:
        taskList, taskService: TaskService(),
        tasksListService: TasksListService(),
        coordinator: self)
        let taskViewController = TaskListViewController
                                (viewModel: viewModel)
        navigationController.pushViewController(taskView
        Controller, animated: true)
    }
```

```
    func gotoAddTask() {
        let addTaskCoordinator = AddTaskCoordinator(n
                                    avigationController:
                                    navigationController,
                                        tasksList: taskList)
        addTaskCoordinator.start()
    }

    func navigateBack() {
        navigationController.popViewController(animated: true)
    }
}
```

By removing the navigation functions from the *TaskListViewController,* your code looks like this (Listing 4-48).

Listing 4-48. AddListViewController code

```
class TaskListViewController: UIViewController {

    private var taskListView: TaskListView!
    private var viewModel: TaskListViewModel!

    init(viewModel: TaskListViewModel) {
        self.viewModel = viewModel
        super.init(nibName: nil, bundle: nil)
    }
    ...
    private func setupTaskListView() {
        taskListView = TaskListView(viewModel: viewModel)
        self.view = taskListView
    }
}
```

Regarding the original *TaskListViewModel* class, we will add a couple of parameters to the Input struct to be able to manage the calls to the Coordinator back to *Home* and access to the *Add Task* screen (Listing 4-49).

Listing 4-49. Use of the Coordinator in the addList and dismiss inputs

```
class TaskListViewModel {

    var output: Output!
    var input: Input!
    let coordinator: TaskListCoordinatorProtocol!

    struct Input {
        ...
        let addTask: PublishRelay<Void>
        let dismiss: PublishRelay<Void>
    }
    ...
    init(tasksListModel: TasksListModel,
        taskService: TaskServiceProtocol,
        tasksListService: TasksListServiceProtocol,
        coordinator: TaskListCoordinatorProtocol) {
        self.tasksListModel = tasksListModel
        self.taskService = taskService
        self.tasksListService = tasksListService
        self.coordinator = coordinator

        // Inputs
        ...
        let addTask = PublishRelay<Void>()
        _ = addTask.subscribe(onNext: { _ in
            coordinator.gotoAddTask()
        })
```

```
    let dismissView = PublishRelay<Void>()
    _ = dismissView.subscribe(onNext: { _ in
        coordinator.navigateBack()
    })
    input = Input(reload: reload,
                deleteRow: deleteRow,
                updateRow: updateRow,
                addTask: addTask,
                dismiss: dismissView)

    ...
}
    ...
}
```

Now we only have to modify in the *TaskListView* the code with which we linked the actions of the *addTaskButton* and the *backButton* with the *TaskListViewModel*. We will now bind them directly to the created inputs, eliminating the use of a delegate that calls the *TaskListViewController* to execute the corresponding navigation (Listing 4-50).

Listing 4-50. Set binding for addList and dismiss input parameters

```
addTaskButton.rx.tap
    .bind(to: viewModel.input.addTask)
    .disposed(by: disposeBag)

backButton.rx.tap
    .bind(to: viewModel.input.dismiss)
    .disposed(by: disposeBag)
```

Add Task Screen

This screen only presents one possible navigation flow: close the screen when adding a task. That is, we will need to add a dismiss method to the Coordinator (Listing 4-51).

Listing 4-51. AddTaskCoordinatorProtocol and AddTaskCoordinator code

```
protocol AddTaskCoordinatorProtocol {
    func dismiss()
}

class AddTaskCoordinator: Coordinator,
AddTaskCoordinatorProtocol {

    var navigationController: UINavigationController
    var tasksList: TasksListModel!

    init(navigationController: UINavigationController,
    tasksList: TasksListModel) {
        self.navigationController = navigationController
        self.tasksList = tasksList
    }

    func start() {
        let viewModel = AddTaskViewModel(tasksListModel:
        tasksList, taskService: TaskService(),
        coordinator: self)
        navigationController.present(AddTaskViewController(view
        Model: viewModel), animated: true)

    }

    func dismiss() {
```

```
        navigationController.dismiss(animated: true)
    }
}
```

By removing the navigation from the *AddListViewController,* your code looks like this (Listing 4-52).

Listing 4-52. AddListViewController code

```
class AddTaskViewController: UIViewController {

    private var addTaskView: AddTaskView!
    private var viewModel: AddTaskViewModel!

    init(viewModel: AddTaskViewModel) {
        super.init(nibName: nil, bundle: nil)
        self.viewModel = viewModel
    }
    ...
    private func setupAddTaskView() {
        addTaskView = AddTaskView(viewModel: viewModel)
        self.view = addTaskView
    }
}
```

In the *AddTaskViewModel,* when integrating the Coordinator, we will not need to generate an output that tells the *AddTaskView* that it should dismiss the View, so we will eliminate the output of the *AddTaskViewModel* and the *viewModel.output.dismiss* of the *AddTaskView* (Listing 4-53).

Listing 4-53. Using the Coordinator in the AddTaskViewModel to close the screen

```
class AddTaskViewModel {

    var input: Input!
    var coordinator: AddTaskCoordinatorProtocol!

    struct Input {
        ...
        let addTask: PublishRelay<Void>
    }

    private var tasksListModel: TasksListModel!
    private var taskService: TaskServiceProtocol!
    private(set) var task: TaskModel!

    init(tasksListModel: TasksListModel,
         taskService: TaskServiceProtocol,
         coordinator: AddTaskCoordinatorProtocol) {
        self.tasksListModel = tasksListModel
        self.taskService = taskService
        self.coordinator = coordinator
        self.task = TaskModel(id: ProcessInfo().
                    globallyUniqueString,
                            icon: "checkmark.seal.fill",
                            done: false,
                            createdAt: Date())

        // Inputs
        ...
        let addTask = PublishRelay<Void>()
        _ = addTask.subscribe(onNext: { [self] _ in
            taskService.saveTask(task, in: tasksListModel)
```

```
        coordinator.dismiss()
    })
    input = Input(icon: icon, title: title, addTask:
    addTask)
  }
}
```

Summary

Similar to what we did with the MVP architecture, in the MVVM architecture we have freed the Controller from the business logic, which we pass to the ViewModel. But unlike in the MVP architecture, the ViewModel is not aware of the existence of the View, which leads to further decoupling.

At the end of this chapter, we have also seen how to further reduce the code in the Controller by passing all the navigation logic to a new class: the Coordinator. This allows the Controller to be reused.

On the one hand, the Data Binding process can be excessive if we are developing a small application (or we are simply making a prototype of our app), and, on the other, the use of libraries such as RxSwift can increase the size of the applications and their performance, and in addition, they present a certain learning curve to apply them conveniently.

Still, the MVVM (and MVVM-C) architecture has many fans, thanks to the separation of responsibilities and ease of use.

In the next chapter, we will see the VIPER architecture that is being used more and more and that fully respects the use of SOLID principles and the separation of responsibilities, allowing for more modular applications, with cleaner code, and easier to maintain.

CHAPTER 5

VIPER: View– Interactor–Presenter– Entity–Router

What Is VIPER?

A Little History

VIPER was introduced in 2014 by Jeff Gilbert and Conrad Stoll and was the first attempt to apply the Clean Architecture (which we saw in Chapter 1), creating a series of components, each of which has a unique responsibility.[1]

VIPER is an acronym for View, Interactor, Presenter, Entity, and Router, and what is achieved is to divide a functionality or implementation into five different layers, gathered within a module (Figure 5-1).

---

[1] www.objc.io/issues/13-architecture/viper/

© Raúl Ferrer García 2023
R. Ferrer García, *iOS Architecture Patterns*, https://doi.org/10.1007/978-1-4842-9069-9_5

How It Works

The use of these components allows us to separate responsibilities within the application, which allows us to comply with the single-responsibility principle. In addition, it will also comply with the interface segregation principle, since we will use protocols (interfaces) to communicate between the layers.

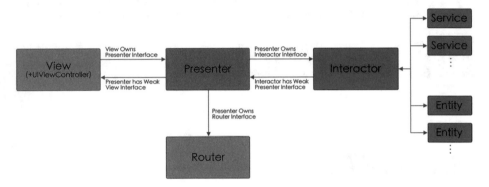

Figure 5-1. *VIPER schema*

Components in VIPER

Now we are going to see in detail each of the components of this architecture.

View

The View, that includes the *UIViewController*:

- It does not contain any logic and is only made up of passive elements: buttons, labels, views…

- It sends the user interactions to the Presenter.

- It knows how to display the information it receives from the Presenter.

- It does not ask the Presenter for information, but it is the Presenter that sends it when the View needs to be updated.

Interactor

The Interactor is the component that contains the business logic:

- It is responsible for receiving the information (models) from the database, servers...

- It is independent of the View.

- It receives actions from the Presenter and, after processing the information, returns the result to the Presenter via a delegate (Delegate Pattern).

- The Interactor never sends entities to the Presenter.

Presenter

The Presenter is the center of the VIPER architecture:

- It acts as a link between the different components.

- It receives user interactions from the View and contains the logic to act on these interactions and request information from the Interactor.

- It receives the information from the Interactor in the form of simple data structures, never the Entities.

- You don't know what components make up the view, but you know what content should be displayed and when.

- It is responsible for passing the information to the View in the most efficient way possible.

- It handles navigation to other screens using the Router.

Entity

Regarding the Entities:

- They are simple object models.

- Usually, they are data structures (*struct*).

- The only one who can work with the Entities is the Interactor.

Router

The Router has several responsibilities regarding the creation and navigation between screens:

- It is in charge of creating the screens (*UIViewController*).

- It is in charge of managing the navigation from one screen to another (it contains the navigation logic).

- It is the owner of the *UINavigationController* and the *UIViewController*.

- It would be like the Coordinator we saw at the end of Chapter 4, in the MVVM-C architecture.

Advantages and Disadvantages of VIPER

When developing a project, the VIPER architecture has many advantages due to the fact that it seeks a "Clean Architecture," but it also has some disadvantages.

Advantages

The main advantages of the VIPER architecture are as follows:

- By having the single-responsibility principle (SRP) as a basic principle, the code is cleaner.

- The code is more decoupled.

- Due to these characteristics, writing unit tests is simpler.

- There is more abstraction when developing the code, so more functionality can be easily added and the product scale.

- The separation of responsibilities between layers means that, for example, the Interactor only contains the business logic and is completely independent of the View, which makes it easier to write automated tests.

- It is considered to be quite useful in the case of complex applications due to, among other things, this isolation of business logic.

- The fact of working with independent modules, with well-defined communication interfaces, allows us to distribute the development of a project among several teams.

Disadvantages

The main disadvantages of the VIPER architecture are as follows:

- The fact that each module contains so many classes: View, Interactor, Presenter, Entities, Router... makes the project end up with a huge amount of code, and classes.

- There is a lot of boilerplate code you must write.

- It is not usually useful for small applications that do not plan to be extended with new functionality.

- Learning VIPER can seem daunting at first, especially for novice developers.

- To facilitate the reuse of modules, it is better not to use navigation between screens using Segue.

VIPER Application

Once we have seen the characteristics of the VIPER architecture, we are going to apply them in the development of our application.

Note   The entire project can be downloaded from the repository of this book. During the explanation of the implementation of the VIPER architecture in our project, we will only show the most relevant parts of the code.

Communication Between Components

As we have explained, the communication between the different components of this architecture is carried out through protocols. We can define each of these protocols based on the flow (*Input/Output*) with respect to the Presenter and then apply it to the appropriate component.

Communication Between Presenter and View

We will establish two protocols between the Presenter and the View: one for Input to the Presenter and one for Output (Listing 5-1).

Listing 5-1. Input/Output protocols of the Presenter with respect to the View

```
// MARK: View Input (View -> Presenter)
protocol ViewToPresenterProtocol {
    var view: PresenterToViewProtocol? { get set }
    var interactor: PresenterToInteractorProtocol? { get set }
    var router: PresenterToRouterProtocol? { get set }
}

// MARK: View Output (Presenter -> View)
protocol PresenterToViewProtocol { }
```

When developing the *Presenter*, we will make it adhere to the input protocol of the *View* with respect to the *Presenter* (*View -> Presenter*). This protocol has three important parameters, which bind you to the *View*, the *Interactor*, and the *Router* (Listing 5-2).

Listing 5-2. Application of the Input protocol between Presenter and View

```
class Presenter: ViewToPresenterProtocol {
    var view: PresenterToViewProtocol?
    var interactor: PresenterToInteractProtocol?
    var router: PresenterToRouterProtocol?
    ...
}
```

On the other hand, when developing the View, we will make it comply with the output protocol of the Presenter to the View (Presenter -> View). To organize the code, we can apply it as an extension (Listing 5-3).

Listing 5-3. Application of the Output protocol between Presenter and View

```
extension ViewController: PresenterToViewProtocol { }
```

Communication Between Presenter and Interactor

We will establish two protocols between the Presenter and the Interactor: one for Input to the Presenter and one for Output (Listing 5-4).

Listing 5-4. Input/Output protocols of the Presenter with respect to the Interactor

```
// MARK: Interactor Input (Presenter -> Interactor)
protocol PresenterToInteractorHomeProtocol {
    var presenter: InteractorToPresenterProtocol? { get set }
}
// MARK: Interactor Output (Interactor -> Presenter)
protocol InteractorToPresenterProtocol: AnyObject { }
```

When we develop the Presenter, we will make it comply with the Output protocol from the Presenter to the Interactor (via an extension) (Listing 5-5).

Listing 5-5. Application of the Output protocol between Presenter and Interactor

```
extension Presenter: InteractorToPresenterProtocol { }
```

On the other hand, when developing the Interactor, it will have to be made to comply with the input protocol between the Presenter and the Interactor (Listing 5-6).

Listing 5-6. Application of the Output protocol between Presenter and Interactor

```
class Interactor: PresenterToInteractorHomeProtocol {

    var presenter: InteractorToPresenterHomeProtocol?
    ...
}
```

Communication Between Presenter and Router

The communication between the Presenter and the Router is unidirectional, so we will only establish an Input protocol between the Presenter and Router.

This protocol contains the main method *createScreen*, which is what allows us to create the *UIViewController* (*View*) (Listing 5-7).

Listing 5-7. Input protocol of the Presenter with respect to the Router

```
// MARK: Router Input (Presenter -> Router)
protocol PresenterToRouterProtocol {
    func createScreen() -> UIViewController
}
```

This protocol will be the one that the Router must comply with (Listing 5-8).

Listing 5-8. Application of the Output protocol between Presenter and Router

```
class Router: PresenterToRouterProtocol {

    static func createScreen() -> UIViewController {
```

```
        let presenter: ViewToPresenterProtocol &
        InteractorToPresenterProtocol = Presenter()
        let viewController = ViewController()
        viewController.presenter = presenter
        viewController.presenter.router = Router()
        viewController.presenter?.view = viewController
        viewController.presenter?.interactor = Interactor()
        viewController.presenter?.interactor?.presenter =
        presenter
        return viewController
    }
}
```

The content that we have shown for these protocols is the basic one, which we will then have to complete (and in some cases, modify) according to the needs of each screen.

VIPER Layers

Unlike the previous architectures in which we organized the files according to their function – view, presenter, viewmodel... – in VIPER, we will divide them by modules, one per screen, which will include the protocols, the view, the introduction of the interactor, and the router; the services that allow us to communicate with the database, and, finally, the component elements: database, UI components, extensions, etc. (Figure 5-2).

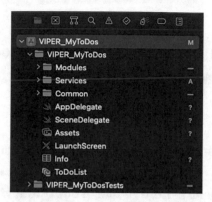

Figure 5-2. *VIPER folder project structure*

Modules

As we just discussed, the Modules folder will contain a subfolder for each screen. Each of these subfolders has five files. Thus, for example, in the case of the *Home* screen, we will have *HomeProtocols, HomeViewController, HomePresenter, HomeInteractor,* and *HomeRouter*.

Services

Here we will have the *TaskService* and *TasksListService* classes, which allow us to send information to the database (create, update, or delete it) or retrieve information from the database and transform it into models.

Common

Core Data

In this folder, we will have the CoreDataManager.swift file, along with the four files automatically created by Xcode for the database entities.

Components

In this folder, we will have those visual elements that we will use in the different screens: labels, buttons, cells, etc.

Models

Here we have the models into which we can transform the database entities. In addition, we will create a protocol that the models must comply with, in order to transform from model to entity and vice versa.

Extensions

In this case, we have created a UIColor extension to be able to easily access the colors created especially for this application and an extension to the NSManagedObject class that will prevent us from conflicting with contexts when we do the test part.

Helpers

They contain the constant parameters that we will use in the application.

MyToDos Application Screens

When we work with the VIPER architecture, it is not only important to be clear about what functions to introduce in each of the components of this architecture, but also to establish the appropriate communication protocols between each component, as we have previously mentioned.

Unlike the architectures that we have seen in previous chapters, in this case, we will join the code of the View and the Controller to simplify the development.

AppDelegate and SceneDelegate

By having a function within the Router class of each screen that instantiates each of the different classes needed to configure the screen, access to the *Home* screen from the *SceneDelegate* is simplified compared to the architectures we have seen previously (Listing 5-9).

Listing 5-9. Access to Home from SceneDelegate

```
func scene(_ scene: UIScene, willConnectTo session:
UISceneSession, options connectionOptions: UIScene.
ConnectionOptions) {
    if let windowScene = scene as? UIWindowScene {
        let window = UIWindow(windowScene: windowScene)
        window.backgroundColor = .white
        window.rootViewController = HomeRouter.createScreen()
        self.window = window
        window.makeKeyAndVisible()
    }
}
```

Home Module

The *Home* module is responsible for displaying the *Home* screen and establishing the different interactions with the user (Figure 5-3).

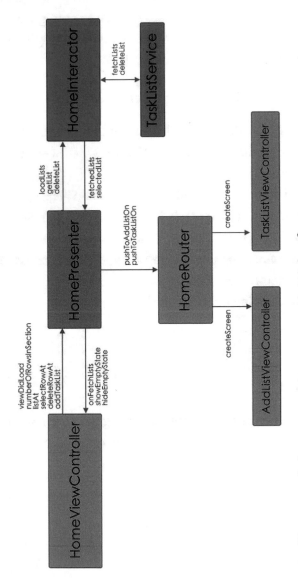

Figure 5-3. Home module components communication schema

Home Protocols

From the diagram of the module corresponding to the *Home* screen and the examples we saw when studying the communication between the different components, we can establish the communication interfaces (protocols) for this case.

The Router only has one input protocol; it contains the static method that creates the screen and the navigation methods for both the *AddListViewController* and the *TaskListViewController* (Listing 5-10).

Listing 5-10. PresenterToRouterHomeProtocol code

```
// MARK: Router Input
protocol PresenterToRouterHomeProtocol {
    static func createScreen() -> UINavigationController

    func pushToAddListOn(view: PresenterToViewHomeProtocol)
    func pushToTaskListOn(view: PresenterToViewHomeProtocol,
    taskList: TasksListModel)
}
```

Regarding the View and the Presenter, we have two protocols: one for Input and one for Output (regarding the View).

The input protocol, *ViewToPresenterHomeProtol*, is what allows us to have the View communicate with the Presenter. Basically, we will have methods related to the construction and actions on the table that shows the task lists (Listing 5-11).

Listing 5-11. ViewToPresenterHomeProtocol code

```
// MARK: View Input
protocol ViewToPresenterHomeProtocol {
    var view: PresenterToViewHomeProtocol? { get set }
    var interactor: PresenterToInteractorHomeProtocol? {
    get set }
    var router: PresenterToRouterHomeProtocol? { get set }

    func viewDidLoad()
    func numberOfRowsInSection() -> Int
    func listAt(indexPath: IndexPath) -> TasksListModel
    func selectRowAt(indexPath: IndexPath)
    func deleteRowAt(indexPath: IndexPath)
    func addTaskList()
}
```

On the other hand, we will have *PresenterToViewHomeProtocol*, the output protocol, which allows the Presenter to communicate with the View (Listing 5-12).

Listing 5-12. PresenterToViewHomeProtocol code

```
// MARK: View Output
protocol PresenterToViewHomeProtocol {
    func onFetchLists()
    func showEmptyState()
    func hideEmptyState()
}
```

Finally, we will have two protocols that relate to the Presenter and the Interactor.

The first one, *PresenterToInteractorHomeProtocol*, shows us how the Presenter communicates with the Interactor (Listing 5-13).

Listing 5-13. PresenterToInteractorHomeProtocol code

```
protocol PresenterToInteractorHomeProtocol {
    var presenter: InteractorToPresenterHomeProtocol? {
    get set }

    func loadLists()
    func getListAt(indexPath: IndexPath)
    func deleteListAt(indexPath: IndexPath)
}
```

The second, *InteractorToPresenterHomeProtocol*, shows the communication from the Interactor to the Presenter (Listing 5-14).

Listing 5-14. InteractorToPresenterHomeProtocol code

```
protocol InteractorToPresenterHomeProtocol {
    func fetchedLists(taskLists: [TasksListModel])
    func selectedList(taskList: TasksListModel?)
}
```

These protocols are the end result of module development. Let's see now where they come from and how we implement them.

HomeRouter

As we have seen, the *HomeRouter* is in charge of instantiating the *Home* screen and the navigation flow between it and other screens.

In the case of the *HomeRouter* class, as shown in Listing 5-15, it must adopt the *PresenterToRouterHomeProtocol* protocol and must implement all of its methods.

Listing 5-15. HomeRouter code, adopting the
PresenterToRouterHomeProtocol

```
class HomeRouter: PresenterToRouterHomeProtocol {

    static func createScreen() -> UINavigationController {

        let presenter: ViewToPresenterHomeProtocol &
        InteractorToPresenterHomeProtocol = HomePresenter()

        let viewController = HomeViewController()
        viewController.presenter = presenter
        viewController.presenter.router = HomeRouter()
        viewController.presenter?.view = viewController
        viewController.presenter?.interactor = HomeInteractor
        (tasksListService: TasksListService())
        viewController.presenter?.interactor?.presenter =
        presenter

        let navigationController = UINavigationController(rootV
        iewController: viewController)
        navigationController.interactivePopGestureRecognizer?.
        isEnabled = false
        navigationController.navigationBar.isHidden = true
        return navigationController
    }

    func pushToAddListOn(view: PresenterToViewHomeProtocol) {
        let addListController = AddListRouter.createScreen()
        let viewController = view as! HomeViewController
        viewController.navigationController?
            .pushViewController(addListController,
            animated: true)
    }
```

```
func pushToTaskListOn(view: PresenterToViewHomeProtocol,
taskList: TasksListModel) {
    let taskListController = TaskListRouter.
    createScreenFor(list: taskList)
    let viewController = view as! HomeViewController
    viewController.navigationController?
        .pushViewController(taskListController,
        animated: true)
    }
}
```

As you can see, we have a first method that creates the module and returns, in this case, a *UINavigationController* component (because it is the application's home screen).

The other two methods, *pushToAddListOn* and *pushToTaskListOn*, are responsible for building and navigating to the *AddList* and *TasksList* modules, respectively. In this way, we again separate the navigation logic from the *UIViewController*, limiting its functionality to the purely visual.

HomeViewController

The *HomeViewController* class is responsible for building and displaying the View with which the user will interact. Since the View interacts with the Presenter, we will have a presenter variable of type *ViewToPresenterHomeProtocol*, which allows the View to communicate with the Presenter (Listing 5-16).

Listing 5-16. HomeViewController code (only the parts in which there is interaction with the presenter are shown)

```
class HomeViewController: UIViewController {
    ...
```

```swift
    var presenter: ViewToPresenterHomeProtocol!

    override func loadView() {
        super.loadView()
        setupHomeView()
        presenter.viewDidLoad()
    }

    ...
}

private extension HomeViewController {
    ...

    @objc func addListAction() {
        presenter.addTaskList()
    }
}

extension HomeViewController: UITableViewDelegate {

    ...

    func tableView(_ tableView: UITableView, didSelectRowAt
    indexPath: IndexPath) {
        presenter.selectRowAt(indexPath: indexPath)
    }
}

extension HomeViewController: UITableViewDataSource {

    ...

    func tableView(_ tableView: UITableView,
    numberOfRowsInSection section: Int) -> Int {
        return presenter.numberOfRowsInSection()
    }
```

```swift
func tableView(_ tableView: UITableView, cellForRowAt
indexPath: IndexPath) -> UITableViewCell {
    let cell = tableView.dequeueReusableCell(withIden
    tifier: ToDoListCell.reuseId, for: indexPath) as!
    ToDoListCell
    cell.setCellParametersForList(presenter.
    listAt(indexPath: indexPath))
    return cell
}

func tableView(_ tableView: UITableView, commit
editingStyle: UITableViewCell.EditingStyle, forRowAt
indexPath: IndexPath) {
    if editingStyle == .delete {
        presenter.deleteRowAt(indexPath: indexPath)
    }
}
}

extension HomeViewController: PresenterToViewHomeProtocol {

    func onFetchLists() {
        tableView.reloadData()
    }

    func showEmptyState() {
        emptyState.isHidden = false
    }

    func hideEmptyState() {
        emptyState.isHidden = true
    }
}
```

In the final part of the code, we can see how the *HomeViewController* adopts the *PresenterToViewHomeProtocol* protocol. This is because, as we will see, the *HomePresenter* is related to the *HomeViewController* through a view variable of type *PresenterToViewHomeProtocol*.

HomePresenter

The *HomeViewPresenter* is bound to the *HomeRouter*, the *HomeViewController*, and the *HomeViewInteractor*. Since the *HomePresenter* receives events from the *HomeViewController* and *HomeInteractor*, two *presenter* variables are created in both classes:

```
// HomeViewController.swift
var presenter:ViewToPresenterHomeProtocol!
```

```
// HomeInteractor.swift
var presenter: InteractorToPresenterHomeProtocol?
```

Therefore, the *HomePresenter* class will need to adopt both protocols in order to communicate with those classes.

So, we can create the class and make it conform to the *ViewToPresenterHomeProtocol*. This protocol includes the methods related to the information displayed in the view (*numberOfRowsInSection, listAt*) or the interaction with it (*selectRowAt, deleteRowAt, addTaskList*). We also introduce a *viewDidLoad* method that will allow us to load the task lists when entering this screen (Listing 5-17).

Listing 5-17. HomePresenter code with the adoption of ViewToPresenterHomeProtocol

```
class HomePresenter: ViewToPresenterHomeProtocol {
    var view: PresenterToViewHomeProtocol?
    var interactor: PresenterToInteractorHomeProtocol?
    var router: PresenterToRouterHomeProtocol?
```

```swift
var lists: [TasksListModel] = [TasksListModel]()

func viewDidLoad() {
    NotificationCenter.default.addObserver(self,
                        selector: #selector(fetchLists),
                        name: NSNotification.Name.NSManaged
                        ObjectContextObjectsDidChange,
                        object: CoreDataManager.shared.
                        mainContext)
    interactor?.loadLists()
}

func numberOfRowsInSection() -> Int {
    lists.count
}

func listAt(indexPath: IndexPath) -> TasksListModel {
    lists[indexPath.row]
}

func selectRowAt(indexPath: IndexPath) {
    interactor?.getListAt(indexPath: indexPath)
}

func deleteRowAt(indexPath: IndexPath) {
    interactor?.deleteListAt(indexPath: indexPath)
}

func addTaskList() {
    router?.pushToAddListOn(view: view!)
}

@objc private func fetchLists() {
    interactor?.loadLists()
}
}
```

On the other hand, and through an extension, we will make the *HomePresenter* conform to the *InteractorToPresenterHomeProtocol* protocol. In this way, when we make calls to the Interactor (such as when loading the lists, selecting a list, or deleting another), the implementation of the methods of this protocol will allow us to receive the information from the Interactor and act accordingly (show the lists or an *EmptyState*, or navigate to the *TaskList* screen), as shown in Listing 5-18.

Listing 5-18. Adoption of the InteractorToPresenterHomeProtocol in the HomePresenter

```
extension HomePresenter: InteractorToPresenterHomeProtocol {

    func fetchedLists(taskLists: [TasksListModel]) {
        lists = taskLists
        taskLists.count == 0 ? view?.showEmptyState() : view?.
        hideEmptyState()
        view?.onFetchLists()
    }

    func selectedList(taskList: TasksListModel?) {
        guard let taskList = taskList else {
            return
        }
        router?.pushToTaskListOn(view: view!, taskList:
        taskList)
    }
}
```

HomeInteractor

The *HomeInteractor* contains the business logic of the application. It is responsible for communicating with the database and returning the necessary information to the *HomePresenter*.

This class must implement the *PresenterToInteractorHomeProtocol* (Listing 5-19).

Listing 5-19. HomeInteractor code implementing the PresenterToInteractorHomeProtocol

```
class HomeInteractor: PresenterToInteractorHomeProtocol {
    var presenter: InteractorToPresenterHomeProtocol?
    var lists: [TasksListModel] = [TasksListModel]()
    var tasksListService: TasksListServiceProtocol!

    init(tasksListService: TasksListServiceProtocol) {
        self.tasksListService = tasksListService
    }

    func loadLists() {
        lists = (tasksListService?.fetchLists())!
        presenter?.fetchedLists(taskLists: lists)
    }

    func getListAt(indexPath: IndexPath) {
        guard lists.indices.contains(indexPath.row) else {
            presenter?.selectedList(taskList: nil)
            return
        }
        presenter?.selectedList(taskList: lists[indexPath.row])
    }

    func deleteListAt(indexPath: IndexPath) {
        guard lists.indices.contains(indexPath.row) else {
        return }
        tasksListService.deleteList(lists[indexPath.row])
    }
}
```

You can see how in the *init* method we inject an instance of *TasksListService* to make requests about task lists to the database.

Add List Module

This screen is responsible for adding task lists and communication between its components. The communication between these components according to the VIPER architecture is shown in Figure 5-4.

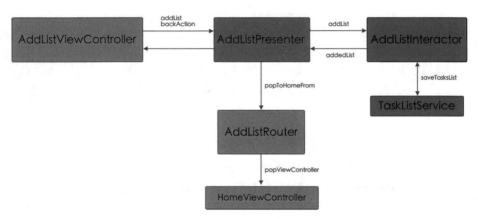

Figure 5-4. *Add list module components communication schema*

AddListProtocols

If we look at the schematic of this module, we can see that the methods used in communication between components have been reduced.

Thus, for example, the *PresenterToRouterAddListProtocol* protocol only has one method, *popToHomeFrom* (to return to the *Home* screen), in addition to the one to create the screen (*createScreen*) (Listing 5-20).

Listing 5-20. PresenterToRouterAddListProtocol code

```
// MARK: Router Input
protocol PresenterToRouterAddListProtocol {
    static func createScreen() -> UIViewController

    func popToHomeFrom(view: PresenterToViewAddListProtocol)
}
```

In the case of the *ViewToPresenterAddListProtocol* protocol, we will have two methods: *addList*, whose function is to send the created list to the database (and which is called when selecting the "Add List" button), and *backAction*, which returns the *Home* (Listing 5-21).

Listing 5-21. ViewToPresenterAddListProtocol code

```
// MARK: View Input
protocol ViewToPresenterAddListProtocol {
    var view: PresenterToViewAddListProtocol? { get set }
    var interactor: PresenterToInteractorAddListProtocol? {
    get set }
    var router: PresenterToRouterAddListProtocol? { get set }

    func addList(taskList: TasksListModel)
    func backAction()
}
```

As in this case the actions carried out on this screen do not require updating, we will not have methods in the *PresenterToViewAddListProtocol* protocol (although we will keep it here to maintain a similar structure to the rest of the modules for its study).

```
// MARK: View Output
protocol PresenterToViewAddListProtocol {}
```

The *PresenterToInteractorAddListProtocol*, which communicates the Presenter with the Interactor, has a single *addList* method, which will tell the Interactor to save the list of tasks passed to it to the database (Listing 5-22).

Listing 5-22. PresenterToInteractorAddListProtocol code

```
// MARK: Interactor Input
protocol PresenterToInteractorAddListProtocol {
    var presenter: InteractorToPresenterAddListProtocol? {
    get set }

    func addList(taskList: TasksListModel)
}
```

Finally, we have the *InteractorToPresenterAddListProtocol* protocol, with a single method, *addedList*, which is used to communicate to the Presenter that the list of tasks has already been added to the database (Listing 5-23).

Listing 5-23. InteractorToPresenterAddListProtocol code

```
// MARK: Interactor Output
protocol InteractorToPresenterAddListProtocol {
    func addedList()
}
```

AddListRouter

The *AddListRouter* adopts the *PresenterToRouterAddListProtocol* protocol, so it must implement its two methods: create the *AddList* module using the *createScreen* method and navigate back to the *Home* screen (when required), going back in the navigation stack using the *popToHomeFrom* method (Listing 5-24).

Listing 5-24. AddListRouter must adopt the
PresenterToRouterAddListProtocol and implement its methods

```
class AddListRouter: PresenterToRouterAddListProtocol {
    static func createScreen() -> UIViewController {
        let presenter: ViewToPresenterAddListProtocol
        & InteractorToPresenterAddListProtocol =
        AddListPresenter()

        let viewController = AddListViewController()
        viewController.presenter = presenter
        viewController.presenter.router = AddListRouter()
        viewController.presenter?.view = viewController
        viewController.presenter?.interactor =
        AddListInteractor(tasksListService: TasksListService())
        viewController.presenter?.interactor?.presenter =
        presenter
        return viewController
    }

    func popToHomeFrom(view: PresenterToViewAddListProtocol) {
        let viewController = view as! AddListViewController
        viewController.navigationController?.
        popViewController(animated: true)
    }
}
```

AddListViewController

As we have seen when commenting on the different protocols used in
this module, the *AddListViewController* does not need to implement the
PresenterToViewAddListProtocol (which is empty, and which we have left

to maintain the structure of the different protocols that are implemented in each module).

The only relationship with the Presenter will be through the variable created and that will allow us to call the *backAction* and *addList* functions of the Presenter (Listing 5-25).

Listing 5-25. AddListViewController implementation

```
class AddListViewController: UIViewController,
PresenterToViewAddListProtocol {

    ...

    var presenter: ViewToPresenterAddListProtocol!

    ...
}

extension AddListViewController {

    ...

    @objc func backAction() {
        presenter.backAction()
    }

    ...

    @objc func addListAction() {
        guard titleTextfield.hasText else { return }
        listModel.title = titleTextfield.text
        listModel.id = ProcessInfo().globallyUniqueString
        listModel.icon = listModel.icon ?? "checkmark.
        seal.fill"
```

```
    listModel.createdAt = Date()
    presenter.addList(taskList: listModel)
}

    ...

}

...
```

AddListPresenter

In the *AddListPresenter*, we have two basic functions. The first is to tell the Interactor that it should add a new task list to the database (*interactor?. addList*), and the other function is to tell the Router that the app should return to the Home screen (*router?.popToHomeFrom*) once a list is added or when the back button is selected (Listing 5-26).

Listing 5-26. AddListPresenter implementation, conforming to ViewToPresenterAddListProtocol and InteractorToPresenterAddListProtocol

```
class AddListPresenter: ViewToPresenterAddListProtocol {

    var view: PresenterToViewAddListProtocol?
    var interactor: PresenterToInteractorAddListProtocol?
    var router: PresenterToRouterAddListProtocol?

    func addList(taskList: TasksListModel) {
        interactor?.addList(taskList: taskList)
    }

    func backAction() {
        router?.popToHomeFrom(view: view!)
    }
}
```

```
extension AddListPresenter:
InteractorToPresenterAddListProtocol {

    func addedList() {
        router?.popToHomeFrom(view: view!)
    }
}
```

AddListInteractor

The code for the *AddListInteractor* is quite simple since you only need to implement the single method of the *PresenterToInteractorAddListProtocol* (*addList*) protocol. In this method, you first tell the database to add a new task list (via the *TasksListService*) and then tell the Presenter that the list has already been added (which will cause the Presenter to tell the Router that returns to *Home*) (Listing 5-27).

Listing 5-27. PresenterToInteractorAddListProtocol implementation, conforming to PresenterToInteractorAddListProtocol

```
class AddListInteractor: PresenterToInteractorAddListProtocol {

    var presenter: InteractorToPresenterAddListProtocol?
    var tasksListService: TasksListServiceProtocol!

    init(tasksListService: TasksListServiceProtocol) {
        self.tasksListService = tasksListService
    }

    func addList(taskList: TasksListModel) {
        tasksListService.saveTasksList(taskList)
        presenter?.addedList()
    }
}
```

Task List Module

This screen is responsible for displaying the tasks that make up a list, marking them as done, deleting them, and adding new ones. The communication between these components according to the VIPER architecture is shown in Figure 5-5.

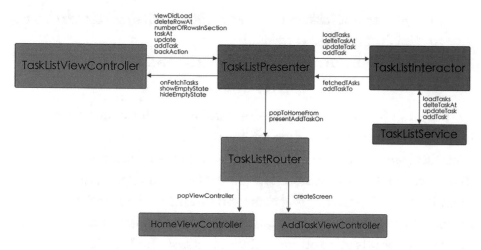

Figure 5-5. *Task list module components communication schema*

TaskListProtocols

The *TaskList* module is the most complex of the four modules that make up the application since it allows greater interaction with the user: updating and deleting tasks, navigating back to Home, or presenting the task creation screen. For this reason, we will see that there are a greater number of methods in the different communication protocols.

In the *TaskListProtocol*, together with the *createScreen* method (which in this case we have modified to pass the list of tasks that we want to show), we will have the *presentAddTaskOn* method, to access the task creation screen. As you can see, we will pass the list of tasks to which to add the created task, and the *popToHomeFrom* method, which we must implement to return to *Home* (Listing 5-28).

Listing 5-28. PresenterToRouterTaskListProtocol code

```
// MARK: Router Input
protocol PresenterToRouterTaskListProtocol {
    static func createScreenFor(list: TasksListModel) ->
    UIViewController

    func presentAddTaskOn(view: PresenterToViewTaskListProtocol,
    forTaskList: TasksListModel)
    func popToHomeFrom(view: PresenterToViewTaskListProtocol)
}
```

If we now look at the two protocols that manage the communications between View and Presenter, we can see that, in the case of the *ViewToPresenterTaskListProtocol* protocol, we have a first method that is executed when the module is loaded (*viewDidLoad*), four methods related to the fact that show and interact with the task list (*numberOfRowsInSection, taskAt, deleteRowAt,* and *update*), and two more methods related to button actions (*addTask* and *backAction*) (Listing 5-29).

Listing 5-29. ViewToPresenterTaskListProtocol code

```
// MARK: View Input
protocol ViewToPresenterTaskListProtocol {
    var view: PresenterToViewTaskListProtocol? { get set }
    var interactor: PresenterToInteractorTaskListProtocol? {
    get set }
    var router: PresenterToRouterTaskListProtocol? { get set }

    func viewDidLoad()
    func numberOfRowsInSection() -> Int
    func taskAt(indexPath: IndexPath) -> TaskModel
    func deleteRowAt(indexPath: IndexPath)
```

```
    func update(task: TaskModel)
    func addTask()
    func backAction()
}
```

Regarding the *PresenterToViewTaskListProtocol* protocol, it will give us the methods that we must implement in the view, both to reload the data to be displayed and to show or hide the *EmptyState* (Listing 5-30).

Listing 5-30. PresenterToViewTaskListProtocol code

```
// MARK: View Output
protocol PresenterToViewTaskListProtocol {
    func onFetchTasks()
    func showEmptyState()
    func hideEmptyState()
}
```

For the interaction between the Interactor and the Presenter, we will use two protocols. The first, *InteractorToPresenterTaskListProtocol*, indicates the methods that the Interactor must implement, all related to the tasks: load, add, update, and delete (Listing 5-31).

Listing 5-31. PresenterToInteractorTaskListProtocol code

```
// MARK: Interactor Input
protocol PresenterToInteractorTaskListProtocol {

    var presenter: InteractorToPresenterTaskListProtocol? {
    get set }

    func loadTasks()
    func deleteTaskAt(indexPath: IndexPath)
    func updateTask(task: TaskModel)
    func addTask()
}
```

In the second protocol, *InteractorToPresenterTaskListProtocol*, we have the methods that we will implement in the Presenter and that will allow us to access the database to obtain the tasks from a list or communicate with the router so that it does not present the add tasks screen (Listing 5-32).

Listing 5-32. InteractorToPresenterTaskListProtocol code

```
// MARK: Interactor Output
protocol InteractorToPresenterTaskListProtocol {
    func fetchedTasks(tasks: [TaskModel])
    func addTaskTo(list: TasksListModel)
}
```

TaskListRouter

As we already know, the *TaskListRouter* class must conform to the *PresenterToRouterTaskListProtocol* protocol and implement its methods. These methods are the ones that will allow us to create the module, present the task creation screen, and return to the *Home* screen (Listing 5-33).

Listing 5-33. Implementation of PresenterToRouterTaskListProtocol on TaskListRuter

```
class TaskListRouter: PresenterToRouterTaskListProtocol {

    static func createScreenFor(list: TasksListModel) ->
    UIViewController {
        let presenter: ViewToPresenterTaskListProtocol
        & InteractorToPresenterTaskListProtocol =
        TaskListPresenter()

        let viewController = TaskListViewController()
        viewController.presenter = presenter
        viewController.presenter.router = TaskListRouter()
```

```
viewController.presenter?.view = viewController
viewController.presenter?.interactor =
TaskListInteractor(taskList: list, taskService:
TaskService())
viewController.presenter?.interactor?.presenter =
presenter
    return viewController
}

func presentAddTaskOn(view: PresenterToViewTaskListProtocol,
forTaskList: TasksListModel) {
    let addTaskController = AddTaskRouter.
    createScreenFor(list: forTaskList)
    let viewController = view as! TaskListViewController
    addTaskController.modalPresentationStyle = .pageSheet
    viewController.present(addTaskController,
    animated: true)
}

func popToHomeFrom(view: PresenterToViewTaskListProtocol) {
    let viewController = view as! TaskListViewController
    viewController.navigationController?.
    popViewController(animated: true)
}
}
```

TaskListViewController

The *TaskListViewController* is in charge of showing us on the screen the tasks that belong to a certain list (or an *EmptyState* in case there is none). This screen presents numerous possibilities for interaction with the user: delete or update a task, press the "*Add task*" button, or press the button to return to Home.

All these actions, and some more (such as configuring the different cells of the table or knowing the number of rows in a table), will be transmitted to the Presenter thanks to the presenter variable that is of the *ViewToPresenterTaskListProtocol* type (Listing 5-34).

Listing 5-34. TaskListViewController code

```
class TaskListViewController: UIViewController {

    ...
    var presenter: ViewToPresenterTaskListProtocol!
    ...
}

private extension TaskListViewController {

    ...

    @objc func backAction() {
        presenter.backAction()
    }

    ...

    @objc func addTaskAction() {
        presenter?.addTask()
    }
}

extension TaskListViewController: UITableViewDelegate,
UITableViewDataSource {
    ...

    func tableView(_ tableView: UITableView,
    numberOfRowsInSection section: Int) -> Int {
        return presenter.numberOfRowsInSection()
    }
```

```swift
func tableView(_ tableView: UITableView, cellForRowAt
indexPath: IndexPath) -> UITableViewCell {
    let cell = tableView.dequeueReusableCell(withIdentifier:
    TaskCell.reuseId, for: indexPath) as! TaskCell
    cell.setParametersForTask(presenter.taskAt(indexPath:
    indexPath))
    cell.delegate = self
    return cell
}

...

func tableView(_ tableView: UITableView, commit
editingStyle: UITableViewCell.EditingStyle, forRowAt
indexPath: IndexPath) {
    if editingStyle == .delete {
        presenter.deleteRowAt(indexPath: indexPath)
    }
}
}

extension TaskListViewController: TaskCellDelegate {

    func updateTask(_ task: TaskModel) {
        presenter.update(task: task)
    }
}
```

On the other hand, the *TaskListViewController* must implement the
PresenterToViewTaskListProtocol protocol, so that the Presenter can make
the necessary calls that update the View (such as reloading the task list or
showing/hiding the *EmptyState*) (Listing 5-35).

Listing 5-35. TaskListViewController must implement
PresenterToViewTaskListProtocol methods

```
extension TaskListViewController:
PresenterToViewTaskListProtocol {

    func onFetchTasks() {
        tableView.reloadData()
    }

    func showEmptyState() {
        emptyState.isHidden = false
    }

    func hideEmptyState() {
        emptyState.isHidden = true
    }
}
```

TaskListPresenter

The *TaskListsPresenter*, due to its relationship with the
TaskListViewController and with the *TaskListInteractor*, must implement
the corresponding protocols.

The first protocol, *ViewToPresenterTaskListProtocol*, forces us to
implement the necessary methods so that the View can send its requests
to the Presenter. Most of these methods are requests that must be passed
to the *TaskListInteractor* to access the database, such as retrieving tasks,
updating them, or deleting them (Listing 5-36).

Listing 5-36. ViewToPresenterTaskListProtocol adoption by
TaskListPresenter

```
class TaskListPresenter: ViewToPresenterTaskListProtocol {

    var view: PresenterToViewTaskListProtocol?
    var interactor: PresenterToInteractorTaskListProtocol?
    var router: PresenterToRouterTaskListProtocol?
    var tasks: [TaskModel] = [TaskModel]()

    func viewDidLoad() {
        NotificationCenter.default.addObserver(self,
                            selector: #selector(fetchTasks),
                            name: NSNotification.Name.NSManaged
                            ObjectContextObjectsDidChange,
                            object: CoreDataManager.shared.
                            mainContext)
        interactor?.loadTasks()
    }

    func numberOfRowsInSection() -> Int {
        tasks.count
    }

    func taskAt(indexPath: IndexPath) -> TaskModel {
        tasks[indexPath.row]
    }

    func deleteRowAt(indexPath: IndexPath) {
        interactor?.deleteTaskAt(indexPath: indexPath)
    }

    func update(task: TaskModel) {
        interactor?.updateTask(task: task)
    }
```

```
    func addTask() {
        interactor?.addTask()
    }

    @objc private func fetchTasks() {
        interactor?.loadTasks()
    }

    func backAction() {
        router?.popToHomeFrom(view: view!)
    }
}
```

The adoption of the *InteractorToPresenterTaskListProtocol* protocol by the *TaskListPresenter* will allow it to respond to requests from the *TaskListInteractor* (Listing 5-37).

Listing 5-37. InteractorToPresenterTaskListProtocol by TaskListPresenter

```
extension TaskListPresenter:
InteractorToPresenterTaskListProtocol {

    func fetchedTasks(tasks: [TaskModel]) {
        self.tasks = tasks
        tasks.count == 0 ? view?.showEmptyState() : view?.
        hideEmptyState()
        view?.onFetchTasks()
    }

    func addTaskTo(list: TasksListModel) {
        router?.presentAddTaskOn(view: view!,
        forTaskList: list)
    }
}
```

TaskListInteractor

The *TaskListInteractor* must implement the
PresenterToInteractorTaskListProtocol protocol. As you can see (Listing 5-38),
most of these methods make calls to the database (via the *TaskService*).

Listing 5-38. TaskListInteractor code

```
class TaskListInteractor:
PresenterToInteractorTaskListProtocol {

    var presenter: InteractorToPresenterTaskListProtocol?
    var tasks: [TaskModel] = [TaskModel]()
    var taskList: TasksListModel!
    var taskService: TaskServiceProtocol!

    init(taskList: TasksListModel, taskService:
    TaskServiceProtocol) {
        self.taskList = taskList
        self.taskService = taskService
    }

    func loadTasks() {
        tasks = (taskService?.fetchTasksForList(taskList))!
        presenter?.fetchedTasks(tasks: tasks)
    }

    func deleteTaskAt(indexPath: IndexPath) {
        guard tasks.indices.contains(indexPath.row) else {
        return }
        taskService.deleteTask(tasks[indexPath.row])
    }
```

```
func updateTask(task: TaskModel) {
    taskService.updateTask(task)
}

func addTask() {
    presenter?.addTaskTo(list: taskList)
}
}
```

Add Task Module

This screen is responsible for adding tasks to a given list. The communication between its components using a VIPER architecture is shown in Figure 5-6.

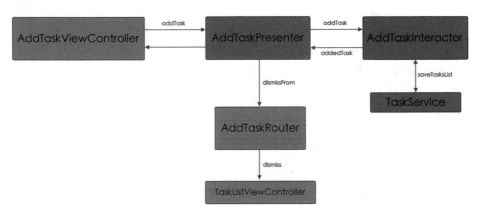

Figure 5-6. *Add task module components communication schema*

AddTaskProtocols

Like the module for adding task lists, this module has few functionalities (basically, adding a task), so we continue to have the same protocols as in the rest of the modules, and the number of methods to apply is smaller.

For example, the *PresenterToRouterAddTaskProtocol* will only present, in addition to the *createScreen* method, the *dismissFrom* method, which is the one that will contain the code to close the add task screen (Listing 5-39).

Listing 5-39. PresenterToRouterAddTaskProtocol code

```
// MARK: Router Input
protocol PresenterToRouterAddTaskProtocol {
    static func createScreenFor(list: TasksListModel) ->
    UIViewController

    func dismissFrom(view: PresenterToViewAddTaskProtocol)
}
```

Of the two protocols associated with the relationship between View and Presenter, only the *ViewToPresenterAddTaskProtocol* will have content (this is the same case as the add task list module). This protocol will be implemented by the Presenter, and together with the variables that allow access to other classes of the module (*view, interactor,* and *router*), it only presents the *addTask* method (to add a new task) (Listing 5-40).

Listing 5-40. ViewToPresenterAddTaskProtocol and ViewToPresenterAddTaskProtocol code

```
// MARK: View Input
protocol ViewToPresenterAddTaskProtocol {
    var view: PresenterToViewAddTaskProtocol? { get set }
    var interactor: PresenterToInteractorAddTaskProtocol? {
    get set }
    var router: PresenterToRouterAddTaskProtocol? { get set }
```

```
    func addTask(task: TaskModel)
}
```

```
// MARK: View Output
protocol PresenterToViewAddTaskProtocol {}
```

The *PresenterToInteractorAddTaskProtocol*, which will implement the *AddTaskInteractor*, presents a single function, *addTask*, which, as we will see later, will tell the database (via the *TaskService*) to add a new task and then tell the Presenter that it has already been added (Listing 5-41).

Listing 5-41. PresenterToInteractorAddTaskProtocol code

```
// MARK: Interactor Input
protocol PresenterToInteractorAddTaskProtocol {

    var presenter: InteractorToPresenterAddTaskProtocol? {
    get set }

    func addTask(task: TaskModel)
}
```

Finally, we will have the *InteractorToPresenterAddTaskProtocol*, which will implement the *AddTaskPresenter*, and whose only method will be *addedTask*, with which we will be telling the *AddTaskPresenter* that the task has already been added (Listing 5-42).

Listing 5-42. InteractorToPresenterAddTaskProtocol code.

```
// MARK: Interactor Output
protocol InteractorToPresenterAddTaskProtocol {
    func addedTask()
}
```

AddTaskRouter

As we have already seen in the previous modules, *AddTaskRouter*
must implement the *PresenterToRouterAddTaskProtocol* protocol and,
therefore, the methods that make it up: *createrScreenFor* and *dismissFrom*
(Listing 5-43).

Listing 5-43. AddTaskRouter class conforming to
PresenterToRouterAddTaskProtocol

```
class AddTaskRouter: PresenterToRouterAddTaskProtocol {

    static func createScreenFor(list: TasksListModel) ->
    UIViewController {
        let presenter: ViewToPresenterAddTaskProtocol
        & InteractorToPresenterAddTaskProtocol =
        AddTaskPresenter()

        let viewController = AddTaskViewController()
        viewController.presenter = presenter
        viewController.presenter.router = AddTaskRouter()
        viewController.presenter?.view = viewController
        viewController.presenter?.interactor =
        AddTaskInteractor(taskList: list, taskService:
        TaskService())
        viewController.presenter?.interactor?.presenter =
        presenter
        return viewController
    }

    func dismissFrom(view: PresenterToViewAddTaskProtocol) {
        let viewController = view as! AddTaskViewController
        viewController.dismiss(animated: true)
    }
}
```

AddTaskViewController

Although it doesn't contain any methods, to keep with the protocol structure, we'll make the *AddTaskViewController* conform to the *PresenterToViewAddTaskProtocol* protocol.

On the other hand, and thanks to the presenter variable (of the *ViewToPresenterAddTaskProtocol* type), we can tell the Presenter that we want to add a task (of the *TaskModel* type) (Listing 5-44).

Listing 5-44. AddTaskViewController class

```
class AddTaskViewController: UIViewController,
PresenterToViewAddTaskProtocol {

    ...

    var presenter: ViewToPresenterAddTaskProtocol!
    ...
}

extension AddTaskViewController {
    ...

    @objc func addTaskAction() {
        guard titleTextfield.hasText else { return }

        taskModel.title = titleTextfield.text
        taskModel.icon = taskModel.icon ?? "checkmark.
        seal.fill"
        taskModel.done = false
        taskModel.id = ProcessInfo().globallyUniqueString
        taskModel.createdAt = Date()
        presenter.addTask(task: taskModel)
    }
```

```
    ...
}

...
```

AddTaskPresenter

The *AddTaskPresenter* must conform to two protocols:
ViewToPresenterAddTaskProtocol (with the method that the View can
call) and *InteractorToPresenterAddTaskProtocol* (with the method that the
Interactor can call).

By conforming to the first protocol, *ViewToPresenterAddTaskProtocol*,
the View will be able to call the *addTask* method and pass it the object
with the tasks that the user wants to create. Then, the Presenter will
communicate to the interactor to be in charge of creating a said task in the
database (Listing 5-45).

Listing 5-45. AddTaskPresenter class conforming to
ViewToPresenterAddTaskProtocol

```
class AddTaskPresenter: ViewToPresenterAddTaskProtocol {

    var view: PresenterToViewAddTaskProtocol?
    var interactor: PresenterToInteractorAddTaskProtocol?
    var router: PresenterToRouterAddTaskProtocol?

    func addTask(task: TaskModel) {
        interactor?.addTask(task: task)
    }
}
```

With the second protocol, *InteractorToPresenterAddTaskProtocol*, the
interactor will be able to tell you that it has already created the task in the
database, and therefore, you can tell the Router to dismiss the *AddTask*
view (Listing 5-46).

Listing 5-46. AddTaskPresenter extension conforming to
InteractorToPresenterAddTaskProtocol

```
extension AddTaskPresenter:
InteractorToPresenterAddTaskProtocol {

    func addedTask() {
        router?.dismissFrom(view: view!)
    }
}
```

AddTaskInteractor

Finally, we have the *AddTaskInteractor* that must conform to the
PresenterToInteractorAddTaskProtocol protocol. This protocol, as we have
seen, consists of a single method (*addTask*), which is what the Presenter
will call to pass the *TaskModel* object that must be created in the database
(Listing 5-47).

Listing 5-47. AddTaskInteractor class conforming to
PresenterToInteractorAddTaskProtocol

```
class AddTaskInteractor: PresenterToInteractorAddTaskProtocol {

    var presenter: InteractorToPresenterAddTaskProtocol?
    var taskList: TasksListModel!
    var taskService: TaskServiceProtocol!

    init(taskList: TasksListModel, taskService:
    TaskServiceProtocol) {
        self.taskList = taskList
        self.taskService = taskService
    }
```

```
func addTask(task: TaskModel) {
    taskService?.saveTask(task, in: taskList)
    presenter?.addedTask()
    }
}
```

VIPER-MyToDos Testing

In the VIPER architecture, the two main components that we are going to test are the Interactors (which are the ones that apply the business logic) and the Presenters (which are the ones in charge of updating the View and communicating with both the Interactor and the Router).

Note   Remember that you can find the complete project code, including the tests, in the repository associated with this book.

Now, as an example, let's see how to set unit tests to the *HomePresenter* and *HomeInteractor* classes of the *Home* module.

HomePresenter

First, we will prepare the setup of our test class. In this class, our *sut* (or *system under test*) will be the *HomePresenter*, but we will also create instances of the different classes to be able to re-create the environment and the different relations between the classes (Listing 5-48).

Listing 5-48. Setup for HomePresenterTest

```
import XCTest

@testable import VIPER_MyToDos

class HomePresenterTest: XCTestCase {
```

```swift
    var sut: HomePresenter!
    var view: HomeViewController!
    var router: MockHomeRouter!
    var interactor: HomeInteractor!

    let taskList = TasksListModel(id: "12345-67890",
                                  title: "Test List",
                                  icon: "test.icon",
                                  tasks: [TaskModel](),
                                  createdAt: Date())

    override func setUpWithError() throws {
        sut = HomePresenter()
        let mockTaskListService = MockTaskListService(lists:
        [taskList])
        interactor = HomeInteractor(tasksListService:
        mockTaskListService)
        interactor.presenter = sut
        view = HomeViewController()
        view.presenter = sut
        router = MockHomeRouter()
        sut.interactor = interactor
        sut.view = view
        sut.router = router
    }

    override func tearDownWithError() throws {
        sut = nil
        super.tearDown()
    }

    ...
}
```

Of all these instances, there is one that we have prepared as a *mock* (not counting *MockTaskListService*), *MockHomeRouter,* so that we can verify where the application would navigate when calling its methods (Listing 5-49).

Listing 5-49. MockHomeRouter code

```
import UIKit

@testable import VIPER_MyToDos

class MockHomeRouter: PresenterToRouterHomeProtocol {
    var isPushedToAddList: Bool = false
    var isPushedToTasksList: Bool = false
    var selectedTaskList: TasksListModel = TasksListModel()

    static func createScreen() -> UINavigationController {
        UINavigationController()
    }

    func pushToAddListOn(view: PresenterToViewHomeProtocol) {
        isPushedToAddList = true
    }

    func pushToTaskListOn(view: PresenterToViewHomeProtocol,
    taskList: TasksListModel) {
        selectedTaskList = taskList
        isPushedToTasksList = true
    }
}
```

As you can see, we have set a couple of variables, *isPushedToAddList* and *isPushedToTasksList,* with an initial value of false, but which change to true when calling the corresponding methods.

Now we can move on to testing the different methods of the
HomePresenter.

First of all, we test that, how we have added a list when creating the
mockTaskListService instance, once the *viewDidLoad* method is called
(which if we look at the *HomePresenter* class calls the *loadLists* method of
the Interactor, which is in charge of retrieving the lists of the database and
return them to the Presenter), the number of rows in the table is 1 and, at
the same time, an object exists in the table (Listing 5-50).

Listing 5-50. Testing the existence of one object in mocked
TaskListService

```
func testNumberOfRows_whenAddedOneList_shouldBeOne() {
    sut.viewDidLoad()
    XCTAssertTrue(sut.numberOfRowsInSection() == 1)
}

func testListAtIndex_whenAddedOneList_shouldExists() {
    sut.viewDidLoad()
    XCTAssertNotNil(sut.listAt(indexPath: IndexPath(row: 0,
    section: 0)))
}
```

Next, we write a test that allows us to verify that if we select a cell
(directly passing the *IndexPath*), on the one hand, the Router redirects us
to the *TaskList* module and, on the other hand, we are passing the object
with the selected list (Listing 5-51).

Listing 5-51. Test for selectRowAtIndex

```
func testSelectRowAtIndex_whenAddedOneList_shouldReturnList() {
    sut.viewDidLoad()
    sut.selectRowAt(indexPath: IndexPath(row: 0, section: 0))
    XCTAssertTrue(router.isPushedToTasksList)
    XCTAssertTrue(router.selectedTaskList.id == "12345-67890")
}
```

Now we will test the ability to delete lists. To do this, we call the
deleteRowAt method (passing the *IndexPath* directly) and then check that
the *lists* variable is empty (Listing 5-52).

Listing 5-52. Test for deleteRowAtIndex

```
func testDeleteRowAtIndex_whenDeleteAList_shouldBeZeroLists() {
    sut.viewDidLoad()
    sut.deleteRowAt(indexPath: IndexPath(row: 0, section: 0))
    XCTAssertTrue(sut.lists.isEmpty)
}
```

With the last test, we will verify that when we call the *addTaskList*
method, the router redirects us to the *TaskList* module (Listing 5-53).

Listing 5-53. Test for addTaskList method

```
func testAddTaskList_whenAddTaskIsCalled_
routerShouldNavigate() {
    sut.addTaskList()
    XCTAssertTrue(router.isPushedToAddList)
}
```

HomeInteractor

The setup of the tests in the *HomeInteractorTest* is similar to that of the *HomePresenterTest*; we create the instances of the different classes that will allow us to configure the environment and its relationships. In the same way as in the *HomePresenterTest*, we will also use the *MockHomeRouter* to simulate the navigation and be able to test it (Listing 5-54).

Listing 5-54. HomeInteractorTest setup

```
import XCTest

@testable import VIPER_MyToDos

class HomeInteractorTest: XCTestCase {

    var sut: PresenterToInteractorHomeProtocol!
    var presenter: HomePresenter!
    var router: MockHomeRouter!
    var view: HomeViewController!
    let taskList = TasksListModel(id: "12345-67890",
                                  title: "Test List",
                                  icon: "test.icon",
                                  tasks: [TaskModel](),
                                  createdAt: Date())

    override func setUpWithError() throws {
        let mockTaskListService = MockTaskListService(lists:
        [taskList])
        sut = HomeInteractor(tasksListService:
        mockTaskListService)
        presenter = HomePresenter()
        router = MockHomeRouter()
        view = HomeViewController()
        presenter.router = router
```

```
        presenter.view = view
        sut.presenter = presenter
    }

    override func tearDownWithError() throws {
        sut = nil
        super.tearDown()
    }
    ...
}
```

Now we start with the tests of the different methods.

With the first test, we verify that when loading the lists from the database, since we use the *MockTaskListService* with a preloaded *TaskListModel* object, we will be returning a single list to the Presenter (Listing 5-55).

Listing 5-55. Testing loadLists method

```
func testLoadLists_whenLoadLists_shouldBeOneList() {
    sut.loadLists()
    XCTAssertTrue(presenter.lists.count == 1)
}
```

In the following method, we will verify that when a list is selected in the Presenter and the *IndexPath* of this list is passed to the Interactor, the latter passes the corresponding list to the Presenter, and said Presenter, in turn, tells the router to call the *TaskList* module by passing the selected list to it (Listing 5-56).

Listing 5-56. Testing navigation to TaskList module on select a list

```
func testGetList_whenGetListIsCalled_shouldRouterNavigate() {
    sut.loadLists()
    sut.getListAt(indexPath: IndexPath(row: 0, section: 0))
    XCTAssertTrue(router.isPushedToTasksList)
    XCTAssertTrue(router.selectedTaskList.id == "12345-67890")
}
```

Finally, we will check the action of deleting a list. To do this, the last test proves that after deleting the only list with which we have preloaded the *MockTaskListService*, the lists variable of the Presenter is empty (Listing 5-57).

Listing 5-57. Test for the deleteList method

```
func testDeleteList_whenListIsDeleted_shouldBeZeroLists() {
    sut.loadLists()
    sut.deleteListAt(indexPath: IndexPath(row: 0, section: 0))
    sut.loadLists()
    XCTAssertTrue(presenter.lists.count == 0)
}
```

Summary

The VIPER architecture was developed keeping in mind the concept of Clean Architecture, in which the application is divided into different layers, each with well-defined responsibilities. This makes the code easily testable and also reusable.

The decoupling and modularization of functionalities allow us to easily add new functions to our project.

As we have seen at the beginning of this chapter, the VIPER architecture has numerous advantages, but also some disadvantages, such as presenting a certain complexity for small projects or presenting a lot of repetitive code (the creation of this repetitive code in VIPER can be facilitated and automated using one of the multiple templates for Xcode that can be found on the Internet).

In the next chapter, we will see a new architecture that follows the principles of clean code: VIP (View–Interactor–Presenter). This architecture, which is starting to have quite a few followers, seeks to solve some of the situations that occurred in the VIPER architecture: for example, it simplifies the flow between components by making it unidirectional, while in VIPER it was bidirectional.

CHAPTER 6

VIP: View–Interactor–Presenter

What Is VIP?

A Little History

Around the year 2015, Raymond Law created what is known as Clean Swift[1] or VIP (View–Interactor–Presenter) architecture with the idea of applying the Clean Architecture (as we saw in Chapter 1) to projects for both iOS and macOS.

The paradigm of this architecture is the unidirectional flow that occurs within the VIP cycle, that is, the information always flows in one direction: from the View to the Interactor, from the Interactor to the Presenter, and from the Presenter to the View.

How It Works

As we just explained, the core of this architecture lies in the one-way loop between the View, Interactor, and Presenter. However, the application of this architecture usually requires the presence of other components

---

[1] https://clean-swift.com/

© Raúl Ferrer García 2023
R. Ferrer García, *iOS Architecture Patterns*, https://doi.org/10.1007/978-1-4842-9069-9_6

(although depending on the complexity of each screen, some may or may not be present): Router, Model, and Worker. Figure 6-1 shows how components are connected.

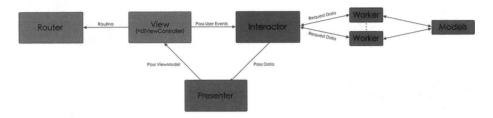

Figure 6-1. *VIP schema*

Components in VIP

Now we are going to see in detail each of the components of this architecture.

Note   As we will see as we go through the study of the VIP architecture, the number of generated classes, repetitive code, and communication protocols is high. If you search the Internet, you will find numerous examples of templates, which, although they all refer to the VIP architecture, may present some variations in their nomenclature, functionalities… due to the fact that they are adapted to different projects.

View (UIViewController)

We can consider that the View (+*UIViewController*) is where each VIP cycle begins and ends (it passes information and events to the Interactor and receives the response from the Presenter):

- The *UIViewController* manages the scene and maintains a strong reference to the View.

- Each *UIViewController* has strong references to the Interactor and the Router.

- Events that occur in the View are passed to the Interactor.

- The View receives the data from the Presenter since the *UIViewController* must conform to the protocol used by the Presenter to send the information.

For example, it shows the initial code that could present the ViewController and the View of a scene (the *Home* screen of our app) (Listing 6-1 and Listing 6-2).

Listing 6-1. The ViewController class contains the Input protocol and references to the Interactor, the Router, and the View

```
import UIKit

protocol HomeViewControllerInput: AnyObject {}

protocol HomeViewControllerOutput: AnyObject {}

final class HomeViewController: UIViewController {
    var interactor: HomeInteractorInput?
    var router: HomeRoutingDelegate?
}

extension HomeViewController: HomeViewControllerInput {}

extension HomeViewController: HomeViewDelegate {}
```

Listing 6-2. The View defines the protocol which connects to the ViewController

```
import UIKit

protocol HomeViewDelegate: AnyObject {}

final class HomeView: UIView {
    var delegate: HomeSceneViewDelegate?
}
```

Interactor

The Interactor is in charge of managing the View requests, obtaining the necessary data (whether from the Database or the Network), and passing it to the Presenter:

- The Interactor contains the business logic of each scene.

- Depending on the requests from the View, the Interactor connects with one or more Workers/Services (which, as we shall see, are in charge of obtaining the data).

- The Interactor maintains a strong reference to the Presenter.

- The Interactor must conform to the protocol that the View uses to send events.

In Listing 6-3, you can see the base code with which we would start working on our *HomeInteractor*.

Listing 6-3. The Interactor class defines its output protocol

```
import Foundation

protocol HomeInteractorOutput: AnyObject {}

typealias HomeInteractorInput = HomeInteractorOutput

final class HomeInteractor {
    var presenter: HomePresenterInput?
}
```

Presenter

The function of the Presenter (Listing 6-4) is to take the information it receives from the Interactor and transform it into information that can be represented by the View (i.e., we transform the information into a ViewModel):

- The Presenter contains the presentation logic.

- It has a weak reference to the View (which acts as an output of the Presenter).

- The Presenter transforms the results of the Interactor into objects renderable by the View.

Listing 6-4. In the Presenter code, we "rename" the HomeInteractorOutput and HomeViewControllerInput to a "Presenter" nomenclature

```
import UIKit

typealias HomePresenterInput = HomeInteractorOutput
typealias HomePresenterOutput = HomeViewControllerInput
```

```
final class HomePresenter {
    weak var viewController: HomePresenterOutput?
}
```

```
extension HomePresenter: HomePresenterInput {}
```

Router

The Router is the component in charge of navigating between ViewControllers and passing information between them (Listing 6-5):

- The Router contains the navigation logic (which causes us to remove it from the ViewController).

- It maintains a weak reference to the View (ViewController).

- This is an optional component, as a scene's ViewController may not have navigation options.

Listing 6-5. HomeSceneRouterLogic structure code

```
protocol HomeRouterDelegate {}
```

```
final class HomeRouter {
    weak var source: UIViewController?
}
```

```
extension HomeRouter: HomeRouterDelegate {}
```

Worker/Service

A Worker/Service is an abstract class that deals, basically, with database information retrieval operations, API requests, and file downloads:

- Each Worker/Service should have a single function (single-responsibility principle).

- An Interactor can call one or more Workers/Services.

- They must be generic so that they can be used by different Interactors.

Model

In the VIP cycle, information flows in one direction: from the View to the Interactor (in the form of a Request), from the Interactor to the Presenter (as a Response), and back to the View (as a ViewModel). Therefore, the use of a Model related to the scene and containing (Listing 6-6) is very established:

- **Request model**: Contains the parameters to allow the Interactor to perform the operations.

- **Response model**: Contains the appropriate data obtained by the Workers and to be passed to the Presenter.

- **ViewModel model**: They are usually primitive-type data, which is passed to the View to update it.

Listing 6-6. Model code structure for the VIP cycle

```
enum HomeModel {
    enum Fetch {
        struct Request {}
        struct Response {}
        struct ViewModel {}
    }
}
```

Configurator

It is an optional component, but it is often used a lot since it allows us to initialize the components of a scene and establish the relationships between them (Listing 6-7):

Listing 6-7. HomeConfigurator class code

```swift
import UIKit

final class HomeConfigurator {

    func configured(_ viewController: HomeViewController) ->
    HomeViewController {
        let interactor = HomeInteractor()
        let presenter = HomePresenter()
        let router = HomeRouter()
        router.viewController = viewController
        presenter.viewController = viewController
        interactor.presenter = presenter
        viewController.interactor = interactor
        viewController.router = router
        return viewController
    }
}
```

Note   As you have seen in the VIPER architecture, here we also have used a protocol nomenclature based on Input/Output terminology to facilitate its recognition and use.

Advantages and Disadvantages of VIP

When developing a project, the VIP architecture has many advantages due to the fact that it seeks a "Clean Architecture," but it also has some disadvantages.

Advantages

The main advantages of VIP architecture are as follows:

- It is based on the principles of Clean Architecture.

- It reduces the size of ViewControllers by passing all logic to Interactors.

- It presents a unidirectional flow of data.

- It is a modular and reusable architecture since the use of numerous protocols allows changes to a single component without affecting the rest of the application.

- The application of the Single-Responsibility principle reduces the size of the methods used, which is also a point in favor of modularity.

- Its structure allows easy maintenance and any error can be easily corrected.

- The implementation of unit tests is simple, which facilitates the development through TDD (test-driven development) and the testability of the application.

Disadvantages

The VIP architecture also has disadvantages, such as follows:

- This architecture is based on a large number of protocols, which can be confusing at first (this can be reduced by using templates).

- The use of so many protocols makes it necessary to write a large amount of code, even for the simplest tasks.

- This large amount of code makes it unsuitable for small applications.

- It may appear as if it has excessive design or complexity.

- Because of all this, it can be unappealing to developers just starting out.

VIP Layers

In a similar way to how we divided the project made with the VIPER architecture into folders in the previous chapter, with the VIP architecture we will do something similar, except that now instead of a folder with modules we have a folder with scenes.

Each scene corresponds to a screen and contains the View (*UIView* and *UIVIewController*), the Interactor, the Presenter, the Configurator, the Router, and the Model. We will also have a folder with the Services or Workers and, finally, a folder with common components (Figure 6-2).

Figure 6-2. *VIP folder project structure*

Scenes

As we just discussed, the Scenes folder will contain a subfolder for each screen. Each of these subfolders has seven files. Thus, for example, in the case of the *Home* screen, we will have *HomeView, HomeViewController, HomePresenter, HomeInteractor, HomeRouter, HomeConfigurator,* and *HomeModel.*

Services/Workers

Here we will have the *TaskService* and *TasksListService* classes, which allow us to send information to the database (create, update, or delete it) or retrieve information from the database and transform it into models.

Common

Core Data

In this folder, we will have the CoreDataManager.swift file, along with the four files automatically created by Xcode for the database entities.

Components

In this folder, we will have those visual elements that we will use in the different screens: labels, buttons, cells...

Models

Here we have the models into which we can transform the database entities. In addition, we will create a protocol that the models must comply with, in order to transform from model to entity and vice versa.

Extensions

In this case, we have created a UIColor extension to be able to easily access the colors created especially for this application and an extension to the *NSManagedObject* class that will prevent us from conflicting with contexts when we do the test part.

Helpers

They contain the constant parameters that we will use in the application.

MyToDos Application Screens

As we have explained, the VIP architecture is based on the View–Interactor–Presenter cycle and on the unidirectional flow of information. From here, we will have other components that will help us with navigation, information retrieval... such as Router, Configurator, and Workers/Services, all of them interconnected through a series of protocols or interfaces.

Like any architecture, if you investigate more about it you will see that the nomenclature of the protocols varies, they use workers or services or use cases, they use configurators or not... The idea is to know the basic idea of the architecture and use the format with which we are most comfortable.

For example, in the nomenclature of protocols, I prefer to use the terminology Input/Output to indicate that they are input or output functions to a component.

AppDelegate and SceneDelegate

To start the application, in the *SceneDelegate* we will create the first scene, the *Home*, by instantiating the *HomeViewController* class (to which we pass an instance of the view, *HomeView*). Next, we configure the *HomeViewController* using the *HomeConfigurator* and pass it to the *UINavigationController* components, which will be the one that holds all the navigation of the application (Listing 6-8).

Listing 6-8. Access to Home from SceneDelegate

```
func scene(_ scene: UIScene, willConnectTo session:
UISceneSession, options connectionOptions: UIScene.
ConnectionOptions) {
    if let windowScene = scene as? UIWindowScene {
        let window = UIWindow(windowScene: windowScene)
        window.backgroundColor = .white
        let homeViewController =
        HomeViewController(homeView: HomeView())
        let navigationController = UINavigationController(r
        ootViewController: HomeConfigurator.configure(homeV
        iewController))
        navigationController.navigationBar.isHidden = true
        navigationController.
        interactivePopGestureRecognizer?.isEnabled = false
        window.rootViewController = navigationController
        self.window = window
        window.makeKeyAndVisible()
    }
}
```

Home Scene

In Figure 6-3, we can see the different components that make up the *Home* Scene, how they are interconnected, the methods that are called, and the direction of the information flow.

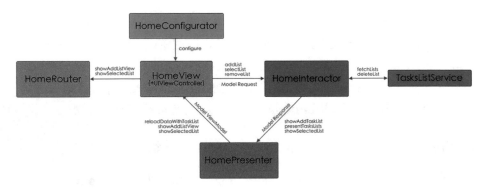

Figure 6-3. *Home scene components and communication schema*

HomeConfigurator

The *HomeConfigurator* is in charge of taking an instance of the *HomeViewController* and establishing all the components of the scene and the dependencies between them.

Thus, in this class, we will instantiate the *HomeInteractor* (to which we pass an instance of the *TasksListService*, which will be the worker or service that will allow us to access the database), the *HomePresenter*, and the *HomeRouter*. Next, we establish the relations of each one of them, to finally return the instance of the *HomeViewController* already configured (Listing 6-9).

Listing 6-9. HomeConfigurator code

```
final class HomeConfigurator {

    static func configure(_ viewController: HomeViewController)
    -> HomeViewController {
        let interactor = HomeInteractor(tasksListService:
        TasksListService())
        let presenter = HomePresenter()
        let router = HomeRouter()
        router.viewController = viewController
        presenter.viewController = viewController
        interactor.presenter = presenter
        viewController.interactor = interactor
        viewController.router = router
        return viewController
    }
}
```

HomeView

The *HomeView* class contains the different elements that make up the graphical interface and that communicate with the *HomeViewController* in two different ways: directly to pass the task lists and display them in the table (*showTasksLists*) and through the methods of the *HomeViewDelegate* protocol, which must implement the *HomeViewController* (Listing 6-10).

Listing 6-10. HomeView class code showing HomeViewDelegate protocol and where their methods are called

```
import UIKit

protocol HomeViewDelegate: AnyObject {
    func addList()
```

```
    func selectedListAt(index: IndexPath)
    func deleteListAt(indexPath: IndexPath)
}

final class HomeView: UIView {

    weak var delegate: HomeViewDelegate?
    ...
    func showTasks(lists: [TasksListModel]) {
        self.lists = lists
        tableView.reloadData()
        emptyState.isHidden = self.lists.count > 0
    }
}

private extension HomeView {
    ...
    @objc func addListAction() {
        delegate?.addList()
    }
    ...
}

extension HomeView: UITableViewDelegate {
    ...
    func tableView(_ tableView: UITableView, didSelectRowAt
    indexPath: IndexPath) {
        delegate?.selectedListAt(index: indexPath)
    }
}

extension HomeView: UITableViewDataSource {
    ...
```

```
func tableView(_ tableView: UITableView, commit
editingStyle: UITableViewCell.EditingStyle, forRowAt
indexPath: IndexPath) {
    if editingStyle == .delete {
        delegate?.deleteListAt(indexPath: indexPath)
    }
  }
}
```

HomeViewController

We can see the *HomeViewController* as the start and end of a VIP cycle.
As we have already seen when explaining the different protocols used in
the VIP architecture, this class will be associated with two protocols: one
with the methods that are used to send requests to the *HomeInteractor*
(*HomeVIewControllerOutput*) and another that will contain the methods
that will be called by the *HomePresenter* and that you will need to
implement the *HomeViewController* (*HomeViewControllerInput*)
(Listing 6-11).

Listing 6-11. HomeViewControllerInput and
HomeViewControllerOutput protocols

```
protocol HomeViewControllerInput: AnyObject {
    func reloadDataWithTaskList(viewModel: HomeModel.
    FetchTasksLists.ViewModel)
    func showAddListView(viewModel: HomeModel.AddTasksList.
    ViewModel)
    func showSelectedList(viewModel: HomeModel.SelectTasksList.
    ViewModel)
}
```

```
protocol HomeViewControllerOutput: AnyObject {
    func fetchTasksLists(request: HomeModel.FetchTasksLists.
    Request)
    func addList(request: HomeModel.AddTasksList.Request)
    func selectList(request: HomeModel.SelectTasksList.Request)
    func removeList(request: HomeModel.RemoveTasksList.Request)
}
```

In the process of instantiating the *HomeViewController*, we pass it an instance of the *HomeView* (we do it in the *HomeConfigurator*) and make its delegate the *HomeViewController*. For that reason, we'll need to make this class conform to the *HomeViewDelegate* protocol (Listing 6-12).

Listing 6-12. HomeViewController init and HomeViewDelegate conformation

```
final class HomeViewController: UIViewController {
    var interactor: HomeInteractorInput?
    var router: HomeRouterDelegate?

    private let homeView: HomeView

    init(homeView: HomeView) {
        self.homeView = homeView
        super.init(nibName: nil, bundle: nil)
    }

    required init?(coder: NSCoder) {
        fatalError("init(coder:) has not been implemented")
    }

    override func viewDidLoad() {
        super.viewDidLoad()
        homeView.delegate = self
        self.view = homeView
```

```
        fetchTasksLists()
    }

    private func fetchTasksLists() {
        let request = HomeModel.FetchTasksLists.Request()
                    Interactor?.fetchTasksLists(request:
                    request)
    }
}

extension HomeViewController: HomeViewDelegate {

    func addList() {
        let request = HomeModel.AddTasksList.Request()
        interactor?.addList(request: request)
    }

    func selectedListAt(index: IndexPath) {
        let request = HomeModel.SelectTasksList.
        Request(index: index)
        interactor?.selectList(request: request)
    }

    func deleteListAt(indexPath: IndexPath) {
        let request = HomeModel.RemoveTasksList.Request(index:
        indexPath)
        interactor?.removeList(request: request)
    }
}
```

As you can see, in each of these three methods of the
HomeViewDelegate, we create a request (in the *addList* method, the
request is empty, but we include it didactically), and then we call the
corresponding methods of the output protocol of the *HomeViewController*,
and that you will need to implement the *HomeInteractor*.

Finally, the *HomeViewController* must conform to the *HomeViewControllerInput* protocol, so that the presenter can pass information to it, either to update the interface or to navigate to another screen (Listing 6-13).

Listing 6-13. HomeViewControllerInput conformation

```
extension HomeViewController: HomeViewControllerInput {

    func showAddListView(viewModel: HomeModel.AddTasksList.
    ViewModel) {
        router?.showAddListView(delegate: viewModel.
        addListDelegate)
    }

    func reloadDataWithTaskList(viewModel: HomeModel.
    FetchTasksLists.ViewModel) {
                        homeView.showTasks(lists: viewModel.
                        tasksLists)
    }

    func showSelectedList(viewModel: HomeModel.SelectTasksList.
    ViewModel) {
        router?.showSelectedList(delegate: viewModel.
        selectedListDelegate, list: viewModel.tasksList)
    }
}
```

HomeInteractor

As we already know, the *HomeInteractor* involves the methods of two protocols: one input, which corresponds to the output protocol of the *HomeViewController* (*HomeViewControllerOutput*), so what we do is rename it as *HomeInteractorInput* (using the *typealias* command), and another output protocol (*HomeInteractorOutput*) with the methods that the *HomeInteractor* will call to pass to the presenter the responses of the requests made in the *HomeViewController* (Listing 6-14).

Listing 6-14. Input/Output protocols for HomeInteractor. The input protocol corresponds to the HomeViewControllerOut, so we changed its name in this class

```
protocol HomeInteractorOutput: AnyObject {
    func presentTasksLists(response: HomeModel.FetchTasksLists.
    Response)
    func showAddTaskList(response: HomeModel.AddTasksList.
    Response)
    func showSelectedList(response: HomeModel.SelectTasksList.
    Response)
}

typealias HomeInteractorInput = HomeViewControllerOutput
```

In the *HomeInteractor* we have the business logic of this scene, and in order to implement it, we will use the *TasksListService* service to be able to access the database in relation to the table that contains the task lists. We will pass the *TasksListService* in the initialization of this class (as we have seen in the *HomeConfigurator*) (Listing 6-15).

Listing 6-15. HomeInteractor initialization

```
final class HomeInteractor {
    var presenter: HomePresenterInput?

    private var lists = [TasksListModel]()
    private let tasksListService: TasksListServiceProtocol!
```

```
    init(tasksListService: TasksListServiceProtocol) {
        self.tasksListService = tasksListService
    }

    func fetchTasksLists() {
        fetchTasksLists(request: HomeModel.FetchTasksLists.
        Request())
    }
}
```

As we already know, the *HomeInteractor* must conform to the *HomeInteractorInput* (which is the name we have given to the *HomeViewControllerOutput* in this class), so we implement its methods (Listing 6-16).

Listing 6-16. HomeInteractorInput conformation

```
extension HomeInteractor: HomeInteractorInput {

    func addList(request: HomeModel.AddTasksList.Request) {
        let response = HomeModel.AddTasksList.
        Response(addListDelegate: self)
        presenter?.showAddTaskList(response: response)
    }

    func fetchTasksLists(request: HomeModel.FetchTasksLists.
    Request) {
        lists = tasksListService.fetchLists()
        let response = HomeModel.FetchTasksLists.
        Response(tasksLists: lists)
        presenter?.presentTasksLists(response: response)
    }
```

```
func selectList(request: HomeModel.SelectTasksList.
Request) {
    let list = lists[request.index.row]
    let response = HomeModel.SelectTasksList.
    Response(selectedListDelegate: self, tasksList: list)
    presenter?.showSelectedList(response: response)
}

func removeList(request: HomeModel.RemoveTasksList.
Request) {
    let list = lists[request.index.row]
    tasksListService.deleteList(list)
    lists.remove(at: request.index.row)
    let response = HomeModel.FetchTasksLists.
    Response(tasksLists: lists)
    presenter?.presentTasksLists(response: response)
}
}
```

Note that in the *addList* method, when preparing the response, we have established the *HomeInteractor* as a delegate (*addListDelegate*), since we must bear in mind that when we add a new list from the *AddListView* scene (as we will see later) we must update the scene Home with the new list.

In these methods, after making the corresponding request (if necessary) to the *TasksListService*, we prepare the response and pass it to the presenter through the corresponding method.

In addition, when creating the response in the *selectList* method, we have also set the *HomeInteractor* as a delegate (*selectedListDelegate*), so that when we modify the tasks of a list in the *TaskList* scene, the Home is also updated.

Therefore, the *HomeInteractor* must conform to the two protocols to which it is a delegate. In both cases, it calls the *fetchTasksLists* method which, as we have seen, is responsible for retrieving the task lists from the database and passing them to *HomePresenter* (Listing 6-17).

Listing 6-17. AddListDelegate and SelectedListDelegate conformation

```
extension HomeInteractor: AddListDelegate {

    func didAddList() {
        fetchTasksLists()
    }
}

extension HomeInteractor: SelectedListDelegate {

    func updateLists() {
        fetchTasksLists()
    }
}
```

HomePresenter

This class is in charge of receiving the responses from the *HomeInteractor*, and processing them so that they can be displayed by the *HomeViewController*, to which they are passed as a ViewModel.

In the HomePresenter, we will also have an input protocol, which corresponds to the output protocol of the *HomeInteractor* (which is why we changed its name), and another output protocol, which corresponds to the input protocol of the *HomeViewController* (and therefore what we also change the name) (Listing 6-18).

Listing 6-18. We changed the names of the **protocols** so that it is easier to see what their function is in the HomePresenter

```
typealias HomePresenterInput = HomeInteractorOutput
typealias HomePresenterOutput = HomeViewControllerInput
```

Finally, we only have to make the *HomePresenter* conform to the *HomePresenterInput* protocol and implement its methods so that the *HomeInteractor* can pass its responses and, after being processed, send them to the *HomeViewController* (Listing 6-19).

Listing 6-19. HomePresenterInput conformation

```
final class HomePresenter {
    weak var viewController: HomePresenterOutput?
}

extension HomePresenter: HomePresenterInput {

    func presentTasksLists(response: HomeModel.FetchTasksLists.
    Response) {
        let viewModel = HomeModel.FetchTasksLists.
        ViewModel(tasksLists: response.tasksLists)
        viewController?.reloadDataWithTaskList(viewModel:
        viewModel)
    }

    func showAddTaskList(response: HomeModel.AddTasksList.
    Response) {
        let viewModel = HomeModel.AddTasksList.
        ViewModel(addListDelegate: response.addListDelegate)
        viewController?.showAddListView(viewModel: viewModel)
    }
```

```
func showSelectedList(response: HomeModel.SelectTasksList.
Response) {
    let viewModel = HomeModel.SelectTasksList.
    ViewModel(selectedListDelegate: response.
    selectedListDelegate, tasksList: response.tasksList)
    viewController?.showSelectedList(viewModel: viewModel)
}
}
```

HomeModel

As we have been seeing in the code of the different components of the *Home* scene, we have done the passing of information in the form of *Request*, *Response*, and *ViewModel* through the *HomeModel*, which contains an enum for each use or request: thus, we have one for the request of the task lists to the database (*enum FetchTasksLists*), another to call the scene that allows us to add a new list (*enum AddTasksList*), and another to call the scene that shows the tasks of a list (*enum SelectTasksList*).

In addition, each of these enums contains, as we discussed at the beginning of the chapter, three structs: *Request* (for requests from the ViewController to the Interactor), *Response* (to pass the responses from the Interactor to the Presenter), and *ViewModel* (to pass the data from the Presenter to the ViewController) (Listing 6-20).

Listing 6-20. HomeModel code

```
enum HomeModel {

    enum FetchTasksLists {
        struct Request {}

        struct Response {
            let tasksLists: [TasksListModel]
        }
```

```swift
    struct ViewModel {
        let tasksLists: [TasksListModel]
    }
}

enum AddTasksList {
    struct Request {}

    struct Response {
        let addListDelegate: AddListDelegate
    }

    struct ViewModel {
        let addListDelegate: AddListDelegate
    }
}

enum SelectTasksList {
    struct Request {
        let index: IndexPath
    }

    struct Response {
        let selectedListDelegate: SelectedListDelegate
        let tasksList: TasksListModel
    }

    struct ViewModel {
        let selectedListDelegate: SelectedListDelegate
        let tasksList: TasksListModel
    }
}
```

```
enum RemoveTasksList {
    struct Request {
        let index: IndexPath
    }

    struct Response {
        let list: TasksListModel
    }
}
}
```

HomeRouter

The *HomeRouter* contains the methods that allow you to navigate from the *Home* to the screen that allows you to add new lists (*AddList* scene) or to the screen that allows you to view the tasks in a list (*TasksList* scene). Both methods are defined in the *HomeRouterDelegate* protocol (Listing 6-21).

Listing 6-21. Definition of HomeRouterDelegate protocol

```
protocol HomeRouterDelegate {
    func showAddListView(delegate: AddListDelegate)
    func showSelectedList(delegate: SelectedListDelegate,
    list: TasksListModel)
}
```

When navigating to a new scene, we must first create the corresponding ViewController, and then we will configure it through its Configurator (Listing 6-22).

Listing 6-22. Conformation of HomeRouter to
HomeRouterDelegate protocol

```
extension HomeRouter: HomeRouterDelegate {

    func showAddListView(delegate: AddListDelegate) {
        let addListViewController = AddListViewController(
        addListView: AddListView())
        viewController?.navigationController?.pushViewController
        (AddListConfigurator.configure(addListViewController,
        delegate: delegate), animated: true)
    }

    func showSelectedList(delegate: SelectedListDelegate,
    list: TasksListModel) {
        let taskListController = TaskListViewController(
        taskListView: TaskListView())
        viewController?.navigationController?.pushViewController
        (TaskListConfigurator.configure(taskListController,
        delegate: delegate, tasksList: list), animated: true)
    }
}
```

In this way, to navigate to the *AddList* scene, we instantiate
the *AddListViewController* and then configure it through the
AddListConfigurator (to which we will pass both the *AddListViewController*
instance and the *AddListDelegate* delegate as parameters).

In the case of navigating to the *TasksListDelegate* scene, we'll
instantiate the *TaskListViewController* and then configure it with the
TaskListConfigurator, to which we'll also pass the list whose tasks we want
to display as the *SelectedListDelegate*.

Note   Remember that both delegates are what will allow us to communicate to the *Home* scene that it should update its view when adding or updating a list.

AddList Scene

This screen is the one that allows us to add new task lists. In Figure 6-4, you can see the components that form it and the connections between them.

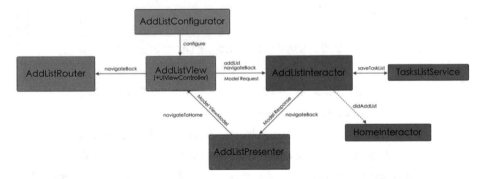

Figure 6-4. *AddList scene components and communication schema*

AddListConfigurator

The *AddListConfigurator* is in charge of taking the instance of the *AddListViewController* that we pass to it from *HomeRouter* (as we have just seen) and configuring it, creating the different components that make up this scene and establishing the different relations between them (Listing 6-23).

Listing 6-23. AddListConfigurator code

```
final class AddListConfigurator {

    static func configure( _ viewController:
    AddListViewController, delegate: AddListDelegate) ->
    AddListViewController  {

        let interactor = AddListInteractor(tasksListService:
        TasksListService(), delegate: delegate)
        let presenter = AddListPresenter()
        let router = AddListRouter()
        router.viewController = viewController
        presenter.viewController = viewController
        interactor.presenter = presenter
        viewController.interactor = interactor
        viewController.router = router
        return viewController
    }
}
```

As you can see, when instantiating the *AddListInteractor* we pass it an instance of the *TasksListService*, since it will be the one that allows us to add new task lists to the database.

AddListView

The *AddListView* contains the graphic elements with which the user interacts to add a new task list or to go back to Home without having added any list. In both cases, the user's actions will be communicated to the *AddListViewController* by implementing the *AddListViewDelegate* protocol (Listing 6-24).

Listing 6-24. AddListView class code showing AddListViewDelegate protocol and where their methods are called

```
protocol AddListViewDelegate: AnyObject {
    func navigateBack()
    func addListWith(title: String, icon: String)
}

final class AddListView: UIView {

    weak var delegate: AddListViewDelegate?

    ...
}

private extension AddListView {

    ...

    @objc func backAction() {
        delegate?.navigateBack()
    }

    ...

    @objc func addListAction() {
        guard titleTextfield.hasText else { return }
        delegate?.addListWith(title: titleTextfield.text!,
        icon: icon)
    }
    ...
}
```

AddListViewController

In the *AddListViewController*, as we already know, we will define the Input and Output protocols with the methods that will allow us to make requests to the *AddListInteractor* or receive calls from the *AddListPresenter*. In this case, we will only have one method in the *AddListViewControllerInput* protocol and two in the case of the *AddListViewControllerOutput* protocol (Listing 6-25).

Listing 6-25. AddListViewControllerInput and AddListViewControllerOutput protocols definition

```
protocol AddListViewControllerInput: AnyObject {
    func navigateToHome()
}

protocol AddListViewControllerOutput: AnyObject {
    func navigateBack()
    func addList(request: AddListModel.AddList.Request)
}
```

In the *AddListViewControllerInput* protocol, we only have the *navigateToHome* method, so the *AddListViewController* communicates to the *AddListRouter* that it should return to the *Home* (this happens both if we add a new list and if we press the back button).

In the case of the *AddListViewControllerOutput*, it has two methods, since we will have two possible requests: add a new list or return to *Home* directly.

In addition to these two protocols, we will create a third protocol, *AddListDelegate*, which, as we saw when describing the components of the *Home* scene, is the one that allows us to indicate to the *Home* that it should update its interface when adding a new list of tasks (Listing 6-26).

Listing 6-26. AddListDelegate definition that allows interaction with the HomeInteractor

```
protocol AddListDelegate: AnyObject {
    func didAddList()
}
```

Next, we develop the part of the code that starts the *AddListViewController*, and that is where we receive the *AddListView* instance, assign it to the *AddListViewcontroller* view, and configure its delegate, so the *AddListViewController* class must conform to the *AddListViewDelegate* protocol (Listing 6-27).

Listing 6-27. AddListViewController initialization

```
final class AddListViewController: UIViewController {
    var interactor: AddListInteractorInput?
    var router: AddListRouterDelegate?

    private let addListView: AddListView

    init(addListView: AddListView) {
        self.addListView = addListView
        super.init(nibName: nil, bundle: nil)
    }

    required init?(coder: NSCoder) {
        fatalError("init(coder:) has not been implemented")
    }

    override func viewDidLoad() {
        super.viewDidLoad()
        addListView.delegate = self
        self.view = addListView
    }
}
```

...

```
extension AddListViewController: AddListViewDelegate {

    func navigateBack() {
        interactor?.navigateBack()
    }

    func addListWith(title: String, icon: String) {
        let request = AddListModel.AddList.Request(title:
        title, icon: icon)
        interactor?.addList(request: request)
    }
}
```

Finally, we create the code for the *AddListViewController* to conform to the *AddListViewControllerInput* protocol (Listing 6-28).

Listing 6-28. AddListViewController conformation to AddListViewControllerInput protocol

```
extension AddListViewController: AddListViewControllerInput {

    func navigateToHome() {
        router?.navigateBack()
    }
}
```

AddListInteractor

We already know that the AddListInteractor involves two protocols, one Input (*AddListInteractorInput*) and another *Output* (*AddListInteractorOutput*), and that the Input protocol corresponds to the output protocol of the *AddListViewController* (*AddListViewControllerOutput*), so we change the name to use it here (Listing 6-29).

Listing 6-29. Definition of the AddListInteractorOutput protocol and renaming the AddListViewControllerOutput to AddListInteractorInput

```
protocol AddListInteractorOutput: AnyObject {
    func navigateBack()
}
```

```
typealias AddListInteractorInput = AddListViewControllerOutput
```

The *AddListInteractorOutput* protocol only has one method, since whether we add a list or want to return to the Home without adding it, we only have to give the *AddListPresenter* the order to return to the *Home*.

The next part of the development of the *AddListInteractor* is the part of its initialization in which we collect both the instance of the *TasksListService* that we pass to it, as well as the delegate that communicates with the *HomeInteractor* (Listing 6-30).

Listing 6-30. AddListInteractor initialization

```
final class AddListInteractor {
    var presenter: AddListPresenterInput?

    private let tasksListService: TasksListServiceProtocol!

    weak var delegate: AddListDelegate?

    init(tasksListService: TasksListServiceProtocol, delegate:
    AddListDelegate) {
        self.tasksListService = tasksListService
        self.delegate = delegate
    }
}
```

Lastly, we implement the code by which we will make the *AddListInteractor* conform to the *AddListInteractorInput* protocol. In the first method (*navigateBack*), what we indicate to the presenter is that we want to return to *Home* (we have paused the back button).

In the second method (*addList*), what we do is create a new task list with the parameters that we have passed through the *AddListModel. AddList.Request* and save it in the database thanks to the *TasksListService* instance.

Next, and thanks to the delegate that we have passed from the *HomeInteractor*, we indicate that the *Home* must update the list of tasks that it must show. Finally, we communicate to the *HomePresenter* that it must return to the *Home* (Listing 6-31).

Listing 6-31. AddListInteractor conformation to AddListInteractorInput

```
extension AddListInteractor
: AddListInteractorInput {

    func navigateBack() {
        presenter?.navigateBack()
    }

    func addList(request: AddListModel.AddList.Request) {
        let list = TasksListModel(id: ProcessInfo().
        globallyUniqueString,
                        title: request.title,
                        icon: request.icon,
                        createdAt: Date())
        tasksListService.saveTasksList(list)
        delegate?.didAddList()
        presenter?.navigateBack()
    }
}
```

AddListPresenter

The *AddListPresenter* presents two protocols: *AddListPresenterInput* (which corresponds to the *AddListInteractorOutput* protocol) and *AddListPresenterOutput* (which corresponds to the *AddListViewControllerInput* protocol) (Listing 6-32).

Listing 6-32. With typealias we rename the protocols to refer to them as Input and Output the AddListInteractor

```
typealias AddListPresenterInput = AddListInteractorOutput
typealias AddListPresenterOutput = AddListViewControllerInput
```

The logic of *AddListPresenter* is quite simple, as you only need to implement the single method of *AddListPresenterInput*, and this is the one that tells the *HomeViewController* to navigate back to the *Home* (Listing 6-33).

Listing 6-33. AddListPresenter code, with AddListPresenterInput protocol conformation

```
final class AddListPresenter {
    weak var viewController: AddListPresenterOutput?
}

extension AddListPresenter: AddListPresenterInput {

    func navigateBack() {
        viewController?.navigateToHome()
    }
}
```

AddListModel

As we have seen in the code of the different components of the *AddList* scene, the *AddListModel* class, with which we pass information in the VIP cycle, we have only used it in the case of passing the *Request* with the title and icon of the created list. However, for didactic purposes, when creating the class, we show all the structs, even if there are a couple of them empty (Listing 6-34).

Listing 6-34. AddListModel code. Only the request has parameters

```
enum AddListModel {

    enum AddList {

        struct Request {
            var title: String
            var icon: String
        }

        struct Response {}

        struct ViewModel {}
    }
}
```

AddListRouter

As we have seen, the *AddListRouter* class will be quite simple, since it has a protocol with a single method (*navigateBack*), which is the one that will implement the return navigation from the *AddList* scene to the *Home* scene (Listing 6-35).

Listing 6-35. AddListRouterDelegate protocol definition and implementation in AddListRouter

```swift
protocol AddListRouterDelegate {
    func navigateBack()
}

final class AddListRouter {
    weak var viewController: UIViewController?
}

extension AddListRouter: AddListRouterDelegate {

    func navigateBack() {
        viewController?.navigationController?.
        popViewController(animated: true)
    }
}
```

TaskList Scene

The *TaskList* scene is the most complex from the protocol point of view since different actions have to be managed: show the tasks in a list, delete them, update them, present the add tasks screen, and navigate back to *Home*.

Also, keep in mind that we have to inform the *Home*, through the *HomeInteractor*'s *selectedListDelegate*, that with each change of a task, the list of tasks in the *Home* scene must be updated. In Figure 6-5, you can see the different components of the *TaskList* scene and the communications between them.

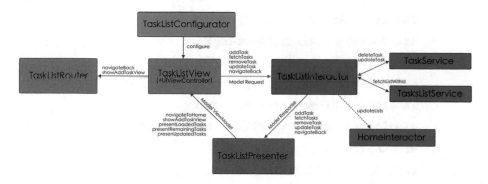

Figure 6-5. *TaskList scene components and communication schema*

TaskListConfigurator

The *TaskListConfigurator* is similar to the ones we have seen so far; it instantiates the different elements of the scene and relates them to each other.

Perhaps, it is worth mentioning the instantiation of the *TaskListInteractor*, since at this point we will have to pass it the list of tasks that we have selected in the *Home*, instances of the *TaskService* and the *TaskListService* for the interaction with the database, and the delegate that allows it to connect with the *HomeInteractor* to tell it to update the *Home* when there is any change in the tasks (Listing 6-36).

Listing 6-36. TaskListConfigurator code

```
final class TaskListConfigurator {

    static func configure( _ viewController:
    TaskListViewController, delegate: SelectedListDelegate,
    tasksList: TasksListModel) -> TaskListViewController {

        let interactor = TaskListInteractor(tasksList:
        tasksList, taskService: TaskService(),
        tasksListService: TasksListService(),
        delegate: delegate)
```

```
        let presenter = TaskListPresenter()
        let router = TaskListRouter()
        router.viewController = viewController
        presenter.viewController = viewController
        interactor.presenter = presenter
        viewController.interactor = interactor
        viewController.router = router
        return viewController
    }
}
```

TaskListView

The *TaskListView* class is quite similar to the *HomeView* since it presents a table with the tasks in a list, it has a button that presents the screen for adding new tasks, tasks can be deleted...

And, in the same way, as in the rest of the Views, it presents a protocol (*TastLisViewDelegate*) that allows communicating the user's interactions to the *TaskListViewController*, which will be in charge of implementing the methods of the said delegate (Listing 6-37).

Listing 6-37. TastLisViewDelegate protocol definition

```
import UIKit

protocol TaskListViewDelegate: AnyObject {
    func navigateBack()
    func addTask()
    func deleteTaskAt(indexPath: IndexPath)
    func updateTask(_ task: TaskModel)
}
```

The tasks that the table must show are passed directly from the *TaskListViewController* through the *show(tasks:_)* method, as shown in Listing 6-38.

Listing 6-38. Tasks to show are passed through the show(tasks:_) method

```
final class TaskListView: UIView {

    weak var delegate: TaskListViewDelegate?
    ...
    func show(tasks: [TaskModel]) {
        self.tasks = tasks
        tableView.reloadData()
        emptyState.isHidden = tasks.count > 0
    }
}
```

Finally, in Listing 6-39, we show the different points of the code in which, through the delegate, we pass the user interactions to the *TaskListViewcontroller*.

Listing 6-39. Calling the protocol methods from the View

```
private extension TaskListView {

    ...
    @objc func backAction() {
        delegate?.navigateBack()
    }

    ...
    @objc func addTaskAction() {
        delegate?.addTask()
    }
```

```
    ...
}

extension TaskListView: UITableViewDelegate,
UITableViewDataSource {

    ...
    func tableView(_ tableView: UITableView, commit
    editingStyle: UITableViewCell.EditingStyle, forRowAt
    indexPath: IndexPath) {
        if editingStyle == .delete {
            delegate?.deleteTaskAt(indexPath: indexPath)
        }
    }
}

extension TaskListView: TaskCellDelegate {

    func updateTask(_ task: TaskModel) {
        delegate?.updateTask(task)
    }
}
```

TaskListViewController

As in the previous cases, we are going to set the input and output protocols for the *TaskListViewController* (Listing 6-40).

Listing 6-40. TaskListViewControllerInput and TaskListViewControllerOutput protocols definition

```
protocol TaskListViewControllerInput: AnyObject {
    func navigateToHome()
    func showAddTaskView(viewModel: TaskListModel.AddTask.
    ViewModel)
```

```
    func presentLoadedTasks(viewModel: TaskListModel.
    FetchTasks.ViewModel)
    func presentRemainingTasks(viewModel: TaskListModel.
    RemoveTask.ViewModel)
    func presentUpdatedTasks(viewModel: TaskListModel.
    UpdateTask.ViewModel)
}

protocol TaskListViewControllerOutput: AnyObject {
    func navigateBack()
    func addTask(request: TaskListModel.AddTask.Request)
    func fetchTasks(request: TaskListModel.FetchTasks.Request)
    func removeTask(request: TaskListModel.RemoveTask.Request)
    func updateTask(request: TaskListModel.UpdateTask.Request)
}
```

In the case of the output protocol, *TaskListViewControllerOutput*, we have defined the methods *navigateBack* (to return to *Home*), *addTask* (to present the screen for adding tasks), *fetchTasks* (to show the tasks in a list), *removeTask* (to delete a task), and *updateTask* (to update a task).

For the input protocol, *TaskListViewControllerInput*, we define the methods *navigateBack* (to return to *Home*), *showAddTaskView* (to show the task addition screen), *presentLoadedTasks* (which returns the tasks of the selected list), *presentRemainingTasks* (which returns the tasks that remain after deleting one of them), and *presentUpdatedTasks* (which returns the tasks when one of them is updated).

On the other hand, we will define a third protocol, *SelectedListDelegate*, which, as you will remember, is the one we use in the HomeInteractor to establish the delegate that will allow us to update the task lists of the *Home* after any change made in this scene (Listing 6-41).

Listing 6-41. SelectedListDelegate protocol definition

```
protocol SelectedListDelegate: AnyObject {
    func updateLists()
}
```

The next step is to prepare the initialization of the *TaskListController*. In the init method, we pass it an instance of the *TaskListView* (we pass it in the *TaskListConfigurator*) and make the *TaskListController* its delegate (so it will need to implement its methods). In addition, we make the first request to the *TaskListInteractor*, which is to retrieve the tasks from the selected list (Listing 6-42).

Listing 6-42. TaskListViewController initialization and TaskListViewDelegate conformance code

```
final class TaskListViewController: UIViewController {
    var interactor: TaskListInteractorInput?
    var router: TaskListRouterDelegate?

    private let taskListView: TaskListView

    init(taskListView: TaskListView) {
        self.taskListView = taskListView
        super.init(nibName: nil, bundle: nil)
    }

    required init?(coder: NSCoder) {
        fatalError("init(coder:) has not been implemented")
    }

    override func viewDidLoad() {
        super.viewDidLoad()
        taskListView.delegate = self
        self.view = taskListView
```

```swift
        fetchTasks()
    }

    private func fetchTasks() {
        let request = TaskListModel.FetchTasks.Request()
        interactor?.fetchTasks(request: request)
    }
}
...

extension TaskListViewController: TaskListViewDelegate {

    func navigateBack() {
        interactor?.navigateBack()
    }

    func addTask() {
        let request = TaskListModel.AddTask.Request()
        interactor?.addTask(request: request)
    }

    func deleteTaskAt(indexPath: IndexPath) {
        let request = TaskListModel.RemoveTask.Request(index:
        indexPath)
        interactor?.removeTask(request: request)
    }

    func updateTask(_ task: TaskModel) {
        let request = TaskListModel.UpdateTask.
        Request(task: task)
        interactor?.updateTask(request: request)
    }
}
```

Finally, since the *TaskListViewController* must conform to the
TaskListViewControllerInput input protocol, we apply its methods
(Listing 6-43).

Listing 6-43. TaskListViewControllerInput conformation code

```
extension TaskListViewController: TaskListViewControllerInput {

    func navigateToHome() {
        router?.navigateBack()
    }

    func showAddTaskView(viewModel: TaskListModel.AddTask.
    ViewModel) {
        router?.showAddTaskView(delegate: viewModel.
        addTaskDelegate, tasksList: viewModel.taskList)
    }

    func presentLoadedTasks(viewModel: TaskListModel.
    FetchTasks.ViewModel) {
        taskListView.show(tasks: viewModel.tasks)
    }

    func presentRemainingTasks(viewModel: TaskListModel.
    RemoveTask.ViewModel) {
        taskListView.show(tasks: viewModel.tasks)
    }

    func presentUpdatedTasks(viewModel: TaskListModel.
    UpdateTask.ViewModel) {
        taskListView.show(tasks: viewModel.tasks)
    }
}
```

TaskListInteractor

Continuing with what we have seen in the other Interactors, the *TaskListInteractor* has two protocols: the input protocol, *TaskListInteractorInput*, which corresponds to the output protocol of the *TaskListViewController* (*TaskListViewControllerOutput*), and the output protocol (*TaskListInteractorOutput*), in which we define the methods which you will need to implement the *TaskListPresenter* (Listing 6-44).

Listing 6-44. Definition of the TaskListInteractorOutput protocol and renaming the TaskListViewControllerOutput to TaskListInteractorInput

```
protocol TaskListInteractorOutput: AnyObject {
    func navigateBack()
    func showAddTask(response: TaskListModel.AddTask.Response)
    func presentTasks(response: TaskListModel.FetchTasks.
    Response)
    func removedTask(response: TaskListModel.RemoveTask.
    Response)
    func updatedTask(response: TaskListModel.UpdateTask.
    Response)
}

typealias TaskListInteractorInput = TaskListViewControllerOutput
```

Once the protocols are defined, we set the initialization of the *TaskListInteractor*. We will modify the *init* method to be able to pass, on the one hand, the list of tasks that we have selected in the *Home*, the two services that allow us to access the database, and the delegate that we pass from the *HomeInteractor* and that will allow us to update the *Home* before any change in the list tasks (Listing 6-45).

Listing 6-45. TaskListInteractor initialization

```
final class TaskListInteractor {

    var presenter: TaskListPresenterInput?

    private var tasksList: TasksListModel!
    private var taskService: TaskServiceProtocol!
    private var tasksListService: TasksListServiceProtocol!
    private var tasks = [TaskModel]()

    weak var delegate: SelectedListDelegate?

    init(tasksList: TasksListModel,
        taskService: TaskServiceProtocol,
        tasksListService: TasksListServiceProtocol,
        delegate: SelectedListDelegate) {
        self.tasksList = tasksList
        self.taskService = taskService
        self.tasksListService = tasksListService
        self.delegate = delegate
    }
}
```

Next, we need to make the *TaskListInteractor* conform to its input protocol, thereby allowing the *TaskListViewController* to communicate with it (Listing 6-46).

Listing 6-46. TaskListInteractorInput conformation code

```
extension TaskListInteractor: TaskListInteractorInput {

    func navigateBack() {
        presenter?.navigateBack()
    }
```

```
func addTask(request: TaskListModel.AddTask.Request) {
    let response = TaskListModel.AddTask.
    Response(addTaskDelegate: self, taskList: tasksList)
    presenter?.showAddTask(response: response)
}

func fetchTasks(request: TaskListModel.FetchTasks.
Request) {
    guard let list = tasksListService.
    fetchListWithId(tasksList.id) else { return }
    tasksList = list
    tasks = tasksList.tasks.sorted(by: { $0.createdAt.
    compare($1.createdAt) == .orderedDescending })
    let response = TaskListModel.FetchTasks.
    Response(tasks: tasks)
    presenter?.presentTasks(response: response)
}

func removeTask(request: TaskListModel.RemoveTask.
Request) {
    let task = tasks[request.index.row]
    taskService.deleteTask(task)
    tasks.remove(at: request.index.row)
    let response = TaskListModel.RemoveTask.
    Response(tasks: tasks)
    presenter?.removedTask(response: response)
    delegate?.updateLists()
}

func updateTask(request: TaskListModel.UpdateTask.
Request) {
    taskService.updateTask(request.task)
    fetchTasks()
```

```
        let response = TaskListModel.UpdateTask.
        Response(tasks: tasks)
        presenter?.updatedTask(response: response)
        delegate?.updateLists()
    }
}
```

If you notice, in the *addTask* method, when creating the response that we will pass to the presenter, we have added the *TaskListInteractor* as a delegate (*addTaskDelegate*). If you remember, we already did this in the *HomeInteractor* so that we can update the *Home* view when adding a new task list in the *AddTaskList* scene or when modifying a task list from a list from the scene we are looking at now.

The last three methods, *fetchTasks*, *removeTask*, and *updateTask*, are the ones that require interaction with the database (through the *TasksListService* and the *TaskService*), and the subsequent call to the *TaskListPresenter* to update the view.

Last but not least, we make the *TaskListInteractor* conform to the *AddTaskDelegate* protocol (which we will create when developing the *AddTask* scene) and which we have just explained is the protocol that will allow us to tell the current scene to update its view when adding a new one (Listing 6-47).

Listing 6-47. AddTaskDelegate conformation code

```
extension TaskListInteractor: AddTaskDelegate {

    func didAddTask() {
        fetchTasks(request: TaskListModel.FetchTasks.Request())
        delegate?.updateLists()
    }
}
```

TaskListPresenter

The first thing we do in the *TaskListPresenter*, as in the previous cases, is to rename the output protocol of the *TaskListInteractor* as the presenter's input protocol and the input protocol of the *TaskListViewController* as output protocol (Listing 6-48). Remember that we do this to have a better view of the Input/Output flow of each component.

Listing 6-48. Renaming protocols with typealias to obtain the TaskListPresenter protocols

```
typealias TaskListPresenterInput = TaskListInteractorOutput
typealias TaskListPresenterOutput = TaskListViewControllerInput
```

Then, we only have to implement the methods of the *TaskListPresenterInput* protocol, to which the *TaskListPresenter* must conform (Listing 6-49).

Listing 6-49. TaskListPresenter conformation to TaskListPresenterInput protocol

```
final class TaskListPresenter {
    weak var viewController: TaskListPresenterOutput?
}

extension TaskListPresenter: TaskListPresenterInput {

    func navigateBack() {
        viewController?.navigateToHome()
    }
}
```

```
func showAddTask(response: TaskListModel.AddTask.
Response) {
    let viewModel = TaskListModel.AddTask.
    ViewModel(taskList: response.taskList, addTaskDelegate:
    response.addTaskDelegate)
    viewController?.showAddTaskView(viewModel: viewModel)
}

func presentTasks(response: TaskListModel.FetchTasks.
Response) {
    let viewModel = TaskListModel.FetchTasks.
    ViewModel(tasks: response.tasks)
    viewController?.presentLoadedTasks(viewModel:
    viewModel)
}

func removedTask(response: TaskListModel.RemoveTask.
Response) {
    let viewModel = TaskListModel.RemoveTask.
    ViewModel(tasks: response.tasks)
    viewController?.presentRemainingTasks(viewModel:
    viewModel)
}

func updatedTask(response: TaskListModel.UpdateTask.
Response) {
    let viewModel = TaskListModel.UpdateTask.
    ViewModel(tasks: response.tasks)
    viewController?.presentUpdatedTasks(viewModel:
    viewModel)
}
}
```

Observe how in the *showAddTask* method, we pass in the *ViewModel* the list to which we want to add the new task and the delegate that will allow us to update the view when adding the said task.

In the last three methods, what we do is pass the tasks of the selected list inside the *ViewModel* (to show them when entering this scene and after deleting or updating some tasks).

TaskListModel

The information exchange model within this scene is shown in Listing 6-50. As you can see, we created a submodel for each of the processes within this scene (*FetchTasks*, *AddTask*, *RemoveTask*, and *UpdateTask*), although some of them have very similar parameters.

Listing 6-50. TaskListModel code

```
enum TaskListModel {

    enum FetchTasks {
        struct Request {}

        struct Response {
            let tasks: [TaskModel]
        }

        struct ViewModel {
            let tasks: [TaskModel]
        }
    }

    enum AddTask {
        struct Request {}
```

```
    struct Response {
        let addTaskDelegate: AddTaskDelegate
        let taskList: TasksListModel
    }

    struct ViewModel {
        let taskList: TasksListModel
        let addTaskDelegate: AddTaskDelegate
    }
}

enum RemoveTask {
    struct Request {
        let index: IndexPath
    }

    struct Response {
        let tasks: [TaskModel]
    }

    struct ViewModel {
        let tasks: [TaskModel]
    }
}

enum UpdateTask {

    struct Request {
        let task: TaskModel
    }

    struct Response {
        let tasks: [TaskModel]
    }
```

```
        struct ViewModel {
            let tasks: [TaskModel]
        }
    }
}
```

TaskListRouter

From what we have been seeing in the development of this scene, we know that we will have to establish two methods in the *TaskListRouter* (through its protocol): one that does not allow us to return to Home (*navigateBack*) and another that presents us with the scene of add new tasks (*showAddTaskView*) (Listing 6-51).

Listing 6-51. TaskListRouterDelegate protocol definition

```
protocol TaskListRouterDelegate {
    func navigateBack()
    func showAddTaskView(delegate: AddTaskDelegate, tasksList:
    TasksListModel)
}
```

The implementation of these methods is similar to that already seen in other cases. To return to *Home*, we simply have to use the *popViewController* method, and to display the *AddTask* scene, we will create and configure the *AddTaskViewController*, to which we will pass the *addTaskDelegate* (which we have already mentioned when developing the *TaskListInteractor*) and the *TasksListModel* object with the list of tasks to which we will add the new task (Listing 6-52).

Listing 6-52. TaskListRouterDelegate conformation code

```
final class TaskListRouter {
    weak var viewController: UIViewController?
}

extension TaskListRouter: TaskListRouterDelegate {

    func navigateBack() {
        viewController?.navigationController?.
        popViewController(animated: true)
    }

    func showAddTaskView(delegate: AddTaskDelegate, tasksList:
    TasksListModel) {
        let addTaskViewController = AddTaskViewController(addTa
        skView: AddTaskView())
        viewController?.present(AddTaskConfigurator.configure(
        addTaskViewController, delegate: delegate, tasksList:
        tasksList), animated: true)
    }
}
```

AddTask Scene

This last screen of the application, AddTask, allows us to add new tasks to a task list. In Figure 6-6, you can see the components that form it and the connections between them.

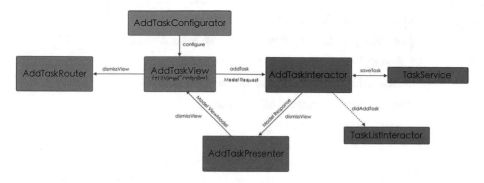

Figure 6-6. *AddTask scene components and communication schema*

AddTaskConfigurator

When developing the *AddTaskConfigurator*, together with the instantiation
of the different components and the connection between them, we must
bear in mind that in the *AddTaskInteractor* instance we must pass both
the list of tasks to which we want to add the new tasks and the delegate
(*AddTaskDelegate*) that will allow us to connect to the *TaskListInteractor* to
update the task list view (Listing 6-53).

Listing 6-53. AddTaskConfigurator code

```
final class AddTaskConfigurator {

    static func configure( _ viewController:
    AddTaskViewController, delegate: AddTaskDelegate,
    tasksList: TasksListModel) -> AddTaskViewController {

        let interactor = AddTaskInteractor(tasksList:
        tasksList, taskService: TaskService(), delegate:
        delegate)
        let presenter = AddTaskPresenter()
        let router = AddTaskRouter()
```

```
        router.viewController = viewController
        presenter.viewController = viewController
        interactor.presenter = presenter
        viewController.interactor = interactor
        viewController.router = router
        return viewController
    }
}
```

AddTaskView

The *AddTaskView* is quite similar in concept to the *AddTaskListView*, with a field to add the task title and an icon picker. But unlike the *AddTaskListView*, which had a button to go back to the previous screen if we didn't want to add any new list, since we now present the screen on the *TaskList* scene and don't navigate to it, we don't need that button, since we can make the screen disappear with a downward swipe gesture.

For this reason, the protocol that will allow us to communicate with the *AddTaskViewController* only has one method (*addTaskWith(title:_, icon:_)*) (Listing 6-54).

Listing 6-54. AddTaskViewDelegate definition and use

```
protocol AddTaskViewDelegate: AnyObject {
    func addTaskWith(title: String, icon: String)
}

final class AddTaskView: UIView {
    weak var delegate: AddTaskViewDelegate?

    ...
}
```

```
extension AddTaskView {
    ...
    @objc func addTaskAction() {
        guard titleTextfield.hasText else { return }
        delegate?.addTaskWith(title: titleTextfield.text!,
        icon: icon)
    }
}
```

AddTaskViewController

By reducing the capabilities of the view, we also reduce the code in the *AddTaskViewController*. Thus, the input and output protocols that we create for these classes, in this case, only contain one method each: *addTask* for output and *dismissView* for input (Listing 6-55).

Listing 6-55. AdTaskViewControllerInput and AddTaskViewControllerOutput protocols definition

```
protocol AddTaskViewControllerInput: AnyObject {
    func dismissView()
}

protocol AddTaskViewControllerOutput: AnyObject {
    func addTask(request: AddTaskModel.AddTask.Request)
}
```

On the other hand, we also define the protocol whose method should be implemented by the *TaskListInteractor* to tell it that it should update the view of the tasks in the list when adding a new one (Listing 6-56).

Listing 6-56. AddTaskDelegate protocol definition to allow AddTask scene to connect to TaskList scene

```
protocol AddTaskDelegate: AnyObject {
    func didAddTask()
}
```

With these protocols defined, we proceed to develop the *AddTaskViewController* initialization code, in which we basically assign the instance that we passed from the *AddTaskView* to the view, assign the delegate to it, and implement the method of the said delegate (Listing 6-57). In this method, what we do is generate a request with the title and icon values of the new task, and we pass it to the interactor.

Listing 6-57. AddTaskViewController initialization code

```
final class AddTaskViewController: UIViewController {
    var interactor: AddTaskInteractorInput?
    var router: AddTaskRouterDelegate?

    private let addTaskView: AddTaskView

    init(addTaskView: AddTaskView) {
        self.addTaskView = addTaskView
        super.init(nibName: nil, bundle: nil)
    }

    required init?(coder: NSCoder) {
        fatalError("init(coder:) has not been implemented")
    }

    override func viewDidLoad() {
        super.viewDidLoad()
        addTaskView.delegate = self
        self.view = addTaskView
```

```
    }
}
...

extension AddTaskViewController: AddTaskViewDelegate {

    func addTaskWith(title: String, icon: String) {
        let request = AddTaskModel.AddTask.Request(title:
        title, icon: icon)
        interactor?.addTask(request: request)
    }
}
```

Lastly, we need to make the *AddTaskViewController* conform to its input protocol, which in this case tells the Router to make the view disappear.

```
extension AddTaskViewController: AddTaskViewControllerInput {

    func dismissView() {
        router?.dismissView()
    }
}
```

AddTaskInteractor

Starting with the *AddListInteractor*, we define the output protocol (*AddTaskInteractorOutput*), which has a single method, and as in the previous cases, we rename the *AddTaskViewControllerOutput* output protocol to *AddTaskInteractorInput* (Listing 6-58).

Listing 6-58. Definition of the AddListInteractorOutput protocol and renaming the AddListViewControllerOutput to AddListInteractorInput

```
protocol AddTaskInteractorOutput: AnyObject {
    func dismissView()
}

typealias AddTaskInteractorInput = AddTaskViewControllerOutput
```

Next, we go to the initialization of this class, in which we pass the *TaskListModel* object where we will add the new task created, the *TaskService* to connect to the database and save the new task, and the delegate that allows us to indicate to the *TaskList* scene that updates the view with the new task (Listing 6-59).

Listing 6-59. TaskListInteractor initialization code

```
final class AddTaskInteractor {
    var presenter: AddTaskPresenterInput?

    private var tasksList: TasksListModel!
    private var taskService: TaskServiceProtocol!

    weak var delegate: AddTaskDelegate?

    init(tasksList: TasksListModel,
        taskService: TaskServiceProtocol,
        delegate: AddTaskDelegate) {
        self.tasksList = tasksList
        self.taskService = taskService
        self.delegate = delegate
    }
}
```

Finally, we need to make the *AddTaskInteractor* conform to the *AddTaskInteractorInput* protocol. This protocol only has one method, *addTask*, to which we pass a request with the title and icon of the new task.

In this method, we first create the *TaskModel* object, which we pass to the *TaskService* for saving to the database. Then we tell the *TaskList* scene to update the task list (via the delegate), and finally, we tell the Presenter to dismiss the View (Listing 6-60).

Listing 6-60. Implementation of the AddTaskInteractorInput protocol

```
extension AddTaskInteractor: AddTaskInteractorInput {

    func addTask(request: AddTaskModel.AddTask.Request) {
        let task = TaskModel(id: ProcessInfo().
        globallyUniqueString,
                        title: request.title,
                        icon: request.icon,
                        done: false,
                        createdAt: Date())
        taskService.saveTask(task, in: tasksList)
        delegate?.didAddTask()
        presenter?.dismissView()
    }
}
```

AddTaskPresenter

The *AddTaskPresenter*, as in the previous cases, acquires its two input and output protocols by renaming the input protocol the *AddTaskViewController* and the output protocol the *AddTaskPresenter* (Listing 6-61).

Listing 6-61. AddTaskPresenter Input/Output protocols

```
typealias AddTaskPresenterInput = AddTaskInteractorOutput
typealias AddTaskPresenterOutput = AddTaskViewControllerInput
```

The conformation to the *AddTaskPresenterInput* protocol is quite simple (Listing 6-62).

Listing 6-62. AddTaskPresenter conformation to AddTaskPresenterInput

```
final class AddTaskPresenter {
    weak var viewController: AddTaskPresenterOutput?
}

extension AddTaskPresenter: AddTaskPresenterInput {

    func dismissView() {
        viewController?.dismissView()
    }
}
```

AddTaskModel

The *AddTaskModel* is quite simple since only the Request presents the fields that are needed to create the task (the rest, although empty, are shown for pedagogical purposes) (Listing 6-63).

Listing 6-63. AddListModel code

```
enum AddTaskModel {

    enum AddTask {
        struct Request {
            var title: String
            var icon: String
        }
```

```
    struct Response {}

    struct ViewModel {}
    }
}
```

AddTaskRouter

The *AddTaskRouter* is also simple, as it only has one method, and that is to dismiss the View (Listing 6-64).

Listing 6-64. AddTaskRouterDelegate and AdTaskRouter code

```
protocol AddTaskRouterDelegate {
    func dismissView()
}

final class AddTaskRouter {
    weak var viewController: UIViewController?
}

extension AddTaskRouter: AddTaskRouterDelegate {

    func dismissView() {
        viewController?.dismiss(animated: true)
    }
}
```

VIP-MyToDos Testing

In the VIP architecture, the three main components that we are going to test are the ViewControllers, the Interactors, and the Presenters as those are the components of the VIP cycle.

Note   Remember that you can find the complete project code, including the tests, in the repository associated with this book.

Now, as an example, let's see how to set unit tests to the *HomeViewController*, the *HomeInteractor*, and the *HomePresenter* classes of the *Home* scene.

In the files of each of the tests for these components, we will also define the mocks of the other components of each scene that are necessary.

HomeViewControllerTest

As we have seen in other cases, the first thing we will do is define the components that we will need in the test. In this case, our *sut* (or *system under test*) is the *HomeViewController*.

As the *HomeViewController* is related to the *HomeInteractor* and the *HomeRouter*, what we will do is define mocks for these classes: *MockHomeInteractor* and *MockHomeRouter* (Listing 6-65).

Listing 6-65. HomeViewControllerTest setup

```
import XCTest
@testable import VIP_MyToDos

final class HomeViewControllerTest: XCTestCase {

    private var sut: HomeViewController!
    private var interactor: MockHomeInteractor!
    private var router: MockHomeRouter!
    private var view: HomeView!
    let taskList = TasksListModel(id: "12345-67890",
                          title: "Test List",
                          icon: "test.icon",
```

```
                    tasks: [TaskModel](),
                    createdAt: Date())

    override func setUpWithError() throws {
        super.setUp()
        interactor = MockHomeInteractor()
        router = MockHomeRouter()
        view = HomeView()
        sut = HomeViewController(homeView: view)
        sut.interactor = interactor
        sut.router = router
    }
    ...
}
```

The *HomeMockInteractor* must conform to the same protocols as the *HomeInteractor* (although we won't use the *didAddList* and *updateList* methods, which connect the *Home* scene to the *AddList* and *TaskList* scenes) (Listing 6-66). What the rest of the methods will do is modify some variables with which we can check if they have been called correctly from the *HomeViewController*.

Listing 6-66. MockHomeInteractor code

```
final class MockHomeInteractor: HomeInteractorInput,
AddListDelegate, SelectedListDelegate {

    private(set) var addListRequest: Bool = false
    private(set) var fetchTasksListRequest: Bool = false
    private(set) var selectTasksListIndex: IndexPath =
    IndexPath(row: 0, section: 0)
    private(set) var deleteTasksListIndex: IndexPath =
    IndexPath(row: 0, section: 0)
```

```
func fetchTasksLists(request: HomeModel.FetchTasksLists.
Request) {
    fetchTasksListRequest = true
}

func addList(request: HomeModel.AddTasksList.Request) {
    addListRequest = true
}

func selectList(request: HomeModel.SelectTasksList.
Request) {
    selectTasksListIndex = request.index
}

func removeList(request: HomeModel.RemoveTasksList.
Request) {
    deleteTasksListIndex = request.index
}

func didAddList() {}

func updateLists() {}
}
```

The *MockHomeRouter* must conform to the *HomeRouterDelegate* protocol. In the same way, as in the *MockHomeInteractor*, we set a series of variables that will allow us to verify that the methods have been called correctly (Listing 6-67).

Listing 6-67. MockHomeRouter code

```
final class MockHomeRouter: HomeRouterDelegate {

    private(set) var navigateToAddList: Bool = false
    private(set) var navigateToTaksList: Bool = false
```

```
private(set) var selectedList: TasksListModel =
TasksListModel()

func showAddListView(delegate: AddListDelegate) {
    navigateToAddList = true
}

func showSelectedList(delegate: SelectedListDelegate,
list: TasksListModel) {
    navigateToTaksList = true
    selectedList = list
}
}
```

Finally, we set the tests for the *HomeViewControllerTest* (Listing 6-68).

Listing 6-68. HomeViewControllerTest test cases development

```
final class HomeViewControllerTest: XCTestCase {
    ...

    func testAddList_whenAddListIsSelected_shoulCallAddList() {
        sut.addList()
        XCTAssertTrue(interactor.addListRequest)
        let viewModel = HomeModel.AddTasksList.
        ViewModel(addListDelegate: interactor)
        sut.showAddListView(viewModel: viewModel)
        XCTAssertTrue(router.navigateToAddList)
    }

    func testSelectedList_whenAListIsSelected_
    shouldCallTasksList() {
        sut.selectedListAt(index: IndexPath(row: 1,
        section: 1))
        XCTAssertEqual(interactor.selectTasksListIndex.row, 1)
```

```
        XCTAssertEqual(interactor.selectTasksListIndex.
        section, 1)
        let viewModel = HomeModel.SelectTasksList.
        ViewModel(selectedListDelegate: interactor, tasksList:
        taskList)
        sut.showSelectedList(viewModel: viewModel)
        XCTAssertTrue(router.navigateToTaksList)
        XCTAssertEqual(router.selectedList.id, taskList.id)
    }

    func testDeleteList_whenAListIsDelete_shouldBeNoLists() {
        sut.deleteListAt(indexPath: IndexPath(row: 1,
        section: 1))
        XCTAssertEqual(interactor.deleteTasksListIndex.row, 1)
        XCTAssertEqual(interactor.deleteTasksListIndex.
        section, 1)
    }
}
```

In the first test, we tested the *AddTaskList* scene call. To do this, we will see if after calling the *addList* method, the *addListRequest* variable of the *MockHomeInteractor* is modified, and then, after calling the *showAddListView* method (and passing it a *ViewModel*), the *navigateToAddList* variable of the *MockHomeRouter* is modified.

In the second test, we test the call to the *TaskList* scene. For this, the tests that we will carry out will be, on the one hand, to verify that we correctly pass the *IndexPath* of a list of tasks to the *HomeInteractor*, and then, that when we indicate to the *HomeRouter* that we want to navigate to the *TaskList* scene, we correctly pass the indicated *TaskListModel* object, and which modifies the *navigateToAddList* variable.

In the last test we will check that when performing the action of deleting a list of tasks, the *IndexPath* that we pass is received correctly.

HomeInteractorTest

As in previous cases, the first step is to create the necessary parameters to start the tests. In the case of the *HomeInteractor*, in addition to the *sut*, we will establish a mock for the *Presenter* (*MockHomePresenter*) and a list of tasks that we will pass to the *MockTaskListService* instance that we will create and pass the interactor (Listing 6-69).

Listing 6-69. HomeInteractorTest setup

```
import XCTest
@testable import VIP_MyToDos

final class HomeInteractorTest: XCTestCase {

    private var sut: HomeInteractor!
    private var presenter: MockHomePresenter!
    let taskList = TasksListModel(id: "12345-67890",
                        title: "Test List",
                        icon: "test.icon",
                        tasks: [TaskModel](),
                        createdAt: Date())

    override func setUpWithError() throws {
    super.setup()
        let mockTaskListService = MockTaskListService(lists:
        [taskList])
        presenter = MockHomePresenter()
        sut = HomeInteractor(tasksListService:
        mockTaskListService)
        sut.presenter = presenter
    }
    ...
}
```

The *MockHomePresenter* must conform to the *HomePresenterInput* protocol. When implementing the protocol methods, we will modify the value of the variables created initially, and that will allow us to verify that *HomeInteractor* has correctly called the methods (Listing 6-70).

Listing 6-70. MockHomePresenter code

```
final class MockHomePresenter: HomePresenterInput {

    private(set) var taskLists: [TasksListModel] =
    [TasksListModel]()
    private(set) var showAddList: Bool = false
    private(set) var selectedList: TasksListModel =
    TasksListModel()

    func presentTasksLists(response: HomeModel.FetchTasksLists.
    Response) {
        taskLists = response.tasksLists
    }

    func showAddTaskList(response: HomeModel.AddTasksList.
    Response) {
        showAddList = true
    }

    func showSelectedList(response: HomeModel.SelectTasksList.
    Response) {
        selectedList = response.tasksList
    }
}
```

Finally, we develop the tests for the different cases that we want to test (Listing 6-71).

Listing 6-71. HomeInteractorTest test cases development

```
final class HomeInteractorTest: XCTestCase {
    ...
    func testPresentList_whenPresentLists_shouldBeOneList() {
        let request = HomeModel.FetchTasksLists.Request()
        sut.fetchTasksLists(request: request)
        XCTAssertEqual(presenter.taskLists.count, 1)
    }

    func testAddList_whenAddListSelected_shouldShowAddList() {
        let request = HomeModel.AddTasksList.Request()
        sut.addList(request: request)
        XCTAssertTrue(presenter.showAddList)
    }

    func testSelectList_whenListIsSelected_shouldBeList() {
        let request = HomeModel.SelectTasksList.Request(index:
        IndexPath(row: 0, section: 0))
        sut.fetchTasksLists()
        sut.selectList(request: request)
        XCTAssertEqual(presenter.selectedList.id, taskList.id)
    }

    func testRemoveList_whenListIsRemoved_shouldBeNoLists() {
        let request = HomeModel.RemoveTasksList.Request(index:
        IndexPath(row: 0, section: 0))
        sut.fetchTasksLists()
        sut.removeList(request: request)
        XCTAssertTrue(presenter.taskLists.isEmpty)
    }
}
```

In the first test, we will verify that we have passed a list of tasks to the Presenter (actually, an array that only contains a list, which is the one that we have passed to the *MockTaskListService* when we have instantiated it).

In the second test, we verify that we have indicated to the Presenter that we want to navigate to the *AddTaskList* scene.

Next, in the third test, we check that if we select a list (passing its *IndexPath*), the selected list is passed to the Presenter.

Finally, in the fourth and last test, we will verify that when deleting a task list (the only one that we have introduced in the *MockTaskListService*), an empty array is passed to the Presenter.

HomePresenterTest

In order to test the *HomePresenter*, we will need to mock the *HomeViewController* (*MockHomeViewController*) and use the *MockHomeRouter* that we created when testing the *HomeViewController* (Listing 6-72).

Listing 6-72. HomePresenterTest setup

```
import XCTest
@testable import VIP_MyToDos

final class HomePresenterTest: XCTestCase {

    private var sut: HomePresenter!
    private var viewController: MockHomeViewController!
    private var router: MockHomeRouter!
    let taskList = TasksListModel(id: "12345-67890",
                        title: "Test List",
                        icon: "test.icon",
                        tasks: [TaskModel](),
                        createdAt: Date())
```

```
override func setUpWithError() throws {
    super.setUp()
    viewController = MockHomeViewController()
    router = MockHomeRouter()
    viewController.router = router
    sut = HomePresenter()
    sut.viewController = viewController
}

    ...
}
```

When setting the *MockHomeViewController*, keep in mind that it must conform to the *HomeViewControllerInput*, *AddListDelegate*, and *SelectedListDelegate* protocols (Listing 6-73).

Listing 6-73. MockHomeViewController code

```
final class MockHomeViewController: HomeViewControllerInput,
AddListDelegate, SelectedListDelegate {

    var router: HomeRouterDelegate?

    private(set) var lists: [TasksListModel] =
    [TasksListModel]()
    private(set) var selectedList: TasksListModel =
    TasksListModel()
    private(set) var showAddList: Bool = false

    func reloadDataWithTaskList(viewModel: HomeModel.
    FetchTasksLists.ViewModel) {
        lists = viewModel.tasksLists
    }
```

```
    func showAddListView(viewModel: HomeModel.AddTasksList.
    ViewModel) {
        showAddList = true
        router?.showAddListView(delegate: self)
    }

    func showSelectedList(viewModel: HomeModel.SelectTasksList.
    ViewModel) {
        selectedList = viewModel.tasksList
        router?.showSelectedList(delegate: self, list:
        viewModel.tasksList)
    }

    func didAddList() {}

    func updateLists() {}
}
```

Finally, we set the different tests for the *HomePresenter* (Listing 6-74).

Listing 6-74. HomePresenterTest test cases code

```
final class HomePresenterTest: XCTestCase {

    ...
    func testPresentLists_whenShouldPresentList_
    reloadDataIsCalled() {
        let response = HomeModel.FetchTasksLists.
        Response(tasksLists: [taskList])
        sut.presentTasksLists(response: response)
        XCTAssertTrue(!viewController.lists.isEmpty)
    }
```

```
func testShowAddTaskList_whenAddTaskListIsSelected_
shouldNavigateToAddTaskList() {
    let response = HomeModel.AddTasksList.
    Response(addListDelegate: viewController)
    sut.showAddTaskList(response: response)
    XCTAssertTrue(viewController.showAddList)
    XCTAssertTrue(router.navigateToAddList)
}

func testShowSelectedList_whenTaskListIsSelected_
shouldNavigateToTasksList() {
    let response = HomeModel.SelectTasksList.
    Response(selectedListDelegate: viewController,
    tasksList: taskList)
    sut.showSelectedList(response: response)
    XCTAssertEqual(viewController.selectedList.id,
    taskList.id)
    XCTAssertTrue(router.navigateToTaskList)
    XCTAssertEqual(router.selectedList.id, taskList.id)
}
}
```

In the first test, we will verify that if we pass an array with a list to the Presenter, it will pass it to the ViewController, and therefore, its lists parameter will not be empty.

In the second test, we will prove that calling the *showAddTaskList* method of the *HomePresenter* will modify the parameters *showAddList* of the *MockHomeViewController* and *navigateToTaskList* of the *MockHomeRouter*.

The last *HomePresenter* test checks that when calling the *showSelectedList* method and passing it a list of tasks (as if we had selected it), the ViewController receives said list, and the Router also receives said list and navigates to the *TaskList* scene.

Summary

The Clean Swift or VIP architecture was thought, mainly, to reduce the massive ViewControllers following the indications of the Clean Architecture and following a unidirectional flow of information (what we have named as VIP cycle). The code is structured around the so-called "scenes," which would correspond to the application screens (similar to the "modules" in the VIPER architecture).

The VIP architecture has many advantages, such as being scalable, easy to maintain, and testable. However, it also has some drawbacks. Perhaps one of the most important is that, because numerous protocols are used for communication, the use of this architecture can be complex at first and can seem overengineered.

To help at this point, it is easy to find templates on the Internet that allow us, once introduced in Xcode, to create all the repetitive code simply by entering the name of the scene we want to create.

With the VIP architecture, we have finished the study of the five most used architectures today, indicating their advantages and disadvantages and applying them to the development of a simple application.

In the next chapter, we will deal with some other somewhat less used architectures, from a more general point of view, seeing what their structure is based on and what their advantages and disadvantages are.

CHAPTER 7

Other Architecture Patterns

Introduction

Until now we have seen the architectures that we can consider most used and known: MVC, MVP, MVVM, VIPER, and VIP. But we can find different proposals, each of which seeks to solve some of the problems that other architectures may present or facilitate the work of developers.

Of the different proposals that can be found, we are going to review the following from the point of view of what its operation is based on, how its components are structured, as well as the advantages and disadvantages of its use:

- RIBs: Router, Interactor, and Builder

- TEA: The Elm Architecture

- Redux

- TCA: The Composable Architecture

© Raúl Ferrer García 2023
R. Ferrer García, *iOS Architecture Patterns*, https://doi.org/10.1007/978-1-4842-9069-9_7

Note   This chapter is only intended to introduce some architectures that may seem less familiar. For this reason, we will simply give an introduction to its origin, components, or operation, without presenting code as we have done in the architectures already seen.

RIBs: Router, Interactor, and Builder
A Little History

This architecture was developed by Uber[1] in 2017 as a solution to a series of situations they faced:

- From a software point of view, the code had grown a lot and many features had been added. This led to Uber's technical debt being enormous, which made it very difficult to add new features, limiting scalability.

- Furthermore, an architecture was needed that could handle multiple states in an application.

- The number of developers working at Uber had increased, so it was necessary to encourage the fact that each team could work on developing components separately without any impediment. That is, a modular architecture was sought.

RIB is a cross-platform architecture developed by Uber for use in mobile applications involving multiple developers and nested states.

Each RIB is made up of three components: Router, Interactor, and Builder, and represents an application state. Keep in mind that in the RIB architecture, since it is guided by business logic and not by views, each of the application's functionalities may or may not have a view.

---

[1] https://github.com/uber/RIBs

This can be seen more clearly if we make a diagram of an application and indicate the different RIBs (Figure 7-1).

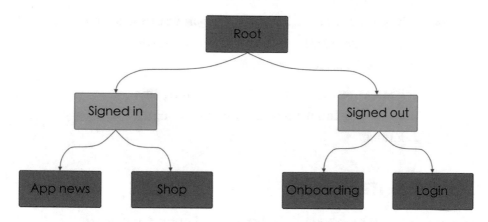

Figure 7-1. *RIB tree example (in red, RIBs without View)*

As you can see in this figure, the *Signed in* and *Signed out* states do not present a view, since they only determine if the user already had an active session (so they continue along that path) or if they did not (so they would continue by the other route).

Each of these states connects to the following states via an interface, with which they can pass whatever dependencies they need. In this way, each of these features can be worked on independently, without the fact of working on one of them affecting the rest (e.g., when each feature is developed by a different team).

How It Works

As we have just seen, we can represent an application and its state using different RIBs interconnected with each other, which we have represented in the form of a tree.

In moving through the application and, therefore, of the different states, these states will be connected and disconnected.

On the other hand, as we move through the RIB tree, information will flow from one RIB to another:

- If it is downstream, that is, from a parent RIB to a child, the direction of communication is usually done as an emission to an Rx data stream.

- If it is ascending, from a child to a parent, this communication usually takes place through a listening interface.

Components

Although we have mentioned the three main components in the RIB architecture (*Router*, *Interactor*, and *Builder*), we can find other components: *Component*, *Presenter*, and *View* (the latter two being optional, since, as we have seen, a RIB does not have to be associated to a View) (Figure 7-2).

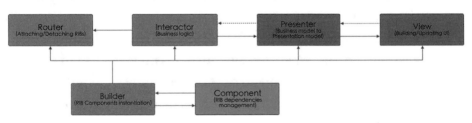

Figure 7-2. *RIB schema*

Router

Routers are in charge of attaching and detaching RIBs based on the events that occur in the Interactors. The presence of the RIBs allows, among other things, to be able to test the Interactors independently (since it is not necessary to know which ones are above or below) or reduce the amount of code of these Interactors by taking the routing part.

Interactor

An Interactor contains the business logic of its RIB, and therefore all functions performed within it can only be limited to its life cycle. In this way, it is possible to avoid that there may be a disconnected RIB (and, therefore, its Interactor), but there are active subscriptions.

An Interactor is the component where Rx subscriptions occur, how their state is changed, or which other RIBs need to connect.

Builder

The Builder of a RIB is like the Configurator that we saw in VIPER: it is in charge of instantiating the different components of the RIB.

Component

A Component is a help for the Builders since they are in charge of managing the dependencies (both internal and external in a RIB). It is common practice to inject the component of a parent RIB into its children so that they have access to its properties.

Presenter

The Presenter, as we already know from other architectures, is in charge of transforming the information that comes from the Interactor into a format that can be displayed by the View (if the RIB has an associated View).

View

As in the case of the Presenter, it is an optional component (for RIBs with an associated View) and it contains the components that define the user interface. They should not have any associated logic and only display information and collect user interaction.

Advantages and Disadvantages

As in any architecture, there are advantages and disadvantages in its application.

Advantages

As advantages of the RIB architecture, we can highlight the following:

- Uber RIBs is an open source project, so we can freely modify and adapt it for our applications.

- This project is accompanied by a series of tools that allow us to quickly generate and configure the RIBs of our application to perform static analysis.

- It is an architecture that can be used on both iOS and Android, which facilitates collaboration between teams on both platforms.

- Thanks to the use of protocols, each RIB is independent of the rest, which allows us to simultaneously develop different RIBs without blocking between them.

- Thanks to this use of protocols, and to the fact that each component of a RIB has clearly defined functions, the testability of each of them is facilitated.

- It has been proven that it is a scalable architecture since, for example, in the case of Uber there are hundreds of developers working on the same source code.

Disadvantages

Among its disadvantages we have the following:

- As in architectures such as VIPER or VIP, a large amount of repetitive code and a high number of components per RIB are generated. This is partially mitigated by the tools provided by Uber to generate these components.

- The learning curve is significant and can be intimidating for developers who are just starting out or with little experience.

- In addition, apart from the documentation (with some tutorials) provided by the project itself, there is not a large bibliography on the Internet, which makes it difficult to learn.

- Communication between RIBs is based on RxSwift for iOS and RxJava or Dagger2 for Android, which can be a problem if we want to use, or already use, another type of reactive library.

The Elm Architecture
A Little History

Elm is a highly typed, pure functional programming language, developed by Evan Czaplicki in 2012,[2] intended for developing graphical user interfaces for web browsers.

---

[2] https://elm-lang.org/assets/papers/concurrent-frp.pdf

The Elm Architecture is born from the use of Elm and is a simple pattern to structure web apps.[3] In this architecture, we have a Model that contains the state of the application, a View that generates the HTML according to the Model, and an Update that transforms the Model. Its first application with Swift was on 2017.[4]

How It Works

The Elm Architecture works according to the following cycle (Figure 7-3):

- In the first place, a Model is passed to the View, which is in charge of representing it.

- When the user interacts with the View, this interaction is transmitted to Runtime as a message, which is relayed to Update along with the current Model.

- The Update is in charge of updating the Model according to the information in the Message and returning it to the Runtime.

- The loop restarts when the Runtime sends the updated Model to the View to update based on the new Model.

Figure 7-3. *The Elm Architecture schema*

---

[3] https://guide.elm-lang.org/architecture/
[4] https://www.youtube.com/watch?v=U805TqsDIV8

Components

In The Elm Architecture, we have (as we just saw) four components: Model, View, Update, and Runtime.

Model

The Model contains the data (as defined) and the state of the application.

View

The View is a function that returns or renders a new view based on the Model (or state) it receives.

Update

An Update is a function that updates the Model (or state) based on the Message it receives.

Runtime

It is what unites and relates the Model, the View, and the Update.

Advantages and Disadvantages

Let's now see some of the advantages and disadvantages of this architecture.

Advantages

As advantages we can highlight the following:

- It is a simple architecture.

- It allows us to develop our views in a declarative way.

373

- The logical definition of each of the components and their behavior allows us to test them easily.

- It uses a one-way data flow (as in VIP).

Disadvantages

Some of the most important disadvantages are as follows:

- Even with its simplicity, it can be complex for developers who are just starting or have little experience.

- Furthermore, apart from some repositories and blogs, there is not a large bibliography on the Internet, which makes it difficult to learn.

Redux

A Little History

Redux is an open source JavaScript library developed by Dan Abramov and Andrew Clark in 2015.[5] What Redux does is manage and centralize the application state, and it is inspired by the Flux architecture developed by Facebook.[6] According to Dan Abramov:[7]

> *And I just, I was trying to make a proof of concept of Flux where I could change the logic. And it would let me time travel. And it would let me reapply the future actions on the code change. So that was like, the goal.*

---

[5] The History of React and Flux with Dan Abramov. `https://threedevsandamaybe.com/the-history-of-react-and-flux-with-dan-abramov/`

[6] `https://facebook.github.io/flux/`

[7] `https://ui.dev/dan-abramov`

How It Works

The Redux architecture is based on the fact that the data only flows in one direction (as we have also seen in The Elm Architecture) and we only have one model (which will act as the source of truth) that will be in charge of storing and modifying the data to be displayed.

The flow in Redux (Figure 7-4) starts with an Action on the View (e.g., clicking a button). This action is passed to the Reducer component, which, based on said Action, is in charge of modifying the state of the application.

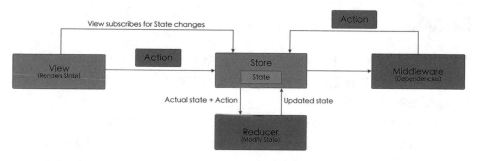

Figure 7-4. *Redux schema*

The change in state causes the View to be updated with the new information (to achieve this we will use the Observer pattern, making the view *subscribe* to state changes).

Components

Let us now see in a little more detail the function of each component.

State

It is the state of the application and there can only be one. That is why we can also indicate that it is the *source of truth*.

Store

The Store contains the State and is in charge of circulating the data. As we have seen, it is in charge of receiving the Action from the View and passing it to the Reducer, along with the state.

Then it receives the new state of the application that the Reducer has generated, and the View, which we have subscribed to the changes of the State, receives it and updates the graphical interface. There is only one Store in the application.

Reducer

A Reducer contains the logic and it is a pure and synchronous function, in charge of modifying the State of the application (they are the only components that can do it).

The Reducer receives the State and the Action of the Store and generates a new State that it returns to the Store. In the case of wanting to divide the logic of an application, it is better to use different Reducers (Composition pattern) than to use different Stores.

Action

An Action is a simple object, which may or may not carry information, and which is sent by the View to change the State of the application. These actions can be caused by various reasons, such as touching a button or receiving the response of a call to an external server.

View

It is what the user sees and is responsible for representing the State of the application. It is subscribed to changes in the State, so it is updated every time the State changes.

Middleware

Middlewares are the components that are responsible for the use of dependencies in the application: database access, calls to servers... since Reducers are pure functions that do not use dependencies. When an action is launched, it passes through the Middlewares along with the application state and, if necessary, they can launch a new action asynchronously.

Advantages and Disadvantages

Like any architecture, Redux has advantages and disadvantages.

Advantages

Using Redux in our projects has some advantages:

- Redux is very lightweight, and there is no need to use external libraries.

- The fact of having a single state favors its debugging.

- In applications we can save the current state locally, which allows us, for example, to return to that state when restarting the application.

- Since the Reducer is made up of pure functions, the business logic is easier to test.

- By separating the business logic (Reducers) from the dependencies (Middlewares), we reduce the number of mocks in the test.

- It has a good separation of responsibilities.

Disadvantages

These are some of its disadvantages:

- As the application grows, since every time an Action is passed the entire State is re-created, the system memory consumption will increase.

- Being such a specific architecture, when we use it in a project, it is practically impossible to transform the project into a different architecture.

- Although it is a well-known architecture in the web world, it is not so well known in iOS development, so it can be complicated for novice developers.

- The fact that Middlewares can launch new Actions asynchronously can lead to, if there are a large number of Middlewares, contradictory actions, infinite loops... that make the system unstable.

- It is a fairly rigid architecture that allows few variations.

TCA: The Composable Architecture
A Little History

The Composable Architecture (TCA) was developed by Brandon Williams and Stephen Celis of Point-Free.[8]

This architecture was born to solve some of the problems that we find when developing our applications:

---

[8] https://github.com/pointfreeco/swift-composable-architecture

- Manage the state of applications in a simple way, and share it between different screens so that any change in state in one of them can be observed by another.

- To be able to divide large functionalities into multiple much smaller and isolated functionalities, but with the characteristic of being able to unite them (compose them) and form a whole again.

- Facilitate the testing of the application, not only at the level of unit tests but also of integration tests and end-to-end tests.

- You may easily get all of this by using a library that offers an API to implement each component.

How It Works

The Composable Architecture is an architecture that works in a declarative way (and not in an imperative way), according to the principles of reactive programming, structuring the code according to Redux patterns. Although fully optimized for use with SwiftUI (which is declarative), it can also be used with UIKit (which is imperative).

TCA derives from The Elm Architecture, but now, for example, TCA works with the idea that each View has its Store, although each of these child stores has a partial copy of the parent view state. Every time an action is sent to a view's Store, it is reactively passed to the parent's stores (Figure 7-5).

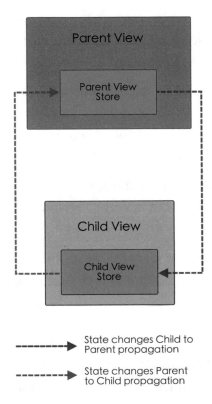

Figure 7-5. *Each View has its Store*

We have seen in Figure 7-5 that in this architecture, each View has a Store. Let's now see what components make up The Composable Architecture (Figure 7-6).

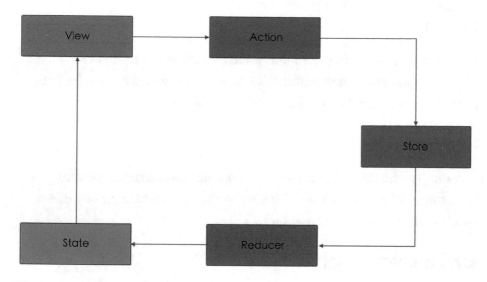

Figure 7-6. *TCA schema*

Components

The Composable Architecture is based on six components: State, View, Action, Reducer, Environment, and Store.

State

It is a set of variables that represent the state of the application and that are necessary to update the View.

View

It is responsible for receiving and representing the data of the State.

Action

It is usually an *enum* that contains as cases all the actions that can occur: events, notifications, user actions…. For example, an action can be both receiving data from a server and touching a button.

Reducer

It is simply a function that takes an Action and the current State and transforms it into a new State. It is also in charge of returning any Effect (such as the call to an external server).

Environment (Effect)

It involves the dependencies that may exist in an application (such as an external call to a server) and contains the logic of interaction with the outside. It is like the Redux Middleware, and it is normally injected (dependency injection) into the Reducer.

The Effect is the result of an Action and is generated by the Reducer (and allows it to connect with the outside). When an Effect completes its work, it can trigger another action for the Reducer.

Store

Store is a combination of State, Action, and Reducer. It receives the user's actions and sends them to the Reducer together with the State. When a new state is generated, the View is updated.

Advantages and Disadvantages

To follow the same line as in the rest of the architectures that we have seen, we are going to see some of the most important advantages and disadvantages.

Advantages

The main advantages of The Composable Architecture are as follows:

- The data flow is unidirectional.

- The Reducers are the only ones that can modify the State, which facilitates testing.

- The application is built with a composition of different functionalities. This allows for designing, developing, and testing each functionality separately.

- In the Environment, we find all the dependencies. This makes the debugging job easier. Also, it is easier to switch from a development environment to a production environment.

- It allows you to develop views in a declarative way.

Disadvantages

The main disadvantages of The Composable Architecture are as follows:

- It is more intended for SwiftUI (declarative UI) than for UIKit (reactive UI).

- By having multiple states, synchronization between them can be complicated.

- In the same way as RIB, TEA, or Redux, it is an architecture that is not as well known as the ones that we have dealt with in depth in the first chapters. This means that not so much information is found and can be intimidating for beginner developers.

Summary

To end the topic of Software Architectures in iOS, we have reviewed some of the lesser known or less used ones (RIBs, TEA, Redux, and TCA). These are more modern architectures, whose bases differ from those we saw initially (MVC, MVP, MVVM, VIP, or VIPER), for example, in the use of states.

The fact that they are little used and even in demand means that the information available is also reduced, which can make access difficult for novice developers. But more than an impediment, we can consider it a learning challenge!

CHAPTER 8

Conclusion

The Importance of Clean Architecture

We have reached the end of this book. I hope that throughout your reading, you have strengthened the importance of, on the one hand, Software Architecture in the development of our applications and, on the other, that this architecture adheres to, as much as possible, the principles of Clean Architecture.

We have worked in some depth on the architectures that today we can consider the most used or most demanded in the development of applications for the iOS operating system: MVC, MVP, MVVM, VIPER, and VIP.

Then we have seen some architectures in a less specific way that, although they are not as well known or used, provide us with other points of view or approaches to the development of applications: RIB, TEA, Redux, and TCA.

As we have been seeing when we have studied the different architectures shown in this book, and we have been seeing the importance of using a Clean Architecture in the development of our applications, the use of Clean Architecture will allow us to:

- Isolate the business logic in a layer so that it is easily testable.

© Raúl Ferrer García 2023
R. Ferrer García, *iOS Architecture Patterns*, https://doi.org/10.1007/978-1-4842-9069-9_8

- Isolate the user interface, so that it is only responsible for displaying the data that is supplied to it. In addition, we must be able to modify it without affecting the rest of the code.

- Be independent of any library used, which should allow us to change one library for another without significantly modifying the application code.

- Be independent of the data sources, so that we can change one data source for another without affecting the business logic.

In a few words, the fact of working with a Clean Architecture should allow us to develop scalable and testable applications, in which any developer can work.

Moving Forward

Now you have a broader understanding of the most commonly used architectures in iOS app development (and how lesser-known ones work).

But this does not end here; to continue advancing, you should apply these architectures in different projects and see for yourself the advantages they provide and the difficulties you may encounter.

Whichever architecture or architectures you choose to develop your applications, I recommend that you delve into it, search for information (books, blogs, videos, conferences...), document yourself, and study projects in which they have been applied. In this way you will be able to see more clearly its advantages and disadvantages, possible problems in its implementation, or solutions to problems that keep you stuck at one point.

Remember that by itself a given architecture is neither bad nor good, they all have advantages and disadvantages. And, although it is a very important part of the development of an application, you should not forget other important points to focus on:

- TDD or test-driven development

- SOLID principles

- Dependency injection

Finally, I hope you have found this book interesting and useful in your development career.

Index

Printed in the United States
by Baker & Taylor Publisher Services